Charles Newhall Taintor

The New York Central and Hudson River Railroad and the Rome

Watertown, and Ogdenburg Railroad ..

Charles Newhall Taintor

The New York Central and Hudson River Railroad and the Rome
Watertown, and Ogdenburg Railroad ..

ISBN/EAN: 9783744791854

Printed in Europe, USA, Canada, Australia, Japan

Cover: Foto ©Andreas Hilbeck / pixelio.de

More available books at **www.hansebooks.com**

NEW YORK CENTRAL
AND HUDSON RIVER RAILWAY.
ROME, WATERTOWN & OGDENSBURG RAILROAD.

New York, Saratoga, Niagara Falls,
THOUSAND ISLANDS, MASSENA SPRINGS.

THE AGENTS OF

The Cheque Bank, Limited, of London,

issue for the special use of American Tourists, Cheques in book form, from £5 upward, payable FREE OF COMMISSIO OR DISCOUNT, in every Town in Europe; also payable ʻt the Bank of Bermuda, Hamilton, and at all the Branches of t Colonial Bank in the West India Islands; also at the Lond Bank of Mexico and South America in Mexico City, and other parts of the world.

Much cheaper than Letters of Credit. Send for particulars to

E. J. MATHEWS & COMPANY, Bankers,
2 Wall Street, New York.

TOURISTS AND INVALIDS
wishing to escape the severity of our Northern Winters, can find no n attractive places than the

BERMUDA ISLAND
— AND —
WEST INDIES.

The Steamship *Orinoco*, 2,000 tons, together with the magnific new Steamship *Trinidad*, 2,160 tons, 1,500 horse power, highest cla: 100 A 1 at Lloyd's, built expressly for this route in 1885, with unsurpass accommodations for passengers, leaves New York and Bermuda eve Thursday during the season.

Steamers for West Indies, St. Kitt's Antigua, Dominica, Martiniq; St. Lucia, Barbados and Trinidad, leave New York and the Islands eve 17 days.

For full particulars, time tables, and descriptive pamphlets, apply tc

A. E. OUTERBRIDGE & CO., Agents,

ARTHUR AHERN, Sec'y, Quebec.   51 Broadway, New Yc

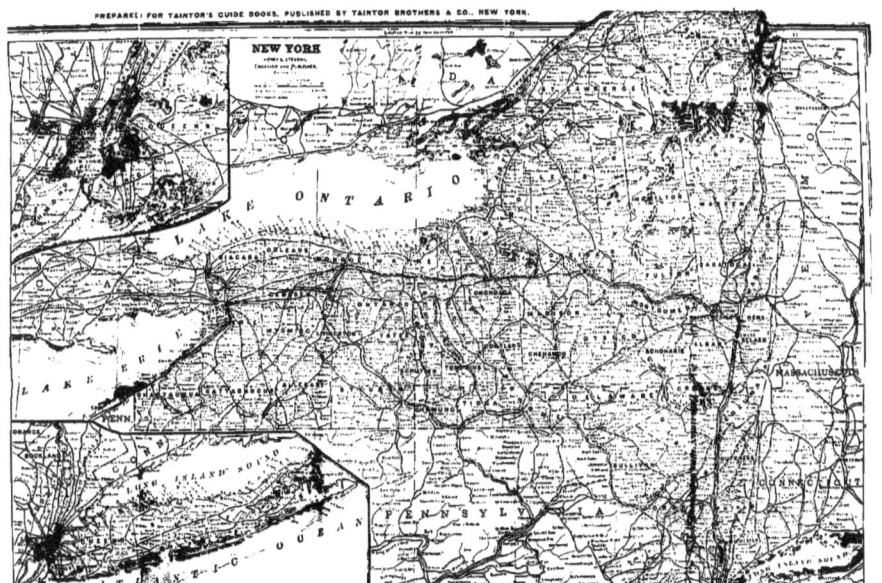

THE

Massachusetts Mutual
LIFE INSURANCE COMPANY
OF
SPRINGFIELD, MASS.

INCORPORATED 1851.

Total Assets, January 1st, 1889, . . $9,565,522.65
Total Liabilities, January 1st, 1889, . . 8,809,995.04
Surplus by Massachusetts Standard, . . . $755,527.61
Number of Policies issued in 1888, **3,631,** insuring 12,007,550.00
Number of Policies in force Dec. 31, 1888, **18,767,** " 49,480,584.00

THE MASSACHUSETTS MUTUAL LIFE INSURANCE COMPANY, of Springfield, is one of the oldest in the United States.

It was incorporated in the year 1851 by the State of Massachusetts, which was the first in the Union to inaugurate an "Insurance Department," thus instituting State supervision over its companies.

It was also the first State to legislate concerning the forfeiture of policies of life insurance; its famous non-forfeiture law was passed in 1861 and amended in 1880. By the recent act of 1887, life insurance legislation has reached a degree of perfection heretofore unknown.

THIS Law requires that all policies issued by THE MASSACHUSETTS MUTUAL LIFE INSURANCE COMPANY shall be non-forfeitable after the payment of two annual premiums, without any further stipulation or act. This makes the amount of paid-up insurance to which the policyholder may be entitled, under any circumstances, **absolutely guaranteed.** He may forget his policy, but his policy will never forget him. Also, that after the payment of two annual premiums, the insured may, on any subsequent anniversary of the date of issue of said policy, surrender the same, and claim and recover from the Company its **"Surrender Value in Cash."** Said Cash Value is fixed by the law itself and **cannot be changed.**

M. V. B. EDGERLY, President.   JOHN A. HALL, Secretary.
HENRY S. LEE, Vice-President.   OSCAR B. IRELAND, Actuary.

MASSASOIT HOUSE,
W. H. CHAPIN,   SPRINGFIELD, MASS

ESTABLISHED 1843

BY

M. & E. S. CHAPIN.

Perfectly Pure Extracts of Choicest Fruits, THE BEST. Unequaled Strength for all. Thousands of gross sold. Winning friends everywhere. DEALERS TREBLE SALES WITH THEM.

    These Delicious Flavors are used at many of the Finest Hotels in the White Mountains, Saratoga Springs, the Catskills, Seaside and Summer Resorts, and in City and Country, and sold by Dealers Everywhere. Wholesale Agents in large cities.

LABORATORY (Home Dept.), WESTFIELD, MASS.
New York Office, 63 Park Place.

ÆTNA LIFE INSURANCE CO.

OF HARTFORD, CONN.

ASSETS, - - - - - $33,819,034.97
SURPLUS, { by Massachusetts and Conn. Standard, 5,566,055.24
{ by New York Standard, 7,325,000.00

CONSERVATIVE, ECONOMICAL, and "SOLID AS GRANITE."

POLICIES NON-FORFEITING AND INCONTESTABLE
after the death of the insured.

All desirable plans of Insurance, including some which are new and especially advantageous.

ADDRESS THE COMPANY OR ANY OF ITS AGENTS.

M. G. BULKELEY, President.

J. C. WEBSTER, Vice-President.   J. L. ENGLISH, Secretary.

WEBSTER'S UNABRIDGED.

WITH OR WITHOUT PATENT INDEX.

A DICTIONARY
118,000 Words, 3000 Engravings,
A GAZETTEER OF THE WORLD
locating and describing 25,000 places,
A BIOGRAPHICAL DICTIONARY
of nearly 10,000 Noted Persons,
A DICTIONARY OF FICTION
found only in Webster,
ALL IN ONE BOOK.

3000 more Words and nearly 2000 more Illustrations than any other American Dictionary. "Invaluable in Schools and Families."

Webster is Standard Authority in the Government Printing Office, and with the U. S. Supreme Court. It is recommended by State Sup'ts of Schools of 36 States.
Published by G. & C. MERRIAM & CO., Springfield, Mass. Illustrated Pamphlet free.

BROTHERHOOD WINES.

Pure Ports, Sherry, and Clarets of our own production for Medicinal or Family uses; endorsed by the Medical Fraternity.

Send for Price-List to our New York House, 26 Vesey Street.

OUR AIMS: | J. M. EMERSON & SON,
Absolute Purity, | Principal Vineyards and Shipping Point,
Natural Flavor, |
Full Strength. | WASHINGTONVILLE, N. Y.

69th ANNUAL STATEMENT, December 31st, 1888.

ÆTNA INSURANCE COMPANY,
HARTFORD, CONN.

CASH CAPITAL	$4,000,000 00
Reserved for Re-Insurance (Fire)	1,906,970 41
" " (Inland)	14,778 70
Unpaid Losses (Fire)	165,586 32
" " (Inland)	22,092 11
All other claims	64,809 15
NET SURPLUS	3,606,514 94
TOTAL ASSETS	**$9,780,751 63**

"AS FOLLOWS":

Cash in Bank	$978,670 57
Cash in hands of Agents	372,910 42
Real Estate	365,000 00
Loans on Bond and Mortgage	43,700 00
Loans on Collaterals	7,770 00
Stocks and Bonds	8,011,751 50
Accrued Interest	949 14
TOTAL ASSETS	**$9,780,751 63**

LOSSES PAID IN 70 YEARS, $63,046,000.

Wm. B. Clark, Vice-Pres.   A. C. Bayne, Sec.   J. Goodnow, Pres.

SCUDDER'S
History of United States.
PRECEDED BY A NARRATIVE OF
THE DISCOVERY AND SETTLEMENT OF NORTH AMERICA,
And of the Events which led to the Independence of the 13 English Colonies.

By HORACE E. SCUDDER.

WITH MAPS AND ILLUSTRATIONS.   PRICE, ONE DOLLAR.

The leading characteristics of this excellent work are :

FIRST.—A Well Considered Text.

SECOND.—A New and Logical Division into Periods, with a Suggestive Method of Treatment.

THIRD.—The insertion of Topical Analyses for Review, as well as a full set of questions on Text and Maps.

FOURTH.—Accurate, Clear, and Distinct Maps, most carefully drawn and engraved, including Six Double Page and Six Single Page Colored Maps.

FIFTH.—Eighty Beautiful Illustrations by eminent artists. Also Superb Portraits of the following representative men : Columbus, the Discoverer; Penn the Founder; Franklin, the Philosopher; Washington the Patriot; Webster, the Statesman, Longfellow, the Poet; engraved by Closson, Johnson, and Kruell, with fifty other Portraits.

SIXTH.—Superior Mechanical Execution, and Low Price.

TEACHERS say : "It is the best equipped school book ever issued in the U. S." "Will both interest and profit our young folks." "The most useful and enjoyable school history." "Simple, accurate, interesting, and impartial."

TAINTOR BROTHERS & CO., Publishers, 18 Astor Place, New York.

CONNECTICUT
FIRE INSURANCE COMPANY,
OF HARTFORD, Conn.

Incorporated 1850. Charter Perpetual

CASH CAPITAL, - - $1,000,000.00
CASH ASSETS, - - 2,260,917.01

WESTERN DEPARTMENT:
A. WILLIAMS, Manager,
155 LA SALLE STREET,
CHICAGO, Ill.

PACIFIC DEPARTMENT:
ROBERT DICKSON, MANAGER
SAN FRANCISCO, Cal.

SCOTT, ALEXANDER & TALBOT, Agents,
45 WILLIAM ST., NEW YORK.

J. D. BROWNE, President, CHAS. R. BURT, Secretary,
L. W. CLARKE, Assistant-Secretary.

THE NEW BOOK OF WORSHIP.
SONGS OF CHRISTIAN PRAISE,
FOR CHOIR AND CONGREGATION.
Published with or without Scripture Selections for Responsive Reading.

EDITED BY REV. CHARLES H. RICHARDS, D.D

SONGS OF CHRISTIAN PRAISE has already been adopted by many churches throughout the country, and has been received with unqualified satisfaction.

Testimonials from the Press.

The New York Observer says: "It contains everything essential to a handbook for general worship and special services. While it is attractively published, it is furnished at a price which is intended to make it popular."

The Interior, Chicago, Ill: "Not burdened with lumber, it is yet large enough for all uses; choice enough to satisfy the most cultivated taste, and popular enough to lead the congregation."

The Congregationalist, Boston, Mass.: "It has been compiled with a discriminating wisdom and taste, and edited with a thoroughness which are uncommon."

The Advance says: "One of the choicest, richest, and most usable hymn-books published."

The Golden Rule, Boston, Mass.: "In its musical part this service-book is probably not surpassed by any other in the language."

The New York Times: "In its mechanical arrangement the book leaves scarcely anything to be desired."

Testimonials from the Pulpit.

Rev. G. L. Spining, D.D., Cleveland, Ohio: "It is the best I have ever seen."

Rev. C. L. Thompson, D.D., Pastor of Presbyterian Church, Kansas City, Mo.: "It is every way an admirable book, convenient in size and shape, rich in hymns and tunes, and fully adapted to all the demands of social and public worship."

Rev. W. E. Knox, D.D., Pastor First Presbyterian Church, Elmira, N. Y.: "Your volume of Christian Praise is very attractive. Mechanically and typographically it is the highest style of art. The hymns I like for their devotional character."

Rev. J. E. Rankin, D.D., Washington, D.C.: "The book is a grand one. Certainly the best of its kind I have ever examined."

Rev. J. Hall McIlvaine, Providence, R.I.. "After two years use, I regard 'Songs of Christian Praise' as beyond comparison with any book that I have ever seen."

Rev. J. G. Vose, D.D., Providence, R.I., says: "Our people are unanimous in its favor, and enjoy it more and more."

Rev. T. M. Monroe, of Akron, Ohio, says: "The book grows upon us, and we heartily commend it."

Rev. W. H. Thomas, says: "Your hymn-book has more than met our expectations. It is a work of merit, and improves with use. It gives perfect satisfaction."

Rev. Frank P. Woodbury, D.D., Rockford, Ill., says: "Our high expectations of the popular acceptance of the book, when, after thorough examination and extensive comparison, we ordered 450 copies, have been more than fulfilled."

Rev. Samuel Conn, D.D., St. Paul, Minn., says: "We decided upon 'Songs of Christian Praise,' after a thorough comparison with several other books. A short trial in actual worship has confirmed our favorable opinion of it."

Rev. L. O. Brastow, D.D., Burlington, Vt., says: "To me personally it is exceedingly satisfactory. It gives satisfaction to the church and congregation."

Rev. Eli Corwin D.D., Racine, Wis., says: "The book is admirable for church service, and is the best for that purpose with which I am acquainted."

Returnable Copies sent free to Pastors or Church Committees desiring books for examination.

A twenty-four page pamphlet, containing specimen pages, testimonials, price lists, etc., mailed free to any address on application to

TAINTOR BROTHERS & CO., Publishers,
18 and 20 Astor Place, New York City.

CONGRESS SPRING.

The Standard Mineral Water.

IT IS A PURELY

NATURAL WATER, CATHARTIC ALTERATIVE,

and slightly stimulating and tonic in its effects, without producing the debility that usually attends a course of medicine. It is used with

Marked Success in Affections of the Liver and Kidneys,

and for **Dyspepsia, Gout, Constipation, and Cutaneous Diseases** it is unrivaled.

It is especially beneficial as a general preservative of the tone of the stomach and purity of the blood, and a

Powerful Preventive of Fevers and Bilious Complaints.

IT IS OF SPECIAL VALUE TO LADIES,

as from its great purifying properties it has good effect in clearing the skin and giving it a healthy, beautiful appearance. In the morning it tones the appetite and promotes digestion. The stomach is cleansed and purified, the nervous and muscular system invigorated, and germs of disease thrown off.

The superior excellence of Congress Water is evidenced in the *happy proportion* of its several ingredients, which combine to make it so efficient, and in the *absolute solution* in which these pure ingredients are *held* when BOTTLED, making it, without doubt, one of the best and *safest saline cathartic waters* ever discovered either in this country or Europe.

As a cathartic water its almost entire freedom from *iron* should recommend it above all others, many of which contain so much of this ingredient as to seriously impair their usefulness.

☞ For sale (in Bottles only) by all leading Druggists, Grocers, Wine Merchants, and Hotels. Address

CONGRESS SPRING CO.,
SARATOGA SPRINGS, N. Y.

1794.   1889.

HARTFORD
Fire Insurance Co

OF HARTFORD, CONN.

STATEMENT JANUARY 1, 1889.

Cash Capital,	$1,250,000 00
Reserve for Re-Insurance (legal standard),	2,014,565 44
Outstanding Claims,	251,532 44
Policy Holders' Surplus,	3,483,982 59
Net Surplus over Capital and All Liabilities,	2,233,982 59
Total Assets,	**$5,750,080 47**
Total Income received during the year,	$2,847,714 62
Increase in Assets,	461,476 50
Increase in Net Surplus,	297,722 78

GEO. L. CHASE, *President.*
P. C. ROYCE, *Secretary.*   THOMAS TURNBULL, *Ass't Secretary.*

WESTERN DEPARTMENT.

G. F. BISSELL, *General Agent.*
P. P. HEYWOOD, *Assistant General Agent.*

CHICAGO, ILL

PACIFIC DEPARTMENT.

BELDEN & COFRON, *Managers.*

SAN FRANCISCO, CAL.

BRANCH OFFICE.

158 BROADWAY,   NEW YORK.

GEORGE M. COIT, *Manager Metropolitan District.*

THE
NEW YORK CENTRAL
AND HUDSON RIVER RAILROAD

AND THE

ROME, WATERTOWN, AND OGDENSBURG RAILROAD.

New York to West Point, Albany, Troy, Saratoga Springs, Utica, Richfield Springs, Trenton Falls, Thousand Islands, Ogdensburg, Massena Springs, Syracuse, Oswego, Rochester, Niagara Falls, and Buffalo.

ILLUSTRATED WITH MAPS, WOODCUTS, Etc.

Copyright, 1889, by
Taintor Brothers & Co.

NEW YORK:
TAINTOR BROTHERS & CO.,
18 and 20 Astor Place.

NATIONAL
Fire Insurance Company
OF HARTFORD, CONN.

STATEMENT, JANUARY 1, 1889.

CAPITAL STOCK, all Cash, - - $1,000,000.00
Funds Reserved to meet all Liabilities:
Re-Insurance Fund, legal standard, $724,429.03 } 819,454.96
Unsettled Losses and other claims, 95,025.93
Net Surplus over Capital and all Liabilities, 507,126.20
TOTAL ASSETS, January 1, 1889, - $2,326,581.16

JAMES NICHOLS, PRES'T.   E. G. RICHARDS, SEC'Y.

FRED. S. JAMES, Chicago, Ill., General Agent Western Department.
GEO. D. DORNIN, San Francisco, Cal., Manager Pacific Department.

The Political Cyclopædia.

If you wish to think, speak, and act intelligently upon the great questions of the day, you need this work, written by the most eminent specialists of this country and Europe: e. g., DAVID A. WELLS discusses the *Tariff and Tariff Legislation* from the standpoint of the free trader, and D. H. MASON from the point of view of the protectionist; E. L. GODKIN writes of *Office Holders;* PROF. ALEXANDER JOHNSTON, the articles on the *Political History of the U. S.;* DORMAN B. EATON, of *Civil Service Reform;* PRES. D. C. GILMAN, of *Universities;* SIMON STERNE, of *Railroads;* PRES. F. A. WALKER, of *Public Revenue and Wages;* EDWARD ATKINSON, of *Banks;* JOHN J. KNOX, of the *Currency,* etc.; THOMAS M. COOLEY, Pres. Interstate Commerce Commission, of *The Bar, Law of Corporation,* etc.; HORATIO C. BURCHARD, ex-Director of the Mint, of *Coinage, Gold, Silver,* etc.

JAMES G. BLAINE writes: "I use it almost daily for reference, and regard it as a model."

THE ATLANTA CONSTITUTION says: "It is doubtful, indeed, if a more important work of reference has ever been prepared," and

THE NEW YORK NATION adds: "We cannot withhold our warm commendation of the industry and discrimination of the editor, and the enterprise of the publishers."

A 16-page Pamphlet Descriptive Sent FREE.

INTELLIGENT SALESMEN AND CANVASSERS who wish to identify themselves with a work of the highest character, and to give their subscribers full value for money received, will do well to correspond with the publishers,

Charles E. Merrill & Co.,
743 BROADWAY, NEW YORK.

INDEX.

	PAGE
Acra	59
Adams	128
Adams' Basin	107
Akin	73
Albany	64
Albion	107, 127
Alder Creek	141
Alexander	102
Alexandria Bay	148
Alverson's	132
Amboy	91
Amsterdam	72
André and Arnold	29
Aqueduct	70
Athens	61
Attica	102
Auburn	97
Aurelius	97
Baggage	13
Barnegat	46
Barrytown	50
Batavia	101
Big Indian	57
Black River	132
Boiceville	56
Bonnie Castle	148
Boonville	141
Brewerton	126
Brier Hill	151
Brockport	107
Buffalo	103
Buffalo Harbor	104
Buffalo to Niagara Falls, Suspension Bridge, & Lewiston	115
Cabs and carriages	13
Cairo	59
Camden	127
Canandaigua	99
Canandaigua to Buffalo & Niagara	109
Canaseraga	86
Canastota	86
Canton	134
Cape Vincent	129
Carleton Island	146
Carmansville	25
Carthage	132-143
Castleton	63

	PAGE
Castor Land	143
Catskill	53
Catskill Station	53
Catskills (the)	55
Cayuga	97
Central Square	127
Charlotte	122
Chittenango	86
Clay	126
Clayton	144
Clifton Springs	99
Clinton	81
Clyde	90
Cocymans	62
Cohoes	70
Cold Spring	42
Commutation rates	18
Cooperstown	76
Cornwall	43
Coxsackie Station	61
Coxsackie Landing	61
Crane's Village	72
Cranston's	39
Crescent	70
Croton	35
Cruger's	37
Deer River	143
De Kalb Junction	134
De Witt	87
Dobbs' Ferry	31
Dunsbeck Ferry	70
Dutchess Junction	44
East Albany	63
East Creek	76
East Palmyra	92
East Stenben	141
East Windham	59
Elevated roads	12
Evan's Mills	133
Fairport	92
Felt's Mills	132
Fishkill Landing	44
Fonda	74
Fort Lee	26
Fort Plain	75
Fort Washington	26
Fox Hollow	57
Frankfort	78
Freehold	59

	PAGE
Fulton	125
Garrison's	39
Gasport	108
Gates	107
Geneva	98
Germantown	52
Glendale	142
Glenwood	29
Goat Island	111, 121
Gouverneur	133
Grand Central Depot	12
Grand Hotel Station	57
Graturck	115
Great Bend	132
Green's Corners	85
Hammond	150
Hastings on Hudson	29
Hastings	127
Haverstraw	34
Herkimer	78
High Bridge	20
Hoffman's	72
Holland Patent	139
Hudson	60
Hudson River	21
Hunter	58
Hyde Park	48
Ilion	78
Indian Head	28
Information for passengers	14
Inwood	25
Irvington	32
Jewett Heights	59
Jordan	90
Kasoag	127
Kingsbridge	20
Kingston	50
Kirkville	87
Lafargeville	144
La Salle	115
Le Roy	109
Lewiston	115-121
Lexington	59
Leyden	141
Linlithgow	53
Little Falls	77
Liverpool	126
Lockport	108

7

INDEX.

	PAGE
Lockport to Buffalo	109
Low Point	45
Lowville	142
Lyons	91
Lyons Falls	142
Macedon	92
Malden	52
Manhattanville	25
Manlius	87
Marcy	139
Marlborough	46
Martinsburg	142
Mary Island	148
Massena Springs	135
M'Connellsville	127
Medina	108
Mexico	125
Middleport	108
Milton	46
Moira	136
Montrose	37
Morris Dock	20
Morristown	151
Mount St. Vincent	27
Mt. Pleasant	56
Newark	91
New Baltimore	62
Newburgh	44
Newfane	122
New Hamburg	45
New Hartford	81
New Haven	125
New Paltz Landing	48
New York	12
New York Central & Hudson River R. R.	9-14
Niagara Falls	110,121
Niagara River	121
Niskayuna	70
Northern Adirondack	136
Northern Tonawanda	115
Norwood	134
Nyack	34
Ogdensburg	151
One Hundred and Twenty-fifth Street	19
One Hundred and Thirty-eighth Street	19
Oneida	85
Ontario Beach	101
Oriskany	84
Oscawana	37
Oswego	123
Otsego Lake	76
Palace cars	14
Palatine Bridge	75
Palenville	58
Palisades	27
Palmyra	92
Parish	127
Paul Smith's	136
Peekskill	37

	PAGE
Philadelphia	133, 144
Phoenicia	56
Phoenix	125
Piermont	32
Pine Hill	57
Port Byron	90
Port Leyden	141
Potsdam	134
Poughkeepsie	46
Prattsville	59
Prospect	140
Prospect Park	114, 146
Pulaski	126
Redwood	150
Remsen	141
Rhinebeck Landing	49
Richfield Springs	82
Richland Junction	126
Riverdale	27
Riverview Station	121
Rochester	93
Rochester & Charlotte Branch	101
Rochester to Buffalo & Niagara Falls	101
Rochester to Niagara Falls	107
Rockland Lake	34
Rome	84
Rome, Watertown & Ogdensburg R. R.	117
Niagara Falls Line	121
Rochester Line	122
Phoenix Line	125
Cape Vincent Div.	129
Carthage, Watertown & Sackett's Harbor Line	131
Carthage to Harrisville	133
Eastern Division	138
Rondout	49
Rose	123
Rossie	150
Round Island	146
Round Island Park	146
Sackett's Harbor	131
Sand Hill	126
Saugerties	51
Savannah	90
Scarborough	34
Schenectady	71
Schodac	62
Scriba	125
Sea Breeze	122
Seneca Falls	98
Shandaken	57
Shokan	56
Sing Sing	34
Skaneateles	96
Skaneateles Junction	96
Sodus Point	123

	PAGE
Sodus Bay	123
Spencerport	107
Sprakers	74
Spuyten Duyvil	20-27
Staatsburg	48
Stages	13
Sterling	123
Sterlingville	144
Stittville	139
St. Johnsville	76
Stockport	61
Stony Point	36
Storm King	44
Stuyvesant	61
Surface roads	12
Suspension Bridge	109, 113
Syracuse	88
Syracuse to Rochester via Auburn	95
Tannersville	58
Tappan Zee	28
Tarrytown	33
The Catskills	55
Theresa Junction	144
Theresa Village	150
Thousand Islands	145
Thousand Island Park	147
Three River Point	125
Tickets	14
Tivoli	51
Tonawanda	115
Trenton	139
Trenton Falls	81, 139
Tribe's Hill	73
Troy	68
Tuscarora Reservation	116
Tyre	98
Utica	79
Van Buren Centre	90
Verona	85
Vestibule trains	14
Victor	100
Wallington	123
Wampsville	86
Warner's	90
Waterloo	98
Waterport	122
Watertown	127
Weedsport	90
Wellesley's Island	147
West Hurley	56
West Kill	59
West Point	41
West Rush	109
Whirlpool	121
Whitesboro	84
Williamstown	127
Windham	59
Wolcott	123
Woodard	125-126
Yonkers	28
Yost's	74

"LACKAWANNA ROUTE."
Delaware, Lackawanna & Western R.R.

THIS Line, which is the shortest running between New York and Buffalo, is noted for its charming and romantic scenery. It runs through the States of New Jersey, Pennsylvania, and New York, passing through the celebrated Delaware Water Gap, the coal fields of Pennsylvania, over the Pocono Mountains (which are 1,970 feet above the level of the sea), and through the rich, fertile, and beautiful valleys of Northern New York. Among the principal points reached by the "Lackawanna" are Delaware Water Gap, Pa.; Scranton, Pa.; Binghamton, N. Y.; Norwich, N. Y.; Richfield Springs, N. Y.; Utica, N. Y.; Syracuse, N. Y.; Oswego, N. Y.; Owego, N. Y.; Ithaca, N. Y.; Waverly, N. Y.; Elmira, N. Y.; Corning, N. Y.; Bath, N. Y.; Dansville, N. Y.; and Buffalo, N. Y.

The **Morris and Essex Division** is noted for its beautiful scenery and sites for suburban residences.

New York City Ticket Office, 429 Broadway, corner of Howard St., where through tickets to all points West, Northwest, and Southwest can be obtained at **Lowest Rates.** Pullman Palace Car accommodations can be secured and baggage called for and checked through to destination.

W. F. HOLWILL, Gen. Pass. Agent, 26 Exchange Place, New York.
N. MULLER, Jr., Gen. Eastern Pass. Agent, 429 Broadway, New York.
HOWARD J. BALL, Gen. Western Pass. Agent, 11 Exchange St., Buffalo, N. Y.
W. C. BRAYTON, Gen. Agent, Pass. Department, Syracuse, N. Y.
W. B. MURRAY, Dis't Pass. Agent, 328 Lackawanna Avenue, Scranton, Pa.

THE newest, latest, and handsomest designed *Pullman Buffet Parlor and Buffet Sleeping Coaches* are attached to all through trains, and particular attention is called to the NEW PARLOR CARS of this Line, furnished as they are with Bay Window Seats, enabling passengers to view the beautiful scenery unobstructed. These cars are also furnished with large Sofas and Lounges, and the latest feature is introduced in the way of Library of the latest novels and standard works of the day for the free use of the patrons of the LACKAWANNA ROUTE.

NEW YORK STATIONS.

UP-TOWN STATION—Foot of Christopher Street. Accessible by Elevated Railroad trains on Ninth Avenue to Christopher Street, within two blocks of Station. Crosstown Street Railroad on Christopher Street connects the Lackawanna Station with the Ninth, Sixth, and Third Avenue Elevated Railways. Christopher Street is convenient to all the principal Up-town Hotels.

DOWN-TOWN STATION—Foot of Barclay Street. Accessible by Elevated Railroad Stations of Sixth Avenue Line at Park Place, and Ninth Avenue Line at Barclay Street, also by Street Cars on West Street. Barclay Street Station is on West Street, North River, convenient to all down-town Ferries, Sound and Ocean Steamers, and the wholesale district of New York.

WESTCOTT'S EXPRESS CO. have agents on all trains to arrange for conveyance of passengers and Baggage to Hotels, Residences, Steamers, Piers, and Railway Depots.

TAINTOR'S GUIDE-BOOKS

TAINTOR BROTHERS & CO., Publishers,
18 & 20 Astor Place, New York.

These Guides describe all Cities, Towns and Stations on the routes, giving items of interest to the traveler for business and pleasure, and are

ILLUSTRATED WITH MAPS AND WOODCUTS.

PRICE, 25 CENTS EACH, BY MAIL.

"**City of New York.**"—Containing descriptions of and directions for visiting the Public Buildings, Places of Amusement, Library, etc. A new Street Directory, Travelers' Directory, and a Map of New York, Brooklyn, Jersey City, Hoboken, etc.

"**Hudson River Route.**"—New York to West Point, Catskill Mountains, Albany, Troy, Saratoga Springs, Lake George, Lake Champlain, Adirondacks, Montreal and Quebec, via Hudson River Steamers.

"**Saratoga Illustrated.**"—The Visitors' Guide to Saratoga Springs, with maps and wood cuts.

"**Saratoga Mineral Waters.**"—Directions for their use by Dr. W. O. Stillman, of Saratoga Springs, N. Y.

Sea-Side Resorts.—A Hand-book for Health and Pleasure Seekers, for the Atlantic Coast from the St. Lawrence to the Mississippi.

"**The Northern Resorts.**"—Boston to the White Mountains, Lake Memphremagog, Green Mountains, Lake Champlain, Sheldon, Massena, Ogdensburgh, Montreal and Quebec.

"**The Pennsylvania Coal Regions.**"—New York and Philadelphia to Easton, Bethlehem, Delaware Water Gap, Mauch Chunk, Scranton, Harrisburg, Williamsport and Elmira.

"**The Erie Route.**"—New York to Ithaca, Watkins' Glen, Rochester, Dunkirk, Buffalo and Niagara Falls, via Erie Railway and branches.

"**New York to Saratoga, Buffalo and Niagara Falls.**"—Via Hudson River and New York Central R.R.

"**The Newport and Fall River Route.**"—New York to Boston, via Newport and Fall River. With descriptions of Newport and Narragansett Bay.

"**Connecticut River Route.**"—New York to the White Mountains, via N. Y. & N. H. and Connecticut River R.R.

"**New York to Philadelphia, Baltimore and Washington.**"

Published by TAINTOR BROTHERS & CO.,
18 and 20 Astor Place, New York.

THE AMERICAN,

BOSTON.

CENTRAL LOCATION.   PERFECT VENTILATION

UNEXCEPTIONABLE TABLE.

PARTICULARLY DESIRABLE

FOR FAMILIES AND SUMMER TOURISTS.

SIX STAIRWAYS FROM TOP TO BOTTOM.
With every security against fire.

Rooms with Meals, { **$3.00 PER DAY** and upwards. } According to Size and Location.

Rooms only. { **$1.00 PER DAY** and upwards. }

THE NEAREST FIRST CLASS HOTEL
TO NORTHERN AND EASTERN DEPOTS,

"It is one of the most attractive and best managed of New England Hotels."—*N. Y. Mail.*

HENRY B. RICE & CO.   *Hanover, near Washington St.*

AS THE QUIETEST
PROFESSIONAL AND BUSINESS MEN
Are as liable as any others to the thousand hazards of life, from morning till night, at home or abroad,

INSURE IN THE TRAVELERS
OF HARTFORD, CONN.

NEW YORK CENTRAL
AND
HUDSON RIVER RAILROAD.

THIS railroad system comprises what was formerly the Hudson River Railway, extending from New York to Albany and Troy, and the New York Central Railroad, having tracks from Albany to Buffalo and Niagara Falls.

The two companies consolidated in 1870, and since that time the growth of passenger and freight traffic has been continuous and rapid. An immense volume of business is now transacted in New York city in connection with these roads, which traverse the most interesting and most populous sections of the State.

The main line of the New York Central & Hudson River Railroad extends from New York city to Buffalo, 440 miles, traversing the eastern and middle portions of the Empire State from the Atlantic Ocean to Lake Erie. It is the only railroad, terminating at the harbor of New York, which reaches the Great Lakes over the territory of a single State, and is the only one having stations on Manhattan Island, or whose rails reach the waters of Long Island Sound. Leaving the Grand Central Station, in the center of the city of New York, it crosses the Harlem River on an iron bridge, follows that stream and Spuyten Duyvil Creek, which forms the northern boundary of Manhattan Island, until it reaches the Hudson, where it joins the original tracks extending along the river's bank to the heart of the business portion of the city, now used for freight trains and for local passenger travel south of Spuyten Duyvil. Having escaped from the boundaries of the metropolis at Yonkers, it traverses the eastern shore of the Hudson— through tunnels, mountains, and over bridges—past cities, towns, and

NEW YORK CENTRAL RAILROAD.

villages—never practically deviating from the dead level of tide flow along its margin, until it crosses the Hudson and enters the capital of the State, 142 miles from its point of departure. In addition to a double track throughout, the Hudson River Division has about 20 miles of third track and 76 miles of sidings.

Ferry connections are made at Tarrytown to Nyack; at Garrison's to West Point; at Fishkill to Newburgh; at Rhinebeck to Kingston, and to the Ulster & Delaware Railroad through the Catskills; at Tivoli to Saugerties; and at Catskill Station to the village of Catskill, where connections are made with the Catskill Mountain Railroad for the Catskill Mountain resorts.

At Dutchess Junction connections are made with the Newburgh, Dutchess & Connecticut Railroad; at Poughkeepsie, with the New York & Massachusetts Railroad; at Rhinebeck, with the Hartford & Connecticut Western Railroad; at Hudson, with the Hudson and Chatham Branch of the Boston & Albany Railroad, and at Albany, with the Boston & Albany Railroad and with the Delaware & Hudson Canal Co.'s Railroad. At Troy, six miles above Albany, it connects with the Hoosac Tunnel route into Massachusetts. Connections are also made at Troy with lines to Montreal and Canada; to Saratoga; to the Adirondacks, and through Vermont and New Hampshire to the White Mountains.

At Albany the line turns almost due west, and follows the natural route of communication between the Hudson and Lake Erie. The only heavy grade, and that insignificant when compared with those on other trunk lines, occurs between Albany and Schenectady, where the Mohawk and Hudson found it necessary to commence operations with inclined planes, but this is soon overcome, and the valley of the Mohawk is reached at Schenectady. This river is followed for 92 miles to near Rome, and there it is deserted for the waters of Oneida Lake, and at Syracuse, 38 miles further, Onondaga Lake is touched. Both of these lakes are drained into Lake Ontario by the Oswego River.

Skirting the Seneca River and its tributaries, which drain Seneca, Cayuga. Owasco, and Skaneateles lakes into the Oswego River, the line reaches Rochester, on the Genesee River, near Lake Ontario, 81 miles from Syracuse. The mountain range which bars the continent from near the Canadian border down to the waters of the Gulf of Mexico, and which is such a serious barrier to every other line of railroad connecting the Atlantic seaboard with the Mississippi Valley, is passed at Little Falls station, midway between Albany and Syracuse, where the Mohawk flows through a natural break in the chain.

From Rochester the main line runs direct to Buffalo, 90 miles distant, while a second line runs, by way of Lockport, to Niagara Falls and Suspension Bridge, connecting there with the Canada railroads, and thence to Buffalo. Between Albany and Buffalo there are four tracks on the main line, and most of the branches have double tracks. At Buffalo the New York Central & Hudson River Railroad unites with the Lake Shore & Michigan Southern, the central link in the Vanderbilt system—which runs through Pennsylvania, Ohio, and Indiana, with branches penetrating all portions of Central and Southern Michigan, to Chicago, Illinois.

At Cleveland, the Lake Shore line connects with the Cleveland, Columbus, Cincinnati & Indianapolis Railway, the Indianapolis & St. Louis Railway, and the Dayton & Union Railroad, which, united under the popular title of the "Bee Line," form the southwestern extension of the Vanderbilt System, reaching all the cities named, and, by connections, every portion of the Mississippi Valley. At Dunkirk, the Dunkirk, Alleghany Valley & Pittsburg Railroad, one of the lines leased by the New York Central & Hudson River Railroad Company, connects with the Lake Shore Railroad.

Connection is also made at Buffalo with the Michigan Central Railroad—another link in the Vanderbilt System, which traverses the Dominion of Canada for 226 miles ; crosses into the State of Michigan at Detroit ; extends northward to the Straits of Mackinac, which unite Lakes Huron and Michigan ; throws out branches to Toledo, in Ohio, and to most of the important towns in Michigan, and continues on to Chicago and Joliet in Illinois.

Minor branch lines of the New York Central & Hudson River Railroad Company are intersected between Albany and Buffalo as follows : Geneva to Lyons, connecting the Auburn and the main lines ; Rochester to Charlotte, on Lake Ontario ; Rochester to Buffalo, via Batavia; Rochester to Canandaigua, connecting with the Northern Central Railroad of the Pennsylvania System ; Batavia to Attica ; Lockport to Tonawanda ; and Suspension Bridge to Lewiston, a port on Lake Ontario.

Along the entire New York Central & Hudson Railroad route, the roadway is substantially constructed. The cars are well equipped, arrangements for public comfort and convenience excellent, and a disposition is evinced by the company at all times to keep pace with requirements.

The New York Central & Hudson River Railroad Company is also the lessee of the West Shore Route, including the "Pacific Express," the "Day Express," and the "Chicago & St. Louis Limited," between New York and Chicago. Boats connecting with the trains start from the foot of Jay Street, North River, and foot of West Forty-second Street, New York. Two of the three trains above referred to stop at West Haverstraw, Cranston's, West Point, Cornwall, Newburgh, Poughkeepsie, Kingston, and Albany, on the Hudson also at other important points, including Rochester and Buffalo.

NEW YORK.

The **Grand Central Depot**, or starting-point for passenger trains on the New York Central & Hudson River Railroad, the Harlem Railroad, and the New York & New Haven Railroad, stands on East Forty-second Street, facing Fourth Avenue. It is one of the largest and most complete structures of the kind in the world, including, as it does, ample office accommodation for administrative purposes, in addition to the usual and ordinary station facilities intended for the convenience and comfort of travelers, who are constantly arriving and departing at all hours of the day and night.

Approaches. Elevated Roads. Trains on the Third Avenue Elevated Road run direct to and from the Grand Central Station. A change of cars is required at junction of the East Forty-second Street branch and main line, at Third Avenue and East Forty-second Street.

Passengers on the Sixth or Ninth Avenue Elevated Roads leave trains at the Forty-second Street station, and reach the Grand Central by cross-town cars or cabs running east on Forty-second Street. The distance can be walked comfortably from Ninth Avenue in fifteen minutes, and from Sixth Avenue in five minutes.

Surface Roads. Fourth and Madison Avenue cars pass the station every few minutes. Forty-second Street cross town cars, and Boulevard line of cars, arrive frequently.

Broadway, Avenue A, Second, Third, Sixth, Seventh, Eighth, and

GRAND CENTRAL DEPOT. Fourth Avenue and 42d Street, New York.

NEW YORK CENTRAL RAILROAD.

Ninth Avenue cars cross Forty-second Street at intervals not exceeding five minutes. The West Side Belt Line crosses Forty-second Street at Tenth Avenue.

Stages. Fifth Avenue stages cross Forty-second Street at short intervals, one block from Grand Central Depot.

Cabs and Carriages. These can be obtained, by order, at any hotel or restaurant. Special rates are made to and from the Grand Central Depot. The usual charges are: For two-seated cabs or hansoms, first mile, 50 cents; for each succeeding mile or any fraction of a mile, 25 cents. For four-seated cabs, first mile, 75 cents; for each succeeding mile or any fraction of a mile, 50 cents. For the use of a cab by the hour, whether for one or more passengers, or whether two-seated or four-seated. $1.00 per hour, and 25 cents for each 15 minutes thereafter, including stops. A charge of 25 cents for each 15 minutes or fraction thereof over 5 minutes is made when cabs are hired by distance. Baggage is carried at 25 cents for each trunk or large portmanteau, and 10 cents for each smaller bundle. In all cases where the hiring of a carriage is not at the time thereof specified to be by the day or hour, it shall be deemed to be by the mile. Whenever a hackney coach or carriage shall be detained, excepting as aforesaid, the owner or driver shall be allowed after the rate of 75 cents an hour.

Waiting-Rooms. Passenger waiting-rooms extend, on the left or west side of the building, from Forty-second Street along Vanderbilt Avenue, each road having separate spaces set apart within the building.

Baggage. The baggage room of the New York Central & Hudson Railroad is at the north end of the station on Vanderbilt Avenue, north of the waiting-rooms, through which a connecting passageway runs to facilitate the checking of trunks after tickets have been secured at the adjacent booking-offices. Outgoing baggage can be checked from hotel or residence by express companies, any of which can be called up by telephone.

One hundred and fifty pounds of baggage will be checked free on each full-rate, regular, or summer excursion ticket on the New York Central & Hudson River Railroad. Seventy-five pounds are allowed on each half-rate ticket.

To ensure forwarding of baggage on same trains by which passage is

INTERIOR VIEW OF GRAND CENTRAL DEPOT.

NEW YORK CENTRAL RAILROAD.

taken, passengers should be at the station at least ten minutes before advertised time for departure of trains, as it is necessary to present passage tickets to the baggage master for checking of baggage.

Tickets. To avoid confusion and disappointment, those who desire to travel in Wagner palace cars or on one of the Wagner vestibuled limited trains must make arrangements to secure accommodation a few hours before the time of starting. The less there remains to be done after arrival at the station, the greater the peace of mind and comfort of the traveler.

Palace Cars. The drawing-room and sleeping-car service of the New York Central and Hudson River Railroad and connecting roads has been entirely reorganized within the past few years. The method of construction secures absolute comfort to the occupants. The cars are elegantly finished and luxuriously appointed.

Vestibule Limited Trains. Each vestibuled train is composed of a buffet, smoking, and library car, two parlor cars, two sleeping-cars, and a dining-car, all of which are united into one continuous covered train by the construction of connecting vestibules upon the platforms. In the smoking and library car are a buffet, movable chairs, and couches tastefully and comfortably upholstered, a secretary supplied with stationery and writing material, and an enclosed reading-room with a well-stocked library, including current newspapers and magazines. A bathroom and an apartment for a "tonsorial artist" are among the latest improvements.

NEW YORK CENTRAL AND HUDSON RIVER RAILROAD.

USEFUL INFORMATION FOR PASSENGERS.

1. Purchase tickets at the ticket office before entering the train. When cash fares are paid on trains, conductors are required to collect an amount in excess of the regular tariff fare.

2. Children between the ages of five and twelve years are charged half fare ; those over twelve, full fare. Children under five, in charge of other passengers, will be carried without tickets.

3. Stop-over will be allowed on all regular full-rate local tickets reading between any two stations on the New York Central and Hudson River Railroad on notice to conductor.

NEW YORK CENTRAL RAILROAD.

4. Round trip limited tickets, unless otherwise specified, are limited going to continuous passage on date of sale; and must be used within the limit prescribed for return passage.

5. Limited tickets to Detroit, Cleveland, Chicago, Cincinnati, St. Louis, etc., are good only for continuous passage on date and train indicated thereon.

6. One hundred and fifty pounds of personal baggage will be checked free on each full ticket, and seventy-five pounds on each half ticket. A reasonable charge will be made for all in excess of that weight.

7. To ensure the forwarding of baggage on same trains by which passage is taken, passengers should be at the station at least ten minutes before advertised time for departure of trains, as it is necessary to present passage ticket to station baggage-masters when baggage is checked.

8. If, upon reaching destination, baggage is not removed from the baggage-room within twenty-four hours, after that time storage will be charged at the rate of twenty-five cents for the first succeeding twenty-four hours, and thereafter ten cents per day until five days have elapsed. If baggage is still unclaimed at the end of that time the rate will be fifty cents per month.

9. Messengers of Westcott Express Co. are on all trains to arrange for the prompt transfer of passengers and baggage to any part of New York, Brooklyn, Jersey City, or Hoboken. Delivery of New York baggage is made from either the 138th Street Station or the Grand Central Station, as requested by passengers. Similar arrangements have been made with C. W. Miller's Transfer Co. for the transfer of passengers and baggage to hotels, residences and depots in Buffalo and Niagara Falls.

10. Package-rooms for the reception of parcels, hand-baggage, etc., will be found in passenger waiting-rooms at Grand Central and Annex Stations, New York, and at Albany, Schenectady, Utica, Syracuse, Rochester, Buffalo, Niagara Falls and Suspension Bridge—under charge of an authorized agent who will issue checks for packages at a nominal rate.

11. The restaurants along the New York Central at Poughkeepsie, Albany, Syracuse and Buffalo, conducted by Johnston Bros., are among the finest and best managed railway restaurants in the East. Moderate charges only are authorized, and prices are posted for the information of the public.

NEW YORK CENTRAL RAILROAD.

SPECIAL INFORMATION FOR TOURISTS.

The special tickets described herein will be sold from June 1st to September 30th, inclusive, and will be available until October 31st, inclusive (except in the case of steamboats or stages that discontinue their trips earlier). The tickets entitle holders to all the privileges of regular first-class tickets.

Children between 5 and 12 years of age, half fare; over 12, full fare.

Stop-over privileges are usually granted on summer tourist tickets; but, to avoid misunderstanding, passengers should notify the proper official of the train or boat of their desire to stop over, as the stop-over regulations of the various lines vary.

Summer excursion tickets during the season will be received for passage on the New York, Chicago & St. Louis Limited, when presented in connection with extra fare tickets, in the case of through tickets from the West; or without extra fare tickets between New York State points, provided the drawing-room or sleeping-car tickets are presented in connection with the summer excursion tickets.

Summer excursion tickets will be available on the New York & Saratoga Limited if presented in connection with drawing-room-car tickets, as no ordinary coaches will be run on the limited trains.

Through tickets by the New York Central & Hudson River Railroad are available between New York and Albany by the Day Line steamers, or all rail, at the option of passengers.

Tickets reading by the Delaware & Hudson Railroad to or from points north of Plattsburg will be accepted for passage between Plattsburg and Fort Ticonderoga, on Lake Champlain steamers, and permit the holder to remain over at Port Kent, thus affording holders an opportunity to visit Au Sable Chasm.

Tickets reading via Glen Falls and Lake George stages, between Lake George and Caldwell, in either direction, will be accepted for passage on the Delaware & Hudson Railroad between the same points.

Tickets to points on the Fall Brook Coal Co.'s R. R., reading to Geneva via Lyons, will be good from the East via Auburn, and from the West via Canandaigua, if desired, without extra charge.

Tickets between Cooperstown and Richfield Springs by the Otsego Lake steamer and stage are for passage only; baggage will be charged extra.

NEW YORK CENTRAL RAILROAD.

Tickets reading by the Grand Trunk or Canadian Pacific Railway, of steamer, between Toronto and Kingston, Kingston and Prescott, Prescott and Montreal, or Montreal and Quebec, are valid either by rail or by the steamers of the Richelieu & Ontario Navigation Company, at the option of passengers.

On tickets reading over Richelieu & Ontario Navigation Company's steamers, meals and berths are extra.

Tickets by Sound Line steamers, between New York and Boston, include a berth.

Summer tourists are reminded that many of the steamers and stage lines cease operations or make irregular trips after October 1st of each year. Passengers should consult local advertising matter for proper information.

"The tourist whose point of departure is the Grand Central Station in the city of New York," writes the author of "The World-famed Hudson," "possesses advantages which are unequaled in this country, and probably in the world. No matter what the motive of his journey may be—whether he be in search of health, recreation, social enjoyment, or all combined, he is able from this point to carry out his plans at a minimum expenditure of time, trouble, and money.

*   *   *   *   *

"Does he long for the combined beauties of hill and dale, mountain and stream? He finds them all at the very outset of his journey, as he is borne along the banks of the world-famed Hudson. Does he find a peaceful enjoyment in the silence of pathless forests, or in floating upon the bosom of placid lakes? If so, the wilds of northern New York will fill the cup of his desire to overflowing. Is he charmed by the majestic grandeur of lofty mountains and deep gorges? Let hi.n hasten to the Adirondacks or the Catskill Mountains. Is he a disciple of Nimrod or Isaak Walton? The North Woods and the St. Lawrence will give him a joyful greeting. Does he seek social intercourse and renewed vigor, or is he an invalid in quest of restored health amid peaceful and attractive surroundings? Saratoga, Richfield, and Sharon throw wide their portals and bid him enter."

NEW YORK CENTRAL AND HUDSON RIVER RAILROAD.

NEW YORK CENTRAL RAILROAD.

BETWEEN GRAND CENT. DEPOT OR THIRTIETH ST. AND	RATES FOR REGULAR TICKETS.			COMMUTATION RATES.												
	Single Trip Tickets (Good until Used)	Strip Tickets, Good Either Way, Limited to 3 Months.	4 Books with 624 Coupons Covering One Year.	Books of 52 Coupons, Good for One Month.									Books of 156 Coupons, Good for 3 Months.			
				1st Month.	2d Month.	3d Month.	4th Month.	5th Month.	6th Month.	7th Month.	8th Month.	9th Month.	10th, 11th and 12th Mos. ea.	1st (quarter)	2d (quarter)	3d (quarter)	4th (quarter)
Spuyten Duyvil	0.22	T'k's 3.60	$ 50.00	6.85	6.55	6.30	5.95	5.70	5.15	4.55	4.00	3.40	2.85	16.95	14.85	12.30	9.00
Riverdale	.24	4.00	52.00	7.20	6.90	6.60	6.20	6.00	5.40	4.80	4.20	3.60	3.00	17.60	15.40	12.65	9.35
Mt. St. Vincent	.26	5.00	54.00	7.55	7.25	6.90	6.60	6.30	5.70	5.05	4.40	3.80	3.15	18.25	15.95	13.10	9.70
Ludlow	.28	5.00	58.00	7.90	7.60	7.25	6.95	6.60	5.95	5.30	4.60	3.95	3.30	19.50	17.10	14.00	10.40
Yonkers	.30	5.00	58.00	7.90	7.60	7.25	6.95	6.60	5.95	5.30	4.60	3.95	3.30	19.50	17.10	14.00	10.40
Glenwood	.30	5.00	60.00	8.25	7.95	7.60	7.25	6.90	6.30	5.50	4.85	4.15	3.45	20.50	17.90	14.70	10.90
Hastings	.38	4.50	65.00	8.30	7.95	7.60	7.25	6.90	6.30	5.50	4.85	4.15	3.45	20.50	17.90	14.70	10.90
Dobb's Ferry	.40	4.90	68.00	9.00	8.65	8.25	7.85	7.50	6.75	6.00	5.25	4.50	3.75	22.10	19.30	15.85	11.75
Irvington	.44	5.25	72.00	9.75	9.20	8.90	8.50	8.10	7.30	6.50	5.65	4.85	4.05	23.05	20.15	16.55	12.25
Tarrytown	.50	6.00	75.00	10.10	9.50	9.25	8.80	8.40	7.55	6.70	5.90	5.05	4.20	24.30	21.20	17.30	12.90
Scarborough	.58	6.75	80.00	10.50	10.35	9.90	9.45	9.00	8.10	7.20	6.30	5.40	4.50	25.30	22.10	18.15	13.45
Sing Sing	.65	7.50	80.00	10.80	10.35	9.90	9.45	9.00	8.10	7.20	6.30	5.40	4.50	26.10	22.80	19.30	14.30
Croton	.68	8.25	85.00	11.15	10.70	10.35	9.75	9.30	8.35	7.45	6.50	5.55	4.65	26.90	23.50	19.30	14.30
Oscawana	.72	9.00	87.00	11.50	11.05	10.55	10.10	9.60	8.65	7.70	6.70	5.75	4.80	28.80	25.75	20.70	15.30
Cruger's	.74	9.00	90.00	11.90	11.40	10.90	10.40	9.90	8.90	7.90	6.95	5.90	4.95	29.45	25.75	21.15	15.65
Montrose	.76	9.75	95.00	12.60	12.10	11.55	11.00	10.50	9.45	8.40	7.35	6.30	5.25	30.40	26.40	21.85	16.15
Peekskill	.82	10.30	100.00	13.35	12.75	12.20	11.65	11.10	10.00	8.90	7.75	6.65	5.55	32.00	28.00	23.00	17.00
West P't or C'n	.98	11.25	105.00	14.05	13.45	12.85	12.30	11.70	10.55	9.35	8.20	7.00	5.85	34.25	29.95	24.60	18.90
Garrison's	.98	11.25	105.00	14.05	13.45	12.85	12.30	11.70	10.55	9.35	8.20	7.00	5.85	35.50	31.10	25.55	18.85
Highlands	.90	11.25	102.00	13.70	13.10	12.55	11.95	11.40	10.25	9.10	8.00	6.85	5.70	34.55	30.25	24.85	18.35

NEW YORK CENTRAL RAILROAD.

The Start. Tourists, gladdened by anticipations of a journey full of pleasant incidents and experiences, and feeling perfectly at ease in all matters relating to their personal comfort and safety, rejoice, in a more or less demonstrative fashion, as they emerge from under the lofty glass roofing of the Grand Central Station, now fairly on their way to visit, perhaps for the first time, scenes rendered famous by important historical events and widely-credited traditions.

125TH STREET. For more than four miles the tracks of the New York Central & Hudson River Railroad run through a straight cutting along Fourth Avenue, between the blocks of city residences, extending northward from Forty-second Street to the Harlem River. The first station reached is used for the convenience of uptown residents. Many who are engaged commercially each day in New York city reside in or near Harlem, a district within easy reach from the business center of the metropolis. Crossing the Harlem River a quarter of a mile above, on one of the most substantial iron bridges in the country, a short distance to the right of which may be seen a handsomely constructed passenger bridge, we arrive at—

138TH STREET. Demand for greater accommodation in this neighborhood, as well as a desire on the part of the railway authorities to encourage residence in the northern suburbs, brought about the erection of a perfectly-appointed station at this point. The building has an imposing appearance, and is considered one of the most elegant and commodious way-stations in the United States. The exterior is of brick and terra cotta, with red Akron tile roof. All fast express trains, excepting the "New York & Chicago Limited," stop here for the service of New York passengers to and from the North and West. It is the most convenient station for passengers going to Mott Haven, Morrisania, and vicinity.

Proceeding through Mott Haven, leaving the Harlem Railroad line on the right, the cars run in a northwesterly direction until a point is reached, nine miles from City Hall, where the New York City & Northern Railroad bridge crosses the Harlem River. The tracks of this road run thence on the right of the New York Central & Hudson River Railroad to Kingsbridge, where the former road separates and proceeds in a northerly direction. Passing under this structure, the train runs north along the right bank of the river to—

HIGH BRIDGE. The bridge, on the left of the station, is 1,450 feet in length and 124 feet high. It is built of granite and cost $900,000. Fourteen piers are used as supports. By means of this bridge the Croton Aqueduct extends across the Harlem River to High Bridge Park Reservoir, thus supplying New York city with water for domestic purposes. It is distant eleven miles from the most southern point of Manhattan Island. Above the bridge is a costly high-service reservoir. The adjacent shores are lofty and well-wooded, forming many picturesque scenes, peculiarly attractive to all admirers of the beautiful in nature. Passing through Highbridgeville and keeping close to the eastern shore of the Harlem River, the next station reached is—

MORRIS DOCK. A station around which a pretty suburban village is rapidly springing up. Thence, having the healthy and growing districts of Tremont, Adamsville, and Fordham on the right, the train proceeds to—

KINGSBRIDGE. At Kingsbridge redoubts were thrown up on both sides of the creek during the Revolutionary War, and on December 19, 1780, an encounter took place between the Americans and a large detachment of British and Hessians, which led to no decisive result. Another skirmish occurred here in 1776, between a party of American stragglers and a Hessian guard, in which the former gained the advantage. Prior to these events, Hendrick Hudson and the Manhattan Indians had a long-sustained fight just at the mouth of the creek, where Hudson anchored the "Half-Moon" in October, 1609. The Indians tried to board the yacht from their canoes, but were repulsed. In the distance, beyond the aqueduct to the right of the station, is Jerome Park, well-known to all sportsmen as an excellent racecourse—one of the best in the country, and yearly becoming more popular among patrons of the turf. After leaving Kingsbridge, the New York Central & Hudson River Railroad rounds a curve, passing on the right of Spuyten Duyvil Creek, thence running across to—

SPUYTEN DUYVIL, on the east bank of the Hudson River, in New York city and county, 12 miles from New York. The cluster of houses on the upper side of the creek and northward bears the name which was originally applied only to the creek itself, which connects Harlem River with the Hudson, thereby forming Manhattan Island. There are fine residences to the north on the heights.

THE HUDSON RIVER.

Among the thousand streams which drain the great Atlantic slope of North America, none is more attractive than the noble river at whose mouth stands the Empire City of the Western World. The European visiting America can have no better introduction to the Western Continent than that which is afforded by a voyage up the Hudson or a journey by rail along its banks; and travelers generally will find that the river and its neighborhood form naturally the first stage of any extended pleasure-tour through the Northern and Eastern States.

Scenery so charming as that of this beautiful river affords a delightful change from the glaring walls and pavements of New York. Before the limits of the metropolis are passed, the eye is charmed by the green wooded hills of Westchester County on the one hand, and by the frowning precipices of the Palisades on the other,—a contrast the like of which is not found so near any other of the world's great capitals.

For twenty miles this mighty dyke of basaltic trap-rock shuts off the western sky, then suddenly disappears, and the view opens upon the rolling hills of Rockland County and the blue outline of the distant Ramapo Mountains; while on the east bank are thriving towns and elegant country seats in almost continuous succession. Here, too, the river widens to the dimensions of a lake, which stretches its beautiful expanse nearly to the magnificent southern portal of the Highlands; when it suddenly contracts to a channel half a mile in width, overhung by the rugged crags of the Donderberg and Anthony's Nose.

For a score of miles above, the river winds amid the grand and rugged mountains of "The Highlands," at whose northern limit another portal opens, through which the traveler is borne to new scenes of beauty stretching far beyond. Above the Highlands the banks continue high and in some places precipitous, opening now and then as if to afford glimpses of the charming country on either side, until some thirty miles more have been passed, when the banks become still less abrupt, and the lofty range of the Catskill Mountains is seen to the westward.

The remote sources of the Hudson are among the highest peaks of

NEW YORK CENTRAL RAILROAD.

the Adirondack Mountains, 4,000 feet above tidewater. Its numerous upper branches unite in the neighborhood of Fort Edward, 180 miles from the ocean, and thence the river follows a southerly course, broken by numerous falls and rapids, to Troy, where it meets tidewater. The principal tributaries are the Mohawk and Hoosick rivers, the former rising in the central part of New York, and the latter in southern Vermont, both joining the Hudson near Troy, below which city the tributaries, though numerous, are small, none of them being navigable for more than two miles.

The mountain-ranges through or near which the Hudson passes are part of the Appalachian system. The Highlands are a continuation of the Blue Ridge, which, after crossing Pennsylvania and New York, ends in the Green Mountains of Vermont and New Hampshire. The Catsbergs and Hilderbergs are continuations of the westward ranges of the Alleghanies. The mean rise and fall of the tide at New York is about five feet, and at Albany two and a half feet.

The commerce of the Hudson River, during the season when it is not obstructed by ice, is extensive and constantly increasing. It is the natural outlet for lumber from the vast forests of the North. This is floated down the main stream and its branches during the high water of early spring, and several millions of feet are every year brought to market in this manner.

The Delaware & Hudson Canal brings vast quantities of coal from Pennsylvania, and keeps numerous barges constantly plying between its junction with the river at Rondout and the various cities reached by water from that point. The Erie Canal, connecting the Great Lakes with the ocean, through the Hudson River, affords means of transportation for Western produce, and for the manufactured goods of the East. The immense " tows " of canal boats ascending and descending the river form an important and interesting feature of its commercial life. Quarries of various kinds of stone, valuable for building, paving, flagging, etc., are found at various points on and near the river; and in Ulster County, water limestone, making the best cement, is found in inexhaustible quantities.

In the vicinity of Haverstraw are extensive beds of clay which give employment to thousands of brickmakers, whose kilns are seen for miles along the river bank. Manufactories, foundries, machine-shops, shipyards, and agricultural products unite to swell the numbers of every sort of vessel suitable for navigating these waters, and the fisheries afford employment to many men. During the winter, many thousand tons of ice are stored for domestic use and for exportation.

In history the river assumes a prominent place in the annals of the country. In September, 1609, when Hendrick Hudson sailed through the Narrows, and anchored his vessel, the "Half-Moon," in New York Bay, the shores were covered with a magnificent forest, unbroken save by natural meadows or by the villages of Indians.

The beautiful bay and river, now one of the busiest scenes of commercial activity in the world, were without signs of human life, except the few canoes of the natives; and Manhattan Island, with its dense population of a million souls, its splendid streets and buildings, and its proud commercial position as the Metropolis of the Western Continent, was a hilly, thickly-wooded island, inhabited by a fierce and warlike race of savages.

Hendrick Hudson was sent out by the Dutch East India Company to search for a northwest passage to India, a problem which tempts explorers even in our own day; and when he looked up the long line of the Palisades, and noted the strong ebb and flow of the tidal currents at the mouth of the river, he thought his object was gained. Accordingly he sailed up the river, viewing, with wonder and delight, the magnificent scenery, and observing the natural wealth of the country, until, on September 21, having reached the present site of Albany, he became convinced that he was following a river, and not a strait.

He was everywhere received with great friendliness by the Indians; but, when returning to the ocean, Hudson's mate shot an Indian for stealing, which caused an immediate collision, and several natives were killed. Hudson returned to Europe, and, in consequence of his reports, trading vessels were soon sent out, and after a few years of traffic in furs, a settlement was made in 1614, on the southern point of Manhattan Island.

During the Revolutionary War the Hudson was the scene of constant activity on the part of both armies. Washington early perceived the strategic importance of the river and its dependencies, and used every means to retain possession. The British, however, in 1776, wrested Manhattan Island from our then inexperienced troops, and retained it during the war. They were unable to effect a permanent lodgment above the island, although they made several successful raids up the river, once as far as Kingston. Fortifications were erected at various commanding points along the river.

The influence which this river has exerted and continues to exert upon the material prosperity of the country is incalculable. New York city undoubtedly owes much of its rapid growth to its position at the mouth of the Hudson River. In the early history of the country, before the railway, navigable bays and rivers were the most important thoroughfares of trade and communication between different sections of the country ; and even now, after the invention of the locomotive, so great are the advantages which such a stream presents to commerce and various industrial interests, that its importance cannot be overshadowed even by the railways. In connection with a splendid system of canals, it affords an immense stretch of inland navigation.

The river itself is navigated by the largest vessels as far as Athens, which is about 117 miles from New York, and about 125 miles from its mouth at the Narrows. Steamboats and schooners ascend to Troy, at the head of tidewater, about 151 miles above New York. Its entire length is something over 300 miles.

As a commercial channel the importance of the Hudson is not excelled by any river of equal length in America. Probably a thousand vessels ply its waters, engaged in the various branches of commerce. The passenger steamboats on the river are numerous. Some of them are of great size, and rank among the finest water-craft in the world.

The name Spuyten Duyvil is ascribed by the veracious Diedrich Knickerbocker (Washington Irving) to Anthony Van Corlear, the redoubtable Dutch trumpeter, who, being bound on an important mission to the mainland, and finding himself unable to procure a boat, swore that "en spuyt den duyvil" he would swim the creek. He plunged in, and when midway across was observed to struggle violently, until, no longer able to resist the duyvil, who was doubtless tugging at his legs, he raised the trumpet to his lips, gave a loud blast and sank forever to the bottom. Opposite Spuyten Duyvil, on the west shore, is Lydecker Peak, one of the highest points of the Palisades. Upon this peak previously stood the magnificent Palisades Mountain House, in full view of the railroad and river. It was one of the finest summer hotels on the Hudson, but was burned on July 3, 1884.

NEW YORK CENTRAL RAILROAD.

In addition to the service of the New York Central & Hudson River Railroad for passengers and freight from the Grand Central Station on East Forty-second Street, New York city, a line, formerly used for general traffic, runs from the freight depot at Thirtieth Street, New York, along Eleventh and Twelfth Avenues, past Riverside Park and along the Hudson River to Spuyten Duyvil. This line is utilized for local passenger traffic, the transportation of emigrants, and the carriage of heavy freight. There are several stations on this line worthy of mention. The first is—

MANHATTANVILLE, New York city and county, 8 miles from City Hall, New York. The name is applied to the neighborhood of One Hundred and Thirty-second Street. The conspicuous building on high ground, a little south of Manhattanville, is the Bloomingdale Insane Asylum, surrounded by about forty acres of ornamental grounds, which are devoted to the use of the inmates. Nearer the river is the Claremont Hotel, where in former years lived Viscount Courtenay, afterwards Earl of Devon. Joseph Bonaparte occupied the house during the first year of his exile in this country. It is now a popular resort for frequenters of the Riverside Drive and Park. The tomb of General U. S. Grant is in Riverside Park, south of Claremont House. Within five minutes' ride of this station, and at the foot of One Hundred and Fifty-second Street is—

CARMANSVILLE, New York city and county, 9 miles from City Hall, New York. In the neighborhood is Trinity Cemetery, Audubon Park (formerly the residence of the late celebrated naturalist), and the New York Institution for the Deaf and Dumb, one of the finest institutions of the kind in the world. On the opposite side of the river, the bank for many miles is formed by the Palisades, a precipitous, rocky cliff of trap-dike formation, from 300 to 500 feet in height. Geologists suppose that ages ago the crust of the earth was ruptured by some cause in the line of this dike, and volcanic matters protruded from below, which, being harder and more durable than the adjacent rocks, have better withstood the slow but constant action of the elements during almost inconceivably long periods of time, but of which the enclosing walls on the east have been removed, leaving the present abrupt precipice.

The next station we come to on our way to Spuyten Duyvil via the eastern shore of the Hudson is—

NEW YORK CENTRAL RAILROAD.

FORT WASHINGTON, New York city and county, 10 miles from City Hall, New York. This extreme northern portion is the most beautiful part of Manhattan Island, and its natural beauties are finely brought out by the good taste and lavish expenditures of the wealthy residents. Splendid river views, rocks, forest trees, winding roads among elegant mansions having beautiful gardens, conservatories, and other attractive and costly surroundings, make it a valuable addition to the Central Park for drives and strolls.

The grading and leveling of city engineers has not yet reached this charming region, although it is penetrated by streets in every direction. The fortification after which this place was named was an extensive earthwork occupying the crown of Washington Heights, and commanding the river above and below, as well as the neighboring country. It formed the end and citadel of an irregular line of works extending along the northern part of the island. The point extending into the river under Washington Heights is Jeffrey's Hook, and among its cedars are mounds which mark the site of a redoubt built at the same time with the neighboring fortifications. These works, with their garrison of 2,700 men, were captured by the British after a sharp resistance, on November 15, 1776. This was the second defeat of the Americans in New York, and was a severe blow to the friends of the republic in this vicinity.

Directly opposite, on the western shore of the Hudson, stands—

* **FORT LEE,** Hudson County, New Jersey,—a village so called because on its site stood, during the last century, a fort bearing that name. The remains of the fort are scarcely discernible, and cannot be seen at all from the river. This fort was occupied by the Americans until after the British had captured Fort Washington in 1776, when it also was abandoned, and the Americans retreated across the State of New Jersey.

The large white building with two towers, standing in the gorge at the beginning of the Palisades, is the Fort Lee Park Hotel. The large octagon building at the base of the hill is a Pavilion.

" From the summit of the Palisades a magnificent view is obtained. High up upon the crest of the great escarpment one may stand, and look far away into the west, and see the most glorious sunsets that ever changed the sky to gold or fire. To the north lie the Highlands we

---

Places marked with a star (*) are on the west side of the Hudson River.

THE PALISADES.

are soon to pass, stretched out in noblest panorama for our view, and to the south the river flows on in a broader stream, until on the eastern side the city of New York begins and the stream changes its aspect, and passes between the crowded shores that send out across it the noisy thunder of their busy life ; and Palisades, and rocky hills, and long reaches of still stream, and green pleasant banks, make a sudden end as the Hudson sweeps grandly and quietly down to the sea."

INWOOD, city and county of New York, 12 miles from City Hall. The former name of this station was "Tubby Hook." It is surrounded with charming villas and picturesque meandering drives.

Having viewed the route to Spuyten Duyvil from the Grand Central Depot *via* Harlem, and taken a brief survey of localities along the old Hudson River line by way of Manhattanville and Fort Washington, we are now at liberty to note the many interesting scenes, historical, legendary, and picturesque, on either bank of that world-famed stream, from the spot near which Anthony the Trumpeter had such a direful experience with " Old Nick," to the lofty Helderberg mountains near Albany, and the council-ground of the Mohegans.

* **The Palisades** are from 250 to 550 feet high, stretching along the west shore of the Hudson from Hoboken to Piermont, with a continuation along the Tappan Zee to Haverstraw and Point No Point. They form an unbroken wall of columnar trap rock, thickly wooded at the summit, and giving a wild, desolate appearance to the locality. One and a half miles north of Spuyten Duyvil station is—

RIVERDALE, in New York city and county, 14 miles from City Hall. This village is composed almost entirely of handsome country residences, the property of New York merchants. It is delightfully located, healthy, and desirable in every way as a rural retreat.

MOUNT ST. VINCENT, a Roman Catholic educational institution, under the immediate control of the Sisters of Charity, who purchased Font Hill, as the place was called, from the celebrated tragedian, Edwin Forrest. The castellated structure of dark stone, built by Forrest as a private residence, is now a part of the Mount St. Vincent Academy, though, unfortunately, the two buildings are architecturally inharmonious. These buildings are at the northern-most limit of the city of New York.

NEW YORK CENTRAL RAILROAD.

Directly across the Hudson from Mount St. Vincent may be seen—

* **INDIAN HEAD**, the highest point of the Palisades, 550 feet above the river. On the same side as Indian Head is the—

* **TAPPAN ZEE**, or Tappan Bay, a "beautiful lake-like widening" of the river, ten miles long and from two to five miles wide. Many legends are related among the country people—even to this day—concerning Tappan Zee. Washington Irving tells the story of a " roystering Dutchman of Spiting Devil," who went out alone in his boat on the bay, spending the whole of one Saturday in going its entire length, after which exploit he attended a quilting party at Kakiat. It was midnight when the frolic ended, and the Dutchman was warned not to enter his boat on Sunday. He was obstinate, however, and swore he'd cross the bay at all hazards. " He was never seen afterwards, but may be heard plying his oars, as above mentioned, being the Flying Dutchman of the Tappan Sea, doomed to ply between Kakiat and Spiting Devil until the day of judgment."

It must not be forgotten that the reader is traveling along the New York Central & Hudson River Railroad on the eastern shore of the Hudson River, brief sketches of points on the opposite side of the river being introduced in order that the panoramic view may be complete. Three miles north of Mount St. Vincent is the thriving town of—

YONKERS, Westchester County, N. Y., 17 miles from New York. Built on a number of hills overlooking the river, it has, since its incorporation in 1855, prospered beyond even the most sanguine expectations of its founders. The population is estimated at 26,000, consisting largely of New York city business men and their families. Gas and water works have been established. An efficient police department has been working for some time. Telegraphic connection is maintained between the police headquarters here and in New York. There are a number of important manufactures carried on within the town limits, including the production of mowers and reapers, silk, carpets, hats, and pencils. Machine shops and elevator works have also been erected, giving constant employment to many skilled artisans. The locality is not without interest from an historical point of view. Hendrick Hudson anchored off Yonkers when ascending the river in September, 1609, and was visited by large numbers of Indians with whom he traded. In the evening the tide set strongly up stream, which confirmed Hudson in the belief that he was in a passage between two oceans. The name Yonkers is derived from the Dutch "Yonk-heer," signifying the heir of a family. The greater part of this region was purchased from the Van der Donck family, to whom it was originally granted by Frederick Philipse.

The old "Philipse Manor" still exists, and is a most attractive object for those interested in relics of the olden time. The manor stands within the town of Yonkers. The older portion was built in 1682, and the more modern portion in 1745. It is probably the finest specimen of an old-fashioned mansion in the country. The interior decorations have been scrupulously preserved and are very quaint and curious. In this old Hall was born Mary Philipse, the belle of her day and the early love of Washington. She chose to marry another, Roger Morris; but it is said that Washington always cherished the memory of the beautiful heiress of Philipse Manor.

GLENWOOD, Yonkers, Westchester County, 18 miles from New York. The name is appropriate and suggestive, as is the place itself, of rustic peacefulness. Leaving Glenwood, a rapid spin of three miles brings into view the quiet village of—

HASTINGS, Greenburg, Westchester County, 21 miles from New York. "Hastings is most romantically situated. The elegant residences of many wealthy New Yorkers can be seen nestling among the trees that crown the hills and afford a beautiful view of the river and the surrounding country." Much Westchester marble is shipped from Hastings. A British force, under Cornwallis, crossed the river at this place in 1776 and joined another force in capturing Fort Lee. Cannonading was kept up from two forts on the heights as the boats got under way, causing much annoyance to the troops on board. Garibaldi, the Liberator of Italy, paid frequent visits to Hastings during his stay in New York. Near Hastings is the stately old Livingston mansion, which was used as the headquarters of Washington and the scene of the official conferences concerning the British evacuation of New York in 1783.

André and Arnold. The story of Arnold's treason and of André's capture and execution is one of the most interesting and at the same time one of the saddest in our history. Benedict Arnold was a major-general in the American army, having won his position by distinguished gallantry and zeal. It is not necessary here to trace the successive steps which led to his fall. Suffice it to say that certain acts of his while in command at Philadelphia led to his trial by court martial. He was sentenced to be reprimanded, but the sentence, mild as it was, embittered him toward his country, and he began to take steps toward opening a correspondence with the enemy.

Assigned to the command of West Point and vicinity, he soon began negotiations for surrender to Sir Henry Clinton. Finally arrangements were made for a meeting with Major John André, Adjutant-General of the British army. The British sloop of war "Vulture" was sent up to Teller's Point with André on board. On the second night he landed on the west side of the river, just below Stony Point, and, meeting Arnold, consulted with him until daylight. Their plans were incomplete when day broke, and Arnold persuaded his companion to go with him to a Tory house near by. Horses were at hand, provided, and the two rode together through the dark woods. Presently they were challenged by a sentry, and then André perceived that he was within the enemy's line. They went on, however, and entered the house. As soon as daylight was sufficiently clear, an American gun opened fire on the "Vulture" from Teller's Point, and the vessel weighed anchor and dropped down the river.

André was in uniform, but in order to provide against discovery he put on a plain coat, and by this act assumed the disguise which deprived him of his official character, and rendered him open to conviction as a spy. In the course of the day plans for the surrender of the garrison about West Point were completed, and André became anxious to regain the British lines. Being unable to get a boat to take him down to the "Vulture," he was forced to take the land route. Accordingly he crossed King's Ferry, and on the strength of Arnold's passes passed all the regular American outposts.

On this particular morning, however, three volunteers had agreed to watch the road at Tarrytown, and on André's appearance halted him, and made him dismount, and discovered inside his stockings the evidences of his mission. André offered bribes to a large amount if they would let him go, but the stern patriots refused, and marched him off to the nearest American post. The commanding officer, Colonel Jamieson, was very near sending prisoner, papers, and all to Arnold, but Major Tallmadge persuaded him to send only a letter detailing the circumstances of the arrest. This Arnold received while at breakfast.

He immediately left the table, ordered his horse, saying that he was wanted down the river, rode to Beverly Dock (see page 39), and, leaping into a boat, went down the river to the "Vulture."

André at once wrote to Washington, frankly telling the whole truth, and closing with the words, "Thus was I betrayed (being Adjutant-General of the B. army) into the vile condition of an enemy in disguise within your posts." Washington convened a court, which tried André at Tappan. The accused so freely admitted all the charges and specifications, that it was not necessary to examine a single witness, and the court, after long deliberation, reluctantly sentenced him to death. Much sympathy was felt for André throughout the American camp, but every one acknowledged that no leniency should be shown. An informal proposition was made to exchange him for Arnold, but neither Washington nor Sir Henry Clinton would officially consider this plan, and on October 2, 1780, André was hung.

In 1832 his remains were removed to England, and a monument stands in Westminster Abbey on which the sad story is inscribed. Arnold was made a Major-General in the British army, and received £10,000, the price of his treason, but was despised even by his brother officers, and died with hardly a friend to mourn his loss. Monuments have been erected to the memory of Paulding and Van Wart, two of the men engaged in André's capture at Peekskill and Tarrytown. In 1878 the Rev. Arthur Penrhyn Stanley, Dean of Westminster, visited this country, and secured permission to have a stone, bearing a suitable inscription, raised to André's memory on the place of his execution.

DOBBS' FERRY, Greenburg, Westchester County, N. Y., 22 miles from New York. A village of considerable size, containing villas and cottages of tasteful and elegant appearance. The village is named after a ferry which was kept in olden times between this place and Piermont, opposite, by one Dobbs, a Swede. An attempt was made some years since to have this name changed to "Paulding," as being both more euphonious and appropriate. The proposition led to quite a controversy in the newspapers; but public opinion decided, for the time at least, in favor of the old Swedish ferryman.

The Palisades, on the opposite side of the river, which for about twenty miles have formed a precipitous river bank, are now suddenly interrupted by the valley through which the Erie Railway was originally built, and they do not again resume their precipitous character.

NEW YORK CENTRAL RAILROAD.

Dobbs' Ferry is well known in Revolutionary annals. The British concentrated their forces here after their dearly-bought victory at White Plains, five miles east. This battle took place in October, 1776. In 1777 a division of the American army, under General Lincoln, was encamped here for several months. Tappan, about three miles southwest of Piermont, was the scene of André's trial and execution during the war of the Revolution. About two years before this event Baylor's regiment of American cavalry was surprised at night at Tappan by the British General Grey, and two thirds of its men were massacred. The Commission sent by Sir Henry Clinton to intercede for the life of the unfortunate spy, Major André, landed here and held a long but unsuccessful consultation with General Greene, the president of the court which condemned him to death. Greene met the Chief of the Commission, by permission of General Washington, only in the character of a private gentleman; but although both friend and foe desired to save André's life, the conference proved unavailing. Dobbs' Ferry was the first place appointed for a meeting between André and Arnold. The plan, however, was not successfully carried out.

IRVINGTON, Greenburg, Westchester County, 24 miles from New York, named for the late Washington Irving, whose estate, called "Sunnyside," is situated a little northeast of the station. The locality has been consecrated by the genius of this most charming writer, and men of wealth and liberal taste have collected about it, laid out beautiful grounds, and erected elegant mansions.

* **PIERMONT**, Orangetown, Rockland County, 24 miles from New York, on the west side of the river, is notable for its pier, one mile long, projecting from the shore to deep water A short distance below Piermont is the boundary line between New York and New Jersey, near which the Palisades recede from the shore and lose their precipitous character. The ridge continues, however, in a series of hills reaching, in some places, a height of nearly seven hundred feet, but nowhere resuming the peculiar palisade formation. We may here call attention to the beautiful "Arbor Vitæ" (Thuja Occidentalis), which is frequently seen, singly or in groves, along the banks. It is, in fact, the common white cedar, which in this vicinity assumes a beautiful pencil-like habit of growth, and forms a distinctive feature of the landscape.

Gliding swiftly past "Sunnyside," we come to—

TARRYTOWN, Greenburg and Mount Pleasant, Westchester County, 29 miles from New York. Tarrytown is delightfully situated on a hillside overlooking the river and the Palisades to the southward, and commanding a distant view of the Ramapo Mountains and Hudson Highlands to the west and north. The whole town is thickly studded with dwellings of every style of beauty. Prominent among these is the white marble edifice known as Paulding Manor, which stands just below the town. This palatial dwelling was built by descendants of Commodore Paulding, and is one of the finest specimens of the Elizabethan style of architecture in this country. It has passed out of the possession of the Paulding family.

A little above Tarrytown is the Pocantico, a small stream flowing through the valley, called by the Dutch "Slaeperigh Haven," and translated into English as "Sleepy Hollow." About half a mile from the mouth of this stream is a Dutch church, which is a curiosity in its way, being the oldest religious edifice in the State of New York. The date of erection is 1699. Its walls contain bricks which were imported from Holland when the church was erected.

The old bell hangs in the belfry, on whose pointed roof an iron vane still turns, bearing the monogram of the founder of the church, Frederick Philipse, whose mansion, known as "Philipse Castle," stands on the banks of the stream not far distant. This is the dwelling whence the Philipse family moved when the mansion at Yonkers was built.

To the eastward of the church is the valley of Sleepy Hollow, and the identical bridge, or at least its successor, over which the Headless Hessian pursued Ichabod Crane, as related by Irving in the "Legend of Sleepy Hollow." Between this bridge and Tarrytown the road crosses André's Brook, and near by stands a monument marking the spot where he was captured. A suitable inscription gives the leading facts connected with that event.

* Nearly opposite Tarrytown, at the foot of a precipitous hill on the western side of the Tappan Zee, the mountains sweep back from Piermont in the form of a semicircle, and meet the river again at the northern extremity of the Zee, in a series of bluffs familiarly known as the Hook, almost as imposing as the Rock of Gibraltar, which it strongly resembles in outline and general appearance. Within this semicircle—one of the loveliest spots on the river—and connected with Tarrytown by a steam ferry, nestles the beautiful village of—

THE STEAMER MARY POWELL ENTERING THE HIGHLANDS OF THE HUDSON RIVER.

NEW YORK CENTRAL RAILROAD.

***NYACK**, which is rapidly growing into a large suburban town. The Rip Van Winkle sleep which seems to have possessed this part of the western shore of the river from time immemorial has been very properly disturbed by the extension of the Northern Railway to Nyack, and now all is bustle and activity. Looking out from the promontory which extends into the "Zee," on a point nearly central between Piermont and the Hook, is the Tappan Zee Hotel.

One mile north of Tarrytown is—

SCARBOROUGH, Ossining, Westchester County, 31 miles from New York; and about the same distance from Scarborough we reach—

SING SING, Ossining, Westchester County, 32 miles from New York. A handsome little city, with a population of 7,000. "The town itself is very beautiful, many elegant residences rising on the long upward slope from the river." One of the New York State prisons is located here. It was built in 1826 by convicts who were brought here for that purpose from Auburn prison. The material is a white marble, quarried near by. There are three buildings, containing one thousand cells for men, and one hundred for women. Croton aqueduct passes through Sing Sing, and is carried over a ravine by a stone arch 70 feet high, having a span of 88 feet. Across the river is Haverstraw Bay, five miles wide—the widest part of the Hudson, extending from Croton Point on the south to Verplanck's Point on the north. The first view of the West Shore Railroad is now obtained from the eastern shore.

Rockland Lake, 150 feet above the river, the source of the Hackensack, and a great ice-quarry in winter, is also opposite Sing Sing, the lake being separated from the Hudson by Hook Mountain, 610 feet in height. The point which abuts on the river is Verdritege Hook, commonly called "Point No Point."

A short distance north of Rockland Lake, on the western shore, is—

HAVERSTRAW, Haverstraw, Rockland County, New York, 36 miles from New York. This village is built on a high bank or plateau Extensive brick-kilns line the river bank close by. Haverstraw is an important station of the West Shore Railroad.

For a few miles below Haverstraw, the summits of the Highlands are distinctly in sight, up the river, although their bases are hidden by intervening hills.

NEW YORK CENTRAL RAILROAD.

The extremity of the tongue of land which projects far into the river from its eastern bank above Sing Sing, from which station we are now proceeding toward Croton, is known as Teller's Point. That portion nearer the shore of the river is termed Croton Point. It separates Tappan Bay from Haverstraw Bay. Off this point the "Vulture" anchored when she brought André to meet Arnold, and from thence the gun was brought to bear which drove that vessel down the river. Croton Point is now occupied by the vineyards of Dr. Underhill, whose pure wines are much used for medicinal purposes. Just below Teller's Point is the mouth of Croton River, which supplies New York with water. This stream has a wide mouth, sometimes called Croton Bay, which was partly filled up in 1841 by the washing away of the Croton Reservoir dam. The work was, however, pressed forward and in 1842 water was supplied to the city through the Croton pipes.

The aqueduct is built of solid masonry, and follows the course of the Hudson at an average distance of about a mile from its shore. This aqueduct is capable of discharging 60,000,000 gallons per day into the receiving reservoir in the Central Park, New York. The entire cost of the Croton works at their completion was about $14,000,000. Since that time great improvements and additions have been made to meet the demands of the growing city. It is estimated that the Croton River will supply water enough for New York even if the city should reach five times its present size. Passing Croton Point at a rapid rate, the cars soon reach—

CROTON, Cortland, Westchester County, New York, 36 miles from New York.

On our way to the next station we can discern, on the opposite shore, Treason Hill, north of Haverstraw, where Arnold met André at Joshua Hett Smith's. Two miles north of Haverstraw, on the same side of the river, is Grassy Point. and a mile farther on is Stony Point, which was stormed by the Americans under General Anthony Wayne on July 15, 1779, with a view to driving the British from their fortifications.

Stony Point, with Verplanck's Point on the eastern shore, form the southern gateways of the Highlands.

CAPTURE OF STONY POINT.

The forts located at Stony Point were held by the Americans until June 1, 1779, when they were simultaneously invested by a British force commanded by Sir Henry Clinton. No direct attack was made on Fort Lafayette, the work on Verplanck's Point, until after the evacuation of Stony Point. The garrison at the latter place numbered only 40 men, and abandoned the work on the approach of an overwhelming force of the British, who quietly took possession, ran up the cross of St. George on the flagstaff, and opened fire on Fort Lafayette with the captured guns.

At the same time Gen. Vaughan attacked on the east side of the river, and the weak garrison of 70 men were soon forced to surrender. The loss of this position was a severe blow to the Americans, compelling them to make a wide détour in order to keep up their communications. General Anthony Wayne at once requested and obtained permission to storm Stony Point, and at midnight on the 15th of July, 1779, led two columns of picked men to the assault. They advanced undiscovered until they were close upon the British picket, which of course gave the alarm, and the garrison turned out.

The parapet was manned, and a scathing fire of grape and musketry swept the hillside; but "Mad Anthony" was at the head of his column, and, within half an hour after the first shot, carried the works at the bayonet's point, capturing the entire garrison with its stores. Wayne was knocked over, but not seriously injured, by a musket ball. The next morning a cannonade was opened on the works at Verplanck's Point, and continued through the day. Re-enforcements were sent to the British, and it soon became evident that sufficient force to hold Stony Point could not be spared by the Americans. They therefore dismantled and abandoned the fort, and it passed again into British hands. They, however, in turn abandoned the position in October, and from that time the Americans retained possession.

On the one hundredth anniversary of the capture of Stony Point, interesting commemorative exercises were held on the spot, and the battle was fought over again in imitation of the original contest, the cadet battalion from West Point participating.

CAPTURE OF STONY POINT BY THE AMERICANS, JULY 16TH, 1779.

OSCOWANA is a small way station, with but few inhabitants. It is the first station north of Croton.

CRUGER'S, Cortland, Westchester County, New York—37 miles from New York. Near the head of Haverstraw Bay, and not far from this station, on our way to view the regions said to be inhabited and ruled by a number of mischievous little goblins in knickerbocker suits, we come to—

MONTROSE, a small, quiet, and unassuming village.

PEEKSKILL, Cortland, Westchester County, New York—43 miles from New York. The village is a pleasant one, standing at the mouth of the romantic Peekskill Hollow, and is within easy reach of all interesting parts of the Highlands. The late Henry Ward Beecher had a country residence a little east of the village. Fort Independence stood, during Revolutionary times, on the point above Peekskill, where its ruins may still be seen. And on the point below is the Franciscan Convent Academy of "Our Lady of Angels." The population of Peekskill is now more than 7,000. It is a bustling and thriving place, having several iron foundries, machine shops and other manufactories, and is surrounded by magnificent river scenery. "Its history dates back to a period anterior to the Revolutionary War, and in that trying time it played an important part. On the old Van Cortland farm, two miles north of the town, yet stands the house in which, for a time, General Washington had his headquarters, and just beyond can be seen the church in which he worshiped."

The village on the point opposite Peekskill is Caldwell's Landing. Above it rise the rocky and weather-beaten crags of the Donderberg, or Thunder Mountain, around which, at the close of a sultry summer day, black clouds are wont to gather, casting a deep inky blackness over mountain and river, while mutterings of thunder are echoed from peak to peak, with such strange and confused rumblings that we can hardly wonder at the superstitions which, according to Irving, peopled the hills with a crowd of little imps in sugarloaf hats and short doublets, who were seen at various times " tumbling head over heels in the rack and mist," and bringing down frightful squalls on such craft as failed to drop the peaks of their mainsails in salute to the Dutch goblin who kept the Donderberg.

On the east shore, on a wide plateau, is the State Encampment, where the regiments of the National Guard of the State of New York encamp once a year, in summer, for drill and inspection.

Above the Donderberg, on the east side of the river, is Anthony's Nose, 1,200 ft. high. In the "History of New York," Irving gives an amusing account of the origin of this name. Another says it was once compared to the nose of one Anthony Hogans, the captain of a sloop, who possessed an unusually large nasal appendage, and thus the name obtained a local currency which eventually became fixed as the title of this majestic hill.

On the west side of the river is Iona Island, on which were formerly extensive vineyards, and which now has a hotel and is a well-known place of resort. This island is the northernmost point which is reached by the sea-breeze. The effect upon vegetation is very noticeable in the spring of the year. The stream which may be seen falling into the river below Anthony's Nose is known as "Brocken Kill." It is full of romantic cascades, almost from its mouth to its sources.

On the west side of the river, nearly opposite to Anthony's Nose, may be seen Fort Montgomery, a small village at the mouth of Montgomery Creek. On the rocky heights above and below the creek, stood Forts Clinton and Montgomery, which were in 1777 the principal defences of the Hudson. They were considered impregnable to an assault from the land side, and with the ordnance of the day they had little to fear from a naval attack. A heavy boom, made of a huge iron chain on timber floats, stretched across the river, and was made fast to the rocks at Anthony's Nose. This, it was thought, would effectually prevent the ascent of a hostile fleet.

On October 6, 1777, Sir Henry Clinton sent a strong detachment around and over the Donderberg, to attack these forts in the rear. A demonstration on the east side of the river had led General Putnam to anticipate an attack on Fort Independence, near Peekskill, and a portion of the garrison at Fort Montgomery was temporarily withdrawn to strengthen that post. The British had a sharp skirmish with an American detachment at Lake Sinnipink, which is still known among the inhabitants as "Bloody Pond."

This attack was the first warning which aroused the garrison at the forts. In the course of the afternoon the forts were attacked, and the garrisons defended themselves gallantly until evening, when, it having become evident that they could not hold out, they took to the mountains, an orderly retreat being impossible, and so the greater part escaped. An American flotilla of two sloops and some smaller craft, which lay above the boom, was abandoned and burned, to prevent its falling into the enemy's hands. The next morning the boom was destroyed, and the British fleet, with a detachment of troops, proceeded up the river. A short time afterward the British received the news of Burgoyne's surrender, and abandoned the forts.

The West Shore R.R. here crosses Montgomery Creek on a fine iron bridge. To the west is the Forest of Dean, and the mountain town of Munroe. The Hudson now bends to the northeast. Far in advance is the ruined height of Fort Putnam, and on the right front is the symmetrical cone of Sugar-loaf Mountain. The Parry House, with ruins of an old mill in front, and Benny Havens's cottage at the waterside, can also be seen in the immediate vicinity.

Still looking across at the western shore, we can there discern, above the points just mentioned, Buttermilk Falls, a series of white rapids on a brook which falls one hundred feet to the river. Here are several large flour mills, and just above is—

*CRANSTON'S, a well-known and much-frequented summer resort. It stands on a lofty bluff overlooking the Hudson, and two hundred and fifty feet above it, with a magnificent view north and south. The village of Highland Falls is just southwest of Cranston's Hotel, but not much of the town can be seen from the river.

By this time, on our journey along the eastern banks, the train has passed Highlands and progressed in a northerly direction as far as—

GARRISON'S, Philipstown, Putnam County, New York, 50 miles from New York. This station, named in honor of a distinguished family of Revolutionary fame, is opposite the military school at West Point. It is surrounded by the most sublime and picturesque scenery of the Hudson, and is associated with some of the eventful scenes of Revolutionary times. On the east bank of the river, about one mile south of the depot, is the Robinson House, where Benedict Arnold received the letter from Colonel Jamieson, informing him of the arrest of André. The General was breakfasting with some distinguished friends when the letter arrived. He immediately left the table, saying that he was wanted down the river, and, ordering his horse, rode to Beverley Dock, and, leaping into his six-oared barge, told his men to pull with all speed down the river to the British man-of-war, the "Vulture," lying off Teller's Point. Thus Arnold escaped, and the glory of an American soldier faded into the infamy of the most noted traitor of history.

This and other places of interest are easily visited from the Highland House, situated about half a mile east of the railroad station, on a plateau commanding one of the most delightful prospects for which the banks of the Hudson are so justly celebrated. It is surrounded on the east and south with mountains abounding in running brooks and wild

INDIAN FALLS, GARRISON'S, N. Y.

shaded glens, and overlooks West Point and the Highlands to the west.

In the vicinity are delightful drives and places of peculiar beauty, among which are Indian Falls, Glen Falls, North and South Redoubt, Anthony's Nose, and Sugar Loaf Mountains on the east side of the river, and West Point and Highland Falls on the west side; while the beautiful Hudson, bright with many a sail and steamer, flows majestically through the mountains toward its ocean home.

The most conspicuous buildings on the opposite side of the Hudson, as we leave Garrison's, are those at—

NEW YORK CENTRAL RAILROAD.

*WEST POINT, Cornwall, Orange County, New York, 51 miles from New York, best known as the site of the United States Military Academy. Located in the very bosom of the Highlands, West Point is their chief attraction. "Its traditions, its relics, its monuments, its dead and living heroes, its romantic 'Flirtation Walk,' all make it a peculiarly fascinating spot. The vicinity abounds in delightful walks and drives, and within easy access are the ruins of several forts. Near by, too, is Bloody Pond, which the simple country folk still believe to be guarded by the ghosts of Hessian soldiers." Before the commencement of the present century, Washington suggested this place as well adapted for the establishment of such an institution, but no formal steps were taken by Congress until 1802. Ten years later, in 1812, the school was fairly established, and has ever since continued to increase in importance and excellence. Few of the academy buildings can be seen from the river, the buildings being situated on an elevated plateau, about 180 feet above the river. This plateau is occupied by the various barracks, schools, arsenals, etc., connected with the institution, bordering a broad parade open for military evolutions, and overlooked by the grand summits of the surrounding hills.

There is no institution in the land better calculated to make a favorable impression on the visitor than this academy. The good order and strict discipline which prevail, however irksome they may be to the cadets, give them a mental and physical training which they never forget. The most accomplished officers of the army are detailed as instructors, with a special professional staff appointed from civil life. Visitors properly introduced may be present at recitations, and, indeed, observe all the elaborate organization that gives this famous military school its well-deserved fame.

The life of a cadet is by no means an easy one. His physique must be perfect, and his mental capacity of no mean order, to enable him to pass successfully through the four years of study and military training. The average number of cadets is about 250. Candidates for admission are nominated by members of Congress and by the President, a certain number being allotted to each Congressional district. These candidates report for examination in June of each year, and, if they are mentally and physically qualified, are admitted as cadets, which is, in military rank, a grade below second lieutenant. The course of instruction is very thorough and complete, especially in mathematics and military tactics.

HUDSON RIVER AT WEST POINT, LOOKING SOUTH.
CRANSTON'S HOTEL IN THE DISTANCE.

NEW YORK CENTRAL RAILROAD.

The best time to visit West Point is during the months of July and August, when the cadets go into camp. Drills, parades, and guard-mountings are the order of the day, all being done in the best manner known to military science.

West Point was the scene of no actual fighting during the Revolution, although it was fortified. A boom similar to that which was prepared at Fort Montgomery was stretched across the river to Constitution Island, which was also heavily fortified toward the latter part of the war, and the remains of the old batteries may still be seen. This island is now owned by, and is the residence of, Miss Warner, author of "The Wide, Wide World," etc. The West Shore Railway passes directly under the West Point parade grounds, through a tunnel beginning on the south, near the boat landing.

Three miles higher up the river on the eastern side is—

COLD SPRING, Philipstown, Putnam County, New York, 54 miles from New York, noted for its iron foundry. Here, under the superintendence of Major Parrot, were cast the celebrated Parrot guns, which did such good service in the war of the rebellion. On an elevated plateau near the village is "Undercliff," the country seat of the late George P. Morris. The mountain immediately above Cold Spring is Bull Hill, or, to give its more classic name, Mt. Taurus. It is 1,586 feet in height. Just above this elevation, and separated from it by a valley, is Breakneck Hill, 1,187 feet high.

It is stated that the former of these hills was once the abode of a wild bull, which became such a source of dread to the inhabitants that they organized a hunt, and drove the animal from his accustomed haunts across the valley to the neighboring hill, where he dashed over the rocks and broke his neck. The two hills were named in honor of this adventure. Breakneck Hill was formerly distinguished by a huge mass of rock bearing a marked resemblance to a human face. This singular formation was for many years one of the sights to be looked at by every passenger up or down the river.

On the west side of the river are Cro' Nest and Butter Hill. The former is the one next above West Point. It is 1,418 feet high, and separated from Butter Hill by a wild and picturesque valley. The name Cro' Nest probably was at first applied to a deep rocky depression which exists near the summit, but it is now understood to mean the mountain itself. The name will recall Joseph Rodman Drake's beautiful poem, "The Culprit Fay," the scene of which is laid among these hills.

The precipice which forms the river-face of Cro' Nest is known as Kidd's Plug Cliff. It owes its name to a singular projecting mass of rock which may be seen near its summit. The neighboring mountain named Klinkersberg by the Dutch, has of late come to be called the Storm King, and as the old name is neither beautiful nor appropriate, it will soon be forgotten. Its summit is 1,529 feet high. To the late N. P. Willis is due the credit of rechristening this grand peak, as well as giving appropriate names to other objects of interest in the vicinity.

* **CORNWALL**, Cornwall, Orange County, New York, 56 miles from New York, a village on the west side of the river in Orange County, is a favorite summer resort. The beauty of its situation renders it a fashionable resort during the summer, when its many beautiful residences are the scene of a constant round of gayety. The entertaining of summer visitors has become the characteristic business of the town. About 5,000 persons annually make their summer abode in this town, and the permanent population has increased within a few years to about 8,000 souls. The hotels and boarding-houses do not reach the magnificent proportions of some of the Saratoga hotels, but are neat and convenient, and, from its nearness to New York and facilities of access, the town has reached a great popularity for summer residence.

There are several schools and churches, a savings bank, public library, and reading-room in the village. "Idlewild," the former residence of N. P. Willis, and where he passed the last fifteen years of his life, is on the road leading from Cornwall to Newburgh. It is scarcely visible from the river. Several other handsome country seats are scattered along the west bank of the river.

Just at the upper entrance to the Highlands is Pollipel's Island, a rocky bit of ground, to which a supernatural origin was ascribed by the Indians. In 1777, a *chevaux de frise*, made of logs with pointed iron heads, was sunk between the island and the mainland to prevent the British ships from ascending the river; but it seems to have proved ineffectual. This island and the neighboring hills have from time to time been searched for deposits of treasure supposed to have been concealed by the almost mythical Captain Kidd. The view down stream from the Breakneck Hill is one of the finest on the river, including several of the grandest peaks of the Highlands, with the noble river flowing at their feet.

STORM KING is the name of a small way-station, three minutes' ride from Cold Spring, and five minutes' from—

DUTCHESS JUNCTION, the connecting point with the New York & New England Railroad, running through Connecticut and Massachusetts to Boston.

From here we are conveyed swiftly along the New York Central & Hudson River route to—

FISHKILL LANDING, better known as Fishkill-on-the-Hudson, Fishkill, Dutchess County, New York, 60 miles from New York. This thriving place is the port, so to term it, of Fishkill, five miles inland. The Matteawan Creek falls into the Hudson at this point. At Fishkill this stream furnishes water-power for several mills and factories of large size. The situation of the town is extremely romantic, being surrounded on all sides by high and rocky hills, which are full of wild and picturesque ravines. Connection is made by ferry with—

***NEWBURGH,** Orange County, New York, 61 miles from New York. This is one of the largest and most thriving cities on the Hudson, being the seat of several large manufacturing enterprises. The water-front is lined with warehouses in which considerable business is transacted. The city stands on an elevation on the west bank of the river, commanding a noble view of the Highlands and of the Matteawan Mountains. The eastern terminus of the Newburgh Branch of the Erie Railway, which joins the main line at Greycourt, nineteen miles west, is at Newburgh. This branch delivers over a million tons of coal here annually for re-shipment. Newburgh is an important station of the New York, West Shore & Buffalo Railway.

The city rises from the river in a succession of terraces, the first plateau being about 130 feet above the water, the second 190 feet, and still further west it reaches an elevation of 300 feet above the Hudson. Newburgh is famed for its oarsmen and its ice-boats. It has several charitable and educational institutions, among which are the Newburgh Almshouse, about two miles west of the center of the city, the Home for the Friendless, on Montgomery Street, and the Theological Seminary of the Associate Reformed (United Presbyterian) Church. This seminary stands on a commanding height, overlooking the city and river. In this institution is a library of over 5,000 volumes, some of which are very rare and valuable.

The Public Schools are excellent, and are attended by about 5,000 children. The Public Library is a beautiful building in the central part of the city, and contains about 10,000 volumes of well-selected books, etc, controlled by the school officers of the city. Newburgh is one of the handsomest cities on the Hudson, and is celebrated as the residence of a wealthy and cultured class of people, some of whom are famous for their literary productions. N. P. Willis, J. T. Headley, and other celebrities, had their country seats in or near Newburgh.

Near a flagstaff standing in the southern part of the town, and distinctly visible from the river, is an old stone house now owned and kept in order by the State, which was occupied by Washington as his headquarters when the army lay at New Windsor, two miles south. This house contains many interesting relics of the Revolutionary War. At the foot of the flagstaff before mentioned, the last surviving member of Washington's Life Guard was buried in 1856, and a monument, with an appropriate inscription, stands over his grave. A short distance south of Newburgh is the site of the American camp, where the troops suffered so severely from smallpox during the winter of 1783.

Six minutes' ride from Fishkill Landing is—

LOW POINT, Fishkill, Dutchess County, New York. 64 miles from New York, built just above a short tunnel, and sometimes termed Carthage Landing.

This is a small village on the east bank of the Hudson. Opposite, on the west bank, is a flat rock, now crowned with cedars, which Hendrick Hudson and his comrades named the Duyvels Dans Kamer, or Devil's Dance-chamber, in consequence of an Indian pow-wow which they witnessed at night, with all its hideous accessories of fire and war-paint. The rock is still known by this name.

Not far from Low Point, on the eastern bank, is the village of—

NEW HAMBURG, Poughkeepsie, Dutchess County, New York, 66 miles from New York, a pretty little village, standing at the mouth of Wappinger's Creek, which falls into the Hudson on the east side. This stream is crossed at its mouth by a long trestle bridge, with a draw in the middle. Wappinger's Falls is on Wappinger's Creek, two miles from New Hamburg village. A ferry plies between New Hamburg and Hampton, opposite. On the heights above the landing are charming views of the Hudson and its surrounding scenery.

*MARLBOROUGH, Marlborough, Ulster County, New York, 66 miles from New York, pleasantly situated on the west bank of the Hudson, overlooking the river and the country beyond. Back of the village are the Shawangunk Mountains, and intervening is a hilly country of great beauty. The West Shore railroad runs along the river bank through Marlborough Landing, a mile east of the village. In this vicinity a beautiful grove of arbor vitæ, or white cedar trees, will be noticed on the west bank above Marlborough, where an entire hillside is covered with the delicate, pencil-like forms of this symmetrical and graceful tree, giving a very picturesque effect to the scenery of this region.

Looking northward above Marlborough, on the same side of the Hudson, can be seen—

*MILTON, or BARNEGAT, Marlborough, Dutchess County, New York, 71 miles from New York. This village is a mile west of the river landing and the West Shore railroad station. A part of it may be seen crowning the steep bank which rises from the western shore of the river. Large quantities of berries and other fruits are raised in this vicinity for the New York market. Just before reaching Poughkeepsie, which city may be seen on the bluff beyond, we pass Locust Grove, the country seat of the late Professor S. F. B. Morse. It can hardly be necessary to remind any one that Professor Morse is the inventor of the Morse alphabet, which made the electric telegraph, of which he was also one of the original discoverers, indispensable to every nation of Christendom.

Eight minutes after leaving New Hamburg, Camelot is passed, and within another ten minutes we reach—

POUGHKEEPSIE, Poughkeepsie, Dutchess County, New York, 75 miles from New York.

The city of Poughkeepsie is built on a table-land located amid a group of hills, at a considerable height, so that its spires and buildings may be seen from a long distance up and down the river. "By day the smoke of its busy mills and factories somewhat mars the scene, but, as night draws on, these light up the river like beacons, and the sound of the ponderous machinery and roaring furnaces greets our ears, and

POUGHKEEPSIE, N. Y.—THE CITY OF SCHOOLS AND BEAUTIFUL RESIDENCES.

tells of the energy of the citizens." The name is a corruption of the Indian name given to the cove which once existed at the mouth of Fall Kill. Poughkeepsie has a population of at least 25,000, contains large manufacturing interests, and is noted for its educational institutions. Two peculiar elevations will be noticed at the river-side, the southern of which bears the name of "Call Rock," from the fact that the inhabitants used to hail passing vessels from its summit.

Poughkeepsie is the shire town of Dutchess County, and contains the usual court and jail buildings. Its streets are beautifully shaded, its situation is very healthful, and everything combines to make it most attractive as a residence. The Vassar Female College, in the eastern part of the city, is the largest and most important of the many excellent educational institutions of Poughkeepsie. The late Matthew Vassar, a wealthy citizen of Poughkeepsie, founded and endowed this extensive college. It is intended for the education of women only, and is the most complete establishment of its kind in the world.

Besides this noble institution there is a Female Academy, the Collegiate Institute, the Military Institute, Riverview Military Academy, Cottage Hill Seminary, Eastman's National Business College, St. Peter's Academy, and numerous other establishments for physical advancement and mental culture. One of the large State asylums for the insane is located at Poughkeepsie.

The place was settled by the Dutch about 1698, and incorporated as a city in 1854. The principal object of interest to the antiquary is the Van Kleck house, a stone structure with loopholes in its walls. It was built in 1705. The State Legislature met in it in 1777 and 1778, when the British held New York, and had burned their former meeting place at Esopus. There also, the State Convention for the ratification of the Federal Constitution met, in 1788. 57 members were present, and after a long debate, in which such men as Governor Clinton, John Jay and Alexander Hamilton took part, the Constitution was ratified by a majority of three.

The Poughkeepsie bridge is a magnificent iron structure, stretching across the Hudson, and forming a connecting-link between New England and the great West.

Huddlestone, the British spy, was executed here in 1780. Andrew Jackson Davis, the "Poughkeepsie Seer," was born here. A steam ferry connects with Lloyd or New Paltz Landing opposite.

THE MEMORIAL FOUNTAIN, POUGHKEEPSIE, N. Y.
Erected by the Hon H G Eastman.

NEW YORK CENTRAL RAILROAD.

***NEW PALTZ LANDING** is opposite Poughkeepsie, and six miles above, on the eastern side, we arrive at —

HYDE PARK, Hyde Park, Dutchess County, New York, 80 miles from New York, named in honor of Sir Edward Hyde, one of the early British Governors of New York. The village is pleasantly situated half a mile east of the river bank, on a beautiful and fertile table-land. The bend in the river between rocky bluffs is known to river men as "Crom Elbow," a combination of the original Dutch name and its English equivalent, "Crooked Elbow." A creek of the same name falls into the river. The point on the east shore is "De Vroos Point." A light iron footbridge will be noticed crossing a deep cutting of the Hudson River Railroad. The house beyond is that of Joseph Boorman, first president of the Hudson River Railroad. Between Hyde Park and Oak Hill, 30 miles above, there are many extensive and ancient country seats, some of them antedating the Revolution.

The beauty of the country seems to have attracted men of taste and wealth in those days to make their homes along this fertile bluff, and in many cases their descendants still occupy the old mansions of their fathers,—a state of things so rare in America as to deserve especial notice. About a mile above Hyde Park landing is "Placentia," the former home of the late James K. Paulding, one of the pioneers of American literature, and the friend of Washington Irving. Opposite, on the west bank, but scarcely in sight from the river, is the famous apple farm of R. L. Pell, Esq. On this farm there are said to be 25,000 bearing apple-trees. The fruit of these trees is packed with the greatest care, and much of it is shipped to Europe.

The river banks are hereafter low and uninteresting, but an air of rich rural peace pervades the country-side, and stately old mansions and neat modern villas are seen on either hand. At the next station —

STAATSBURG, Hyde Park, Dutchess County, New York, 85 miles from New York, the railroad leaves the river for a short distance, striking through a little valley which affords a more direct course. The banks of the Hudson running northward now lose the precipitous character which has marked them thus far, and slope less abruptly from the river. Two miles above Hyde Park, Esopus Island will be noticed near the east banks. Just below, on the west side of the river,

VIEW IN THE GROUNDS OF EASTMAN PARK, POUGHKEEPSIE, N. Y.

is the Astor residence. Opposite are two fine estates, the lower owned by Dr. Hussack, and the upper by Mrs. M. Livingston.

Not far above Staatsburg, on the east side of the river, is the country seat known as Wildercliff. It is by no means so elegant as many of the neighboring estates ; but to members of the Methodist Church in America it is interesting, as having been built by Freeborn Garrettson, the eminent preacher who married a sister of Chancellor Livingston, and to whose energy is due much of the prosperity of that branch of the Christian Church. The place may be recognized by the broad lawn which lies in front of the house.

Next above this place is Ellerslie, the residence of Hon. William Kelley, long prominent in political life. His estate contains about 600 acres, much of which is devoted to gardens and ornamental grounds, and the rest is highly cultivated as a farm. The quaint stone house on a hill near Rhinebeck Landing is the Beckman house, built prior to 1700. It served as a church and as a fort during early times, when the Indians were hostile and powerful.

RHINEBECK LANDING, Rhinebeck, Dutchess County, New York, 90 miles from New York, is two miles west of the village of Rhinebeck, which cannot be seen from the steamer.

The first settlement was by William Beckman, who brought several German families with him in 1647. Within the limits of the town there is an extensive vein of gold-bearing quartz, which yields the precious metal in paying quantities. The western terminus of the Hartford & Connecticut Western Railroad is at Rhine Cliff, on the Hudson, close to Rhinebeck station. This railroad forms a direct route between Connecticut and Rhode Island and the Catskill Mountains, and other points on the Hudson. A steam ferry connects here with—

***RONDOUT,** Kingston, Ulster County, New York, 90 miles from New York. Rondout is now a part of the city of Kingston, with which it was incorporated in 1878. From it, the Ulster & Delaware R. R., which has its terminus here, runs in a northwesterly direction into the Catskill Mountain regions.

It is the point of departure from the Hudson River to the southern part of the Catskill range, including the Overlook Mountain. Hudson River R. R. passengers land at Rhinebeck, and cross the river by steam ferry to Rondout, thence by rail to the Catskills and Delaware

The SIDEWALK APPROACH to and MARBLE WALL fronting EASTMAN PLACE, the Residence of the Hon. H. G. Eastman, Poughkeepsie, N. Y

County. The Wallkill Valley R. R. runs southwest from Rondout, connecting with Erie R. R. for New York or the West.

Rondout Creek enters the Hudson from the westward. Its mouth is the eastern end of the Delaware & Hudson Canal, which joins the creek two and a half miles above. This canal, finished in 1828, extends to the vicinity of the Pennsylvania coal-fields; and every provision is made at Rondout for the trans-shipment of vast quantities of coal.

*KINGSTON, the capital of Ulster County, is on Esopus Creek, which at that point approaches within about two miles of Rondout, and then curves to the northward, entering the Hudson twelve miles above. The population of Kingston, including Rondout, is 20,000. It is "a bustling, pushing town," having a front of four miles on the Hudson. Beautiful scenery abounds in the vicinity, and there are many pleasant and romantic drives in the neighboring country. Kingston is one of the principal points of departure to the Catskill region from the West Shore Railway, which connects with the mountain railroads. Kingston was settled in 1614, and was thrice destroyed by Indians before a permanent footing was obtained by the Europeans.

In 1777 the State Legislature met and formed a constitution. In the autumn of the same year soon after the capture of Forts Montgomery and Clinton by the British, General Vaughan, with 3,000 troops, landed at Rondout, marched to Kingston (then Esopus), and sacked and burned the town, remaining until he received the news of Burgoyne's surrender, when he at once retired to New York, abandoning all that he had gained. While Esopus (Kingston) was burning, the inhabitants fled to Hurley, a neighboring village, where the small force of American troops tried and hung a messenger who was caught carrying despatches from Clinton to Burgoyne. When first caught, this man swallowed a silver ball, which an emetic brought again to light, and which was found to contain the fatal despatch.

Six miles above Rhinebeck Landing, on the New York Central & Hudson River Railroad, we arrive at—

BARRYTOWN, Red Hook, Dutchess County, New York, 96 miles from New York, formerly known as Lower Red Hook Landing. A little above Rhinebeck is the residence of William B. Astor. It may be recognized by its tower and pointed roof. This estate is named "Rokeby," and is one of the finest on the river. Next above is the estate known as Montgomery Place, surpassing in beauty, if possible, the last one mentioned. The house was built by the wife of General Montgomery, who fell in the assault on Quebec in 1775. His remains are deposited under the monument erected by the Continental Congress in 1776, and since built into the wall of St. Paul's church, which fronts on Broadway, New York city, where it attracts the attention of all observant strangers who pass. Mrs. Montgomery was a sister of Chancellor Livingston, and Montgomery Place still remains in the Livingston family; her brother, Edward Livingston, succeeded her in the ownership of the place, and his family still occupies it.

Near the eastern shore, two miles above Barrytown, is Cruger's Island, a spot made beautiful by nature and art. In a grove near the southern end stands a ruin which was imported from Italy by the former proprietor of the island. Its broken arches may be seen among the trees as the boat passes, forming a singular contrast with the modern architecture of the neighboring house. The latter, however, is not in sight from the boat at the same time with the ruin. A glimpse of it may be caught in passing, a short distance above.

Within ten minutes from the time we leave Barrytown, we find ourselves alongside the platform at—

TIVOLI, Red Hook, Dutchess County, New York, 100 miles from New York. There is a village of growing importance surrounding the railway station. It is connected with Saugerties on the west bank of the river by a steam ferry. It is one of the stations at which passengers leave the railroad trains who desire to go to the famous Overlook Mountain House—one of the finest mountain hotels in the Catskills.

Near the village is an old mansion, now owned by Col. De Peyster, which was built before the Revolution by one of the Livingston family. The British, on their way to burn Claremont, a little above, in 1777, stopped here under the impression that this was the house to be destroyed. The proprietor, however, aided by his well-stocked wine-cellar, convinced them of their mistake, and they left him unmolested.

* SAUGERTIES, Saugerties, Ulster County, New York, 101 miles from New York, is an important village of about 4,000 inhabitants, on the New York, West Shore & Buffalo Railroad. The village is about one mile from the steamboat landing, with which it is connected by stages that meet all passenger boats and trains. Saugerties is near the mouth of Esopus Creek, which is navigable to the village. There are extensive iron works and paper mills at this place, and large quantities of flagging-stone are quarried in the vicinity. The Bigelow Blue Stone Co. employ in their various quarries in Ulster County 3,500 men, and quarry 200,000 tons of stone annually. "Plattekill Clove," which lies back of this place, in the mountains, is a remarkably wild and rugged chasm, affording scenery of varied grandeur and beauty. A road winds through this gorge, up to the Catskill Mountain House region beyond.

* **MALDEN,** a small village on the same side, with Plattekill Clove on the west. The Bigelow Blue Stone Company's works are carried on here; several thousand men and a considerable fleet of vessels being employed. Higher up the Hudson, on the east, our train reaches—

GERMANTOWN, Germantown, Columbia County, New York, 105 miles from New York. This village was settled in 1710 by German emigrants, under the patronage of Queen Anne, who caused land to be purchased from Robert Livingston for them.

The view of the Catskill Mountains is here very fine. The entire range can be seen. Germantown is not directly upon the river bank, and cannot be seen from the river. The large white building on a hill near the landing is the "Riverside Seminary," established by Philip Rockafellow.

A few miles above Germantown is the mouth of Roeleff Jansen Kill, where the original Livingston Manor House stood. Robert R. Livingston, Chancellor of New York, built an elegant house a little south of the old one, where his mother continued to reside. Chancellor Livingston's active sympathy with the cause of the Republic during the Revolution made him so obnoxious to the British, that when General Vaughan burned Esopus he sent an expedition up the river to burn Claremont—the name of the Livingston estate. They burned both the houses, but new and more elegant ones were at once erected near the ruins, and Claremont is still one of the finest country-seats on the river.

Chancellor Livingston's name will always be associated with that of Robert Fulton. The experiments of Fulton would probably have been delayed for years had it not been for the generous aid of Chancellor Livingston. After a series of discouraging failures in Paris and New

CATSKILL MOUNTAIN HOUSE.

York, their efforts were crowned with success, and in September, 1807, the "Claremont" made her first trip from New York to Albany, bearing Fulton, the Chancellor, and others.

A short distance northward we pass—

LINLITHGO, a small way station, and the last before we arrive at—

CATSKILL STATION, Greenport, Columbia County, New York, 111 miles from New York. A steam ferry runs from a point near the station to—

* **CATSKILL,** Catskill, Greene County, New York, 111 miles from New York. Catskill Landing is at the end of a long causeway reaching across the shallows, on the western shore. But little of the town can be seen from the river. Cats Kill enters the Hudson near by, winding through rocky bluffs, with a deep channel which is navigable for large vessels a mile from its mouth. The Catskill Mountain Railroad runs from Catskill to Palenville, at the foot of the mountains. Passengers for Mountain, Kaaterskill, and Laurel Houses take this railroad at the landing. The West Shore Railway crosses Catskill Creek on a high bridge in the western part of the village.

It also connects with the Catskill Mountain railroad. The Prospect Park Hotel, on the high bluff overlooking the river and village, is the leading resort hotel of the town, and its commanding position and excellent management have made it a popular summer resort. From the Prospect Park Hotel the views of the mountains on either side of the river are really sublime, and the combination of mountain, river, and intervale scenery is marvelously beautiful and charming. The rapidly-passing commerce of the Hudson adds a panoramic effect, enlivening the scene and delighting the spectator with ever-varying views. The Prospect Park Hotel opens about the middle of June for the season. The Irving House is a new, commodious hotel, in the center of the village of Catskill, affording very good accommodations for very moderate prices It is kept open throughout the year.

Hendrick Hudson anchored the "Half-Moon" at the mouth of Cats Kill, on the 20th of September, 1609, and was visited by large numbers of friendly Indians, who brought provisions of all sorts, in return for which, as is stated by Juet, the historian of Hudson's voyage, some of them were made drunk. Thomas Cole, one of the pioneers of American Landscape Art, had his studio in this vicinity, where he could

CASCADE IN PLATTEKILL CLOVE.

study nature in her most beautiful forms. Here he painted the celebrated allegorical series of pictures known as "The Voyage of Life." Church, the great landscape painter, has a beautiful country-seat on the summit on the east side of the Hudson, opposite Catskill. It commands some of the sublimest river views.

On a sort of terrace, twenty-two hundred feet above the river, about 12 miles back from it, and near the edge of an abrupt precipice, is built the "Mountain House," a spacious building, which is distinctly visible for a considerable distance along the river. The coolness and exhilarating quality of the air, the grandeur of the view, and the comfortable accommodations of the hotel, attract numerous visitors in the summer

The mountain rises behind the hotel to a height of thirty-eight hundred feet above the river. One of the many attractions in the vicinity is the Catskill Falls. Kaaterskill Creek, a branch of Catskill Creek, starting high up in the mountain, as an outlet for two ponds, here dashes over two perpendicular precipices, one a hundred and the other eighty feet in height, and, passing through a precipitous and romantic ravine, called "The Clove," reaches the lower valley of the Hudson.

THE CATSKILLS.

The Catskill Mountains have probably been seen and admired, if not visited, by more travelers than any other mountain group on the American continent. Approaching within ten miles of a great natural highway, they have, since the earliest days of the settlement of the country, commanded the attention of all voyagers on the Hudson River, and, since the enormous increase of travel induced by modern multiplication of railroads and steamboats, they are annually seen by millions and visited by thousands.

Moreover, they have been celebrated in song and story, and one of the most popular and successful actors of our time has made Irving's character of Rip Van Winkle, with the mountain region where he lived and slept, familiar to the English-speaking world. The group of summits known under this name lies within the counties of Greene, Ulster, and Delaware, in New York. They are a part of the great mountain system which follows the Atlantic seaboard from the Arctic regions almost to the Gulf of Mexico, and known at different parts of its course as the White Mountains, the Green Mountains, the Blue Ridge.

In ascending the Hudson, the first point of divergence for mountain travel is Rondout (city of Kingston). Here is the terminus of the Ulster & Delaware Railroad, following up the valley of the Esopus, which skirts and penetrates the southern and western portion of the mountains. The opening of this road rendered access to this portion of the mountains so easy, that numerous and excellent hotels have been built in localities which the traveler could formerly reach only by a long and tedious stage route.

The track rises by a steep gradient 184 feet above the river, and almost immediately comes in sight of Overlook Mountain. In the nine miles which are passed before reaching West Hurley, the train climbs 530 feet above the river. Before reaching the station, the Overlook Mountain House may be seen perched upon the shoulder of the mountain, and seeming much nearer than the railway will seem when viewed from above. The profile of the range is exceedingly fine from this point of view, and there are many who derive more enjoyment from looking *at* a mountain range than in looking *from* it. The stage road tends in

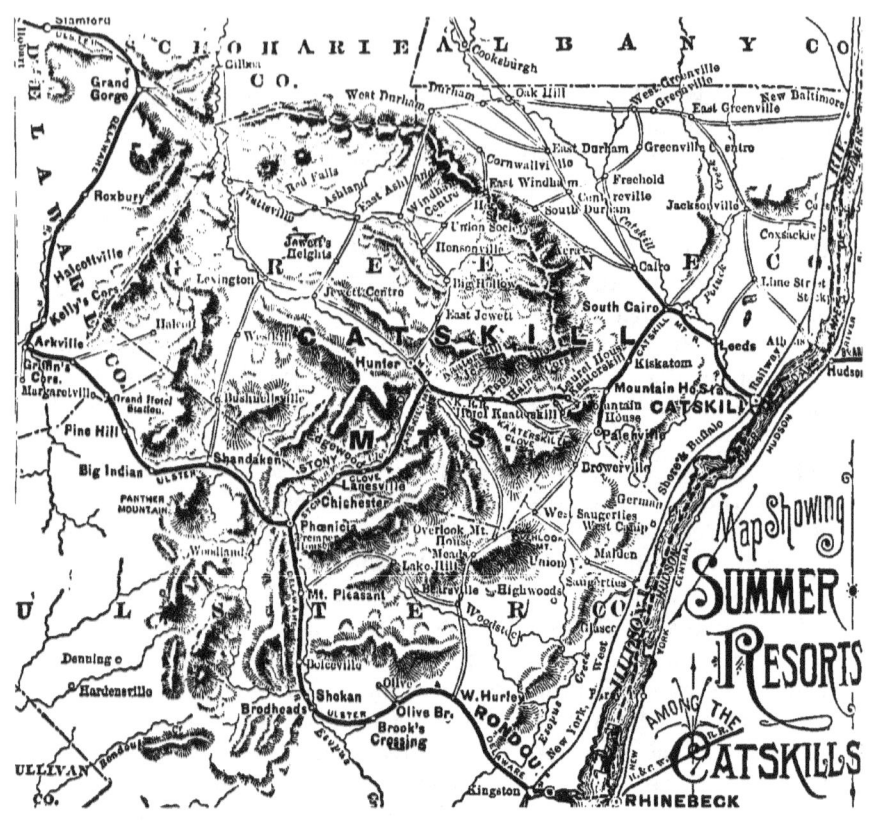

a northerly direction after leaving the station, leaves the outlying range with its three summits, Tonche Hook, Ticetenyck, and Little Tonche on the left, and soon begins the long ascent of Overlook Mountain.

The hotel stands on a plateau 3,000 feet above tidewater, and a little below the highest point of the mountain, and commands views toward all points of the compass; that toward the south embracing a large portion of the Hudson Valley, and those in other directions commanding mountain and valley scenery in great variety and picturesqueness. In Plattkill Clove, three miles north of the hotel, is a succession of waterfalls, and in every direction there are charming walks to many points of interest. From

WEST HURLEY the railroad follows a westerly course, passing Brodhead's Bridge, where there are fine falls on the Esopus, and an attractive view from the bluffs above the creek.

SHOKAN is picturesquely situated at a mountain gateway through which the Esopus rushes in rapids. High Point Mountain, 3,100 feet high, is seen to the southward. The valley here takes a more northerly course, and on the west side of the track is seen a group of fine summits. The northernmost is the Wittenberg, and the next Mt. Cornell. The walk to the summit of these peaks is a favorite one with mountain climbers. At—

BOICEVILLE the road reaches an elevation of 615 feet above tidewater.

MT. PLEASANT, 24 miles from Rondout, and 700 feet above the river, is the opening of the Shandaken Valley, a mountain depression full of the most enchanting natural scenery.

PHŒNICIA, 27 miles from Rondout, and nearly 800 feet above the Hudson, is a place of considerable resort, and the point of departure for Hunter and Tannersville, through Stony Clove, a remarkable ravine, where it is said snow and ice can be found the year through.

Tremper House is at the entrance to Stony Clove. It is on a terrace 300 feet broad and 1,500 long, and almost between Slide Mountain and Hunter Mountain, two of the highest peaks of the Catskills. The hotel will accommodate 200 guests. A carriage road ascends to the summit of Mt. Tremper, affording a superb view of Shandaken Valley, the

NEW YORK CENTRAL RAILROAD.

Lake Mohonk Gap, Wittenberg, Cross Mountain, and an assembly of mountains, too many for enumeration here. At—

FOX HOLLOW the elevation is 999 feet. Before reaching the station a bridge is crossed at the entrance of Woodland Valley. On the northern side of the road are Mts. Sheridan and North Dome.

SHANDAKEN is 33 miles from the river, and 1,060 feet above it. Here passengers for West Kill, Lexington, and Jewett Heights leave the cars and take stages for their destinations.

BIG INDIAN (36 miles) is 1,202 feet above the river. A bridge here crosses the Esopus, from which a fine view is obtained up Big Indian Valley. This station is nearest to Slide Mountain, and from it parties usually start for the ascent of that peak. Carriages can go without especial difficulty within five miles of the summit, and here parties can remain overnight. Dutchers is the name of the place. The view from Slide Mountain is one of the finest in the Catskills.

PINE HILL, 1,660 feet above the sea, is 39 miles from Rondout. Half a mile from Pine Hill station is the Guigou House. After passing over the Grand Horseshoe Curve the train reaches—

GRAND HOTEL STATION, 1,889 feet above the Hudson River at Rondout, which is the highest point on the Ulster & Delaware R. R.

The new Grand Hotel stands on Summit Mountain, about one eighth of a mile from the station, and 2,500 feet above the level of the sea. It is in a remarkably picturesque and healthy part of the mountains, and commands a view of marvelous beauty and grandeur. Summit Mountain is in the center of a group of peaks made celebrated by artists, writers, and historic associations. Around it are the Panther Mountain, 4,000 feet high ; the Belle Air Table and Slide Mountain, 4,220 feet high, the highest mountain in the Catskills, and whose crest pierces the clouds. It has a frontage of 650 feet, with piazzas along the front of the main buildings.

Parlor cars run on the West Shore Railroad direct to the Grand Hotel station.

Catskill Mountain House is reached by the Ulster & Delaware Railroad to Kaaterskill station, thence by stage one mile ; or by the Catskill Mountain Railway from Catskill to Mountain House station, thence up the mountain by stage ; or by carriage all the way from Catskill.

The Laurel House commands magnificent views down the famous Kaaterskill Clove. The hotel has recently been greatly enlarged and improved by the introduction of modern improvements. Piazzas commanding the grandest views of mountain scenery surround the house. The famous Kaaterskill Falls and Clove, and many other of the most charming attractions of the Catskills are near the Laurel House. The great beauty of this locality is so well known that a description is unnecessary. To the lovers of quiet, its secluded walks afford delightful retreats ; while the drives in the vicinity—especially through the Cloves—are remarkably beautiful. There is also good trout-fishing in the neighborhood. The Laurel House is reached by stages and carriages from Mountain House Station of the Catskill Mountain R. R. from Catskill. Carriages, and an authorized agent, are also in attendance at the cars and boats at Catskill.

PALENVILLE is at the lower entrance of Kaaterskill Clove. It is 10 miles by railroad from Catskill village, 3 miles below the falls, and has a number of excellent hotels and boarding-houses.

TANNERSVILLE is 15 miles from Catskill Village, high up in the Kaaterskill Clove, on the way to Hunter. It is surrounded on all sides by towering summits and wild ravines. The Stony Clove Railroad runs from Phœnicia to Tannersville Junction and Hunter through the famous Stony Clove. A branch runs to Hotel Kaaterskill, which stands on the summit of Kaaterskill Mountain, 3,000 feet above the sea, commanding the most extensive view of any hotel in the Catskill Mountains. The view embraces 60 miles of the Hudson River and valley, High Peak and Round Top mountains, Kaaterskill Clove, Sunset Rock, and many other noted and interesting objects. The mountain drives are numerous and particularly charming. Hotel Kaaterskill is reached by the Ulster & Delaware Railroad from Rondout, N. Y., on the Hudson River, to Phœnicia and the Stony Clove Railroad to Tannersville Junction, thence five miles by Kaaterskill Railroad to Hotel Kaaterskill.

HUNTER, 1,600 feet above the Hudson River, is about 4 miles west of Tannersville, and, while it is a village of a somewhat more prominent character, possesses, in the main, similar natural advantages. The Hunter House, Breeze Lawn Hotel, Central House, Villa Du Bois, and Ripley House are among the most prominent abiding-places for summer visitors.

CAUTERSKILL FALLS, CATSKILL MOUNTAINS,
Near Laurel House.   J. L. Schutt, Proprietor.

NEW YORK CENTRAL RAILROAD.

LEXINGTON is 9 miles from Hunter, and 10 miles from railway connections on the Ulster & Delaware Railroad. The O'Hara House and the Douglass House will be found comfortable stopping-places.

WEST KILL, 4 miles from Lexington, is near Deep Hollow Gorge, in some parts of which the sun never shines.

CAIRO is 10 miles from Catskill, near Round Top Mountain, and facing the Hudson Valley. Merritt's Grand View House and the Webster House are among the principal hotels. The surroundings are highly picturesque and attractive.

FREEHOLD is a resort of considerable popularity. It is reached by stage from Catskill or Athens, and commands a very fine view of the mountain range,—Black Head, 3,965 feet high, being the nearest and most conspicuous.

ACRA is on the road from Catskill northward. Mott's Sunside Farm is one of the resorts of the vicinity.

EAST WINDHAM is reached by a good road from Catskill. Lamoreau's Summit House is the principal hotel. From here it is said that the Adirondacks and White Mountains can at times be seen.

WINDHAM, a delightful village 25 miles from Catskill, is beautifully situated, amid lovely mountain scenery. Reasonably good roads lead in all directions. The Windham House is one mile from the village.

JEWETT HEIGHTS is a small village in full sight of the Catskill range, and commanding a wide view of the Hudson. The Jewett Height House is available for boarders.

PRATTSVILLE is situated on Schoharie Hill, with well-shaded streets and the purest of mountain air. There is a daily line of stages from Catskill and from Stratton's Falls on the Ulster & Delaware Railroad. The village contains several excellent hotels and boarding-houses.

NEW YORK CENTRAL RAILROAD.

The New York Central & Hudson River route continues on the eastern shore of the Hudson River.

HUDSON, Hudson City, Columbia County, New York, 115 miles from New York. The city of Hudson, incorporated in 1785, is the capital of Columbia County, and occupies a site of great beauty, being built upon a promontory jutting into the Hudson River, and commanding the most extensive and charming views in every direction. Upon the summit of the bluff overlooking the river, a public square and a broad street or promenade have been laid out, and ornamented with trees and shrubbery. Fine views are afforded of the city, the river, and the country on the opposite shore, with the Catskill Mountains in the background. The city extends up the slope of Prospect Hill, which rises to a height of 200 feet. The elevation just below Hudson landing is Mount Merino. It is cultivated over almost its whole surface of 600 acres. Hudson, being at the head of ship navigation, was of great importance in the early commerce of the river, and it rapidly grew to be a place of considerable size and wealth. Population, 15,000. Considerable business is now done in the manufacture of iron, and the export of agricultural staples. The Claverack Creek, a romantic stream, is a little east of Hudson, and, running northward, joins other streams, forming Columbiaville Creek.

The Hudson & Chatham Railway, leased by the Boston & Albany R.R. Co., has its western terminus here, and connects at Chatham with the Boston & Albany and the Harlem railways.

The sect known as "Shakers," made so conspicuous a few years ago by Hepworth Dixon in his "New America," may be seen at their headquarters, a few miles from Hudson. Tourists wishing to visit them can take a train from Hudson to Chatham, thence, by the Boston & Albany line, direct to the village in which these peculiar people live. Those who have visited Mount Lebanon declare that the settlement of the Shakers is well worthy of inspection. Strangers are always well received, and invariably receive courteous and hospitable treatment.

The "quaint old village" of Claverack, in Columbia County, is located four miles inland from Hudson. Descendants of the Muhlers, Ostranders, and Van Rensselaers reside at Claverack, in the houses occupied by their forefathers. There is a "Spook Rock" in the neighborhood, which is said to turn in its bed when the bell of an adjacent schoolhouse rings. Directly opposite Hudson is the village of—

* ATHENS, Athens, Greene County, New York, 115 miles from New York. This village was originally fixed upon as the eastern terminus of the Erie Canal, but the project was abandoned. The inhabitants are largely engaged in shipbuilding and brickmaking. The West Shore Railroad runs through West Athens, one mile west of Athens, with which it connects by stage. A ferry connects Athens with Hudson. Above Athens and Hudson, on the east side of the river, is Roger's Island, behind which the shipping of New York merchants was concealed during the Revolutionary War. At that time the island was densely wooded, and formed an effectual screen.

STOCKPORT, Stockport, Columbia County, New York, 119 miles from New York. Columbiaville is the name of the village at the station. It is in the township of Stockport, at the mouth of Kinderhook River. Five miles up this river is Lindenwald, in Kinderhook township, the former residence of Martin Van Buren. The Columbia Sulphur Springs near Stottsville have a fine hotel and bathing-houses, and have become quite a popular place of resort for invalids and others.

The next place of interest, north of Athens, on the eastern bank, is—

COXSACKIE STATION, Stuyvesant, Columbia County, New York, 123 miles from New York, formerly called Kinderhook Station, which is connected by ferry with—

* COXSACKIE LANDING, Coxsackie, Greene County, New York, 123 miles from New York. This village is on the west side of the river, and is a station of the West Shore Railway. Its name is derived from an Indian word signifying "cut banks." The chief occupations of the inhabitants are shipbuilding, farming, and shad-fishing. The headland nearly opposite is Newtown Hook.

STUYVESANT, Stuyvesant, Columbia County, New York, 125 miles from New York, possesses a foundry and flouring-mill. At Stuyvesant Falls, on Kinderhook River, in the south-east part of the township, there are several cotton and woolen mills, and other manufactories. The landing-place or station is five miles from the ancient Dutch inland hamlet of Kinderhook—a Dutch word meaning "Children's Point," and said to have been given by Hendrick Hudson on seeing crowds of Indian children watching him from the banks. Martin Van Buren, eighth President of the United States, was born at Kinderhook in 1782.

NEW YORK CENTRAL RAILROAD.

*NEW BALTIMORE, New Baltimore, Albany County. New York, 127 miles from New York, is opposite the middle of Schodack Island, which is three miles long. The chief business of this place is shipbuilding. There are several yards with complete sets of ways, etc. Schooners, sloops, and barges are the craft which are built. The West Shore Railroad runs through the village.

Here begin the Government dikes. As early as 1790 State appropriations were made for the purpose of improving the channel, but all efforts were unavailing until the present system of dikes was commenced. Mr. A. Van Santvoord and others caused the subject to be brought before the State Legislature, and work was begun in 1863. In 1868 the United States Government assumed the work of completing the dikes. They now extend several miles along the river, effectually accomplishing the purpose for which they were intended.

Near this point may be seen Beeren, or Bear Island—meeting-point of the four counties of Albany, Rensselaer, Columbia, and Greene—site of the "Castle of Rensselaerstein," from whose wall Nicholas Kroon, the agent of Killian Van Rensselaer, the Patroon, compelled passing vessels to dip their colors and pay tribute, or take the chances of being sunk by the ordnance of the fort.

SCHODAC, Schodac, Rensselaer County, New York, 132 miles from New York. A small village on the east bank of the river. Good farming lands lie along the river, and the surrounding region is a pleasant rolling country. The name is from Is-cho-da, a "fire-plain." Schodac was the council-ground of the Mohegans. Here their great Sachem Aepgin sold his dominions on the east bank of the Hudson to Killian Van Rensselaer in 1680. "The Mohegans originally occupied the east bank of the Hudson from Germantown to its head waters, and the west bank from Cohoes to Catskill. They suffered from the attacks of the Mohawks and the early encroachments of the Dutch, and moved east into Massachusetts, and afterwards west to Wisconsin."

*COEYMAN'S, Coeyman's, Albany County, New York, 132 miles from New York, on the west bank of the river. Its name (pronounced Que-mans) is that of one of its early settlers. The mountains seen to the westward are the Helderbergs. Coeyman's is the junction of the Albany Branch with the main line of the New York, West Shore & Buffalo Railway. The main line diverges northwestward to central New York and Buffalo.

NEW YORK CENTRAL RAILROAD.

CASTLETON, Schodac, Rensselaer County, New York, 135 miles from New York, is a small and compact village, built upon a steep hillside on the eastern bank of the river, which at this point passes through meadow lands and is quite shallow. To navigators, the Hudson at Castleton was formerly known as the "Overslaugh." Many attempts have been made to deepen the channel, but without permanent success. This sand-bar, as it is termed, has proved fatal to more steamboats and other vessels than any known place on the continent.

Nine miles north of Castleton, on the east bank, is—

EAST ALBANY, Greenbush, Rensselaer County, New York, 144 miles from New York, connected with Albany by two fine railroad bridges. This is the point of separation for those traveling still further north, and those westward bound, the former continuing on to Troy and other northern points, while the latter are borne across one or other of the stupendous bridges that span the Hudson and form a connecting link between East Albany and the State Capital.

KENMORE HOTEL, ALBANY, N. Y.
Located on North Pearl Street, convenient to Capitol, Depots, Boat Landings, and Post Office. Elevator, steam heat, and all modern appliances for elegance and comfort. Now under the proprietorship of H. J. ROCKWELL, also of the well-known Wayside Hotel, Lake Luzerne, N.Y.
F. W. ROCKWELL, Manager. H. J. ROCKWELL, Proprietor.

ALBANY.

Albany County, New York, 144 m. fr. New York. Pop. 90,758.
HOTELS : *Delavan, Kenmore, Brunswick, and American.*

This city, the capital of the State of New York, and eastern terminus of the New York Central and Hudson River Railroad, lies on the west bank of the Hudson River, near the middle of the county, in the midst of a fertile and well-cultivated section, and embraces a strip of land about one and a half miles wide, extending thirteen and a half miles in a northwest direction, to the northern boundary of the county. Before incorporation it was known under the names of "Beverwyck," "William Stadt," and "New Orange." The seat of the State Government, originally fixed at New York city, was removed to this place in 1798. After Jamestown, Va., and St. Augustine, Fla., Albany is the oldest town in the Union, having been founded by the Dutch in 1623. It was called Albany in 1664, in honor of the Duke of York and Albany. The early growth of the city was exceedingly slow ; its population numbering less than 10,000 at the end of a century from its incorporation, which was in 1686. In 1714, when a century old, it contained only 3,329 inhabitants, nearly 500 of whom were slaves. Steam navigation, originated by Fulton on the Hudson in 1807, and the completion of the Erie Canal in 1825, each gave powerful impulses to its growth, and in less than half a century it added more than 50,000 to its population.

The whole city, comprised within the limits of Pearl, Steuben, and Beaver Streets in 1676, was surrounded by wooden walls, with openings for musketry. There were six gates to the city, and the maintenance of these fragile defenses was the source of unceasing contention between the authorities and the inhabitants. A portion of these walls were remaining so late as 1812. They were thirteen feet in height, and made of timber about a foot square. The city has many handsome avenues, and the walks and drives about the city are beautiful. A walk of half a mile from the city brings to view the verdure-clad mountains of Vermont and the towering Catskills.

The first railroad in the State of New York, and the second in the United States, was opened from Albany to Schenectady in 1831. The commerce of Albany is considerable. Besides the great natural means of communication which the river affords, in Day Line and

NEW YORK CENTRAL RAILROAD.

People's Line of steamers, the city is connected with New York by three lines of railroad, the Hudson River, the Harlem, and the West Shore. The New York Central and West Shore Railroads and the Erie Canal connect it with the Great Lakes. It communicates with Northern New York, Vermont, and Canada by the Delaware and Hudson Canal Co.'s Railroad, and by the way of Troy by the Troy and Boston Railway, and by the Champlain Canal. By the Boston and Albany Railway it communicates with the New England States, and by the Albany and Susquehanna division of the Delaware and Hudson Canal Co.'s R.R. with Binghamton on the Erie Railway, and the coal regions of Pennsylvania.

The two railroad drawbridges across the Hudson are each over 4,000 feet in length, one at the northern part of the city, now used entirely for freight trains, and the magnificent new iron bridge at the central part of the city, at the west end of which is the passenger depot for the city of Albany, and at the east end is the station for East Albany. The bridge cost nearly $2,000,000.

The manufactures are extensive and varied. Its numerous stove foundries and breweries are on an immense scale. Seventy thousand barrels of ale are made annually at one brewery. The workshops of the N. Y. C. & H. R. Railroad, at West Albany, give employment to more than two thousand persons. Its other manufactures are varied and extensive. The sales of barley amount to more than 2,000,000 bushels per annum, most of which is consumed by the brewers. Lumber is another very important article of trade. Albany is also one of the leading cattle marts of the country. The markets at Bull's Head, in New York, and at Brighton, near Boston, receive many of their supplies from here.

The State buildings include the new Capitol, a magnificent structure at the head of State Street, State Hall, State Library, Geological and Agricultural Hall, Normal School, and State Arsenal and Armory. The City Hall is an elegant structure, faced with Sing Sing marble, and surmounted by a gilded dome. The new post-office is located on Broadway, at the foot of State Street, and in architectural beauty is one of the finest post-offices in the State. The Albany County Almshouse is the magnificent brick building observed on the west bank of the Hudson just before reaching Albany. The Penitentiary is in the west part of the city.

Besides Public Schools, the Educational Institutions are the Albany Academy, Albany Female Academy, Albany Female Seminary, Albany Institute, and the Albany Industrial School. The public schools afford instruction to 25,000 children of both sexes, and are conducted at an annual expense of $100,000. There are two Christian Associations, Protestant and Catholic, the former being the oldest institution of the kind in the United States. The Dudley Observatory, on an eminence in the northern border of the city, was incorporated April 2, 1852; it was founded through the munificence of Mrs. Blandina Dudley, who gave $90,000 for its construction and endowment. The building, constructed in the form of a cross, is admirably arranged, and is furnished with some of the largest and finest instruments ever constructed. It has an extensive library attached.

The Albany Medical College and the Law School of the University of Albany are on Eagle Street, and have all the facilities for teaching the respective sciences. The Albany Almshouse, Insane Asylum, and a Fever Hospital are located upon a farm of 116 acres, one and a half miles southwest of the city, and are under the management of the city authorities. The Industrial School building is located on the same farm. The Albany City Hospital, on Eagle Street, was incorporated in 1849. The Albany Orphan Asylum, on Washington Street, at the junction of the Western Turnpike, was incorporated in 1831; it was erected, as was the City Hospital, by private subscription; it is now aided by State funds. The St. Vincent Orphan Asylum, incorporated in 1849, is under the charge of the Sisters of Mercy. The male department, two miles west of the Capitol, is under the charge of the Christian Brothers.

The first church (Ref. Prot. D.) was formed in 1640. A Lutheran Church existed in 1680. The first Protestant Episcopal Church (St. Peter's) was erected in 1715; it stood in the center of State Street, opposite Chapel Street. The communion plate of this church was presented to the Onondagas by Queen Anne. The most costly edifices are the Catholic Cathedral of the Immaculate Conception, corner of Eagle and Lydius Streets, and the St. Joseph's (R. C.) Church.

Water is supplied to the city from Rensselaer Lake, about five miles west of the City Hall, and 225 feet above the level of the water of the Hudson. This lake covers thirty-nine acres, and its capacity is 180,000,000 gallons. A brick conduit conveys the water to Bleecker Reservoir, on Patroon Street, whence it is distributed through the city. This reservoir has a capacity of 30,000,000 gallons. The cost of the construction of these works was upwards of $1,000,000.

The Delavan House, on Broadway, adjoining the New York Central and Hudson River R. R. Depot, is one of the finest hotels in the country. It has long been celebrated for its excellent cuisine

and fine furnishings. It is kept by T. Roessle, and its management is very efficient and remarkably popular.

The Hotel Kenmore is a new house, kept by H. J. Rockwell, and is situated on North Pearl Street, two blocks from the N. Y. Central R. R. Depot, and a short distance from the Capitol. It is fitted up in modern style, with elevator, hot and cold running water, and steam heaters ; telephone connected with the office in each room. It is strictly first class in all respects.

North of the city is the ALBANY RURAL CEMETERY, one of the most beautiful rural cemeteries in the country, abounding in romantic dells, shaded ravines, cascades, miniature lakes, rustic bridges over forest streams, etc. It is a place of rare picturesque beauty.

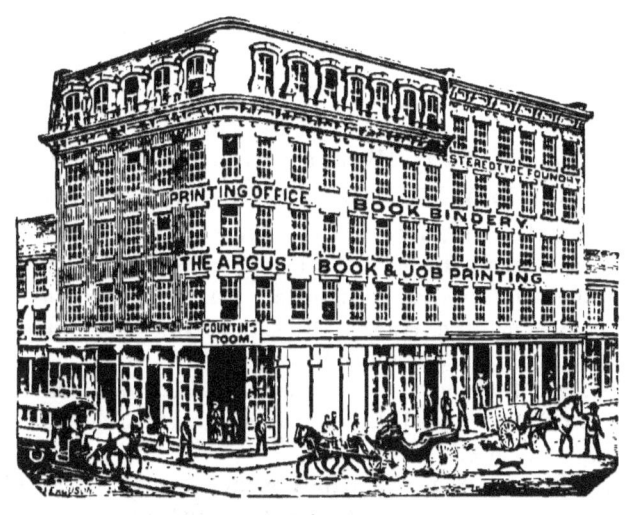

The Argus

ESTABLISHED 1813.

DAILY, WEEKLY AND SEMI-WEEKLY,

Cor. BROADWAY and BEAVER STREET, ALBANY, N. Y.

The Cheapest and Most Widely-Circulated Democratic Newspaper in the United States.

PRICES.

Daily, $8. Daily, with Sunday Edition, $10. Semi-Weekly, $2.25. Weekly, $1. Sunday Edition, $2.

CLUBS AT REDUCED RATES.

Payments always in Advance.

The Argus Company are fully prepared to do all kinds of

Printing, Binding, Stereotyping, and Electrotyping,

IN THE BEST MANNER AND AT THE LOWEST RATES.

All correspondence should be addressed to

THE ARGUS COMPANY,
Albany.

TROY.

Rensselaer Co., N. Y., 150 *m. fr. New York. Pop.*, 56,747.

HOTELS : *Troy House, American, and Mansion House.*

The capital of Rensselaer County is situated at the head of navigation on the Hudson River, and famous for its manufactures.

It is principally located upon an alluvial flat, three-fourths of a mile wide, between the Hudson River and the high bluffs which bound it on the east. The bluff directly east of the city is known as Mount Ida, and that on the northeast as Mount Olympus. Mount Ida is principally composed of clay, and has been the scene of several destructive landslides.

Poesten Kill and Wynant's Kill, breaking through these hills in narrow ravines, form a series of cascades which afford an excellent water-power. The city charter was granted April 12, 1816. A terrible fire in 1862 destroyed forty acres of its dwellings. The total property destroyed amounted to more than $3,000,000, one half of which was covered by insurance.

The city contains a very handsome court-house of Sing-Sing marble, wide and well-paved streets, planted with shade-trees, extensive water-works, gas-works, and other improvements usual in a prosperous modern city. The Troy water-works were built by the city in 1833–1834, and have since been extended. The water is drawn from the Piscawin Creek, and the reservoir is sufficiently high to raise it to the tops of most of the houses.

There are twenty-two factories operated by water-power, a part of which is afforded by a dam thrown across the Hudson, which also renders the river above navigable for canal-boats. Numerous iron-foundries and machine-shops afford employment to large numbers of the inhabitants. Some of these are of great magnitude, and in the aggregate employ 3,000 men. The establishment of Messrs. Winslow, Griswold, & Holly, where the Bessemer cast-steel is manufactured, is the largest of the kind in the United States.

The famous original "Monitor" was constructed by these gentlemen ; they also had a contract subsequently to build six other iron-clad vessels. The Troy horseshoe, railroad-spike, and nail manufactory is one of the largest in the State. The manufacture of cotton and woolen goods is also conducted on a large scale. The railway-car manufactory here is the largest in the State. Paper, hosiery, carriages, clothing, shirts, collars, mathematical instruments, etc., are largely manufactured. Breweries, distilleries, flour and grist-mills, are many in number.

The educational institutions, besides the public schools, are the Troy Academy, incorporated in 1834; the Troy Female Seminary, first established at Middlebury, Vt., in 1813, removed to Waterford in 1819, and thence to this place in 1821, incorporated in 1837. This institution gained a national reputation under the charge of Mrs. Emma Willard. Upwards of 7,000 pupils have been educated here. The Rensselaer Polytechnic Institute, organized in 1824, was endowed by Stephen Van Rensselaer. It was formed for the purpose of teaching the application of mathematics to civil engineering and the natural sciences. Next to West Point this institute has the best reputation in its special departments of any school in America. The Troy Lyceum of Natural History was incorporated in 1820. St. Peter's College is built on Mount St. Vincent. The college building, in process of erection, was destroyed by a landslide in 1859; has since been rebuilt. St. Joseph's Academy was founded in 1842.

The charitable institutions are many. The Troy Hospital, in the care of the Sisters of Charity, was incorporated in 1851. The Marshall Infirmary, incorporated in 1851, was built at an expense of $35,000, which was donated by Benj. Marshall, Esq. The Troy Orphan Asylum, incorporated in 1835, situated on Grand Division Street, is built of brick, and supported by private donations and State appropriations. Children between three and nine years are received, and dismissed at ten, when suitable situations can be obtained. St. Mary's Orphan Asylum, connected with St. Mary's Church (R. C.), is under the care of the Christian Brothers and Sisters of Charity. The Warren Free Institute, a school for indigent female children, was incorporated in 1846. It was endowed by the Warren family. A free church for the pupils and their parents is connected with the Institute.

Troy being at the head of tidal waters, steamers run to it daily. Besides the Hudson River, the Erie Canal, and the Champlain, giving water communication of vast extent, railroads connect the city with every part of the country. The Union Railway Depot is used for the

NEW YORK CENTRAL RAILROAD.

joint accommodation of the great railroads that center here, viz.: the New York Central & Hudson River (uniting at Schenectady with the other branch from Albany), the Delaware & Hudson Canal Co.'s R.R., the Troy & Boston Railway, the two latter running northerly through eastern New York and western Vermont, and connecting with roads to Plattsburgh, Burlington, Montreal, etc. The Central Vermont R.R. forms a direct connection here for Bennington, Manchester, Rutland, Burlington, St. Albans, Montreal, etc. The Troy & Boston Railway forms a direct route to Boston *via* Hoosac Tunnel, one of the long tunnels of the world.

Fifteen minutes after leaving Troy, on our way to Syracuse, Rochester, Buffalo, Niagara Falls, and the Suspension Bridge, via Schenectady, we arrive at—

COHOES, Watervliet, Albany County, New York, 153 miles from New York, an important manufacturing city on the Mohawk River. An extensive dam creates an immense water-power here, comprising the whole body of the Mohawk River, with a total descent of 103 feet. The railroad bridge across the Mohawk is 900 feet in length, and is in full view of the Cohoes Falls, about three-fourths of a mile above. The river here flows over a rocky declivity 78 feet in height, of which 40 feet is a perpendicular fall. The main fall is 900 feet wide, and the banks above and below are wild and precipitous. The Erie Canal rises by a series of 18 locks from the Hudson River, through the village of Cohoes, to the northerly part of the town of Watervliet, three miles above, at which point it crosses the river in a stone aqueduct, 1,137 feet long, 26 feet high, and resting on 26 piers.

The products of the knitting and cotton mills, axe and edge tool, and other factories, amount to over $2,000,000 per annum. In recent excavations made in the rocky bank of the Mohawk, for the foundation of a new mill, the fossil remains of a gigantic mastodon were discovered. The Harmony Mills Co. of Cohoes have liberally donated this interesting relic of the earth's ancient history to the State collection at Albany. It is considered as the most perfect skeleton of the mastodon ever discovered. Leaving Cohoes, and passing

CRESCENT, DUNSBECK FERRY, NISKAYUNA, and **AQUEDUCT,** which are unimportant way stations along the Mohawk River and valley, a forty-five minute run brings us to—

SARATOGA SPRINGS.

Saratoga Co., N. Y.—182 m. fr. New York. Population, 10,000.

But little of the town can be seen from the railroad, as the traveler approaches Saratoga Springs. It is somewhat irregularly laid out, and many of its streets are pleasantly shaded. The land on which the town proper stands is sufficiently level to render all parts of the place of easy access on foot or in a carriage, and yet is broken into low, rolling hills, so that the monotony of a dead level is pleasantly relieved. The population is about 10,000 during the winter, and rather more than double that number in the summer.

Saratoga abounds in magnificent hotels, handsome villas, and a multitude of boarding-houses. The town devotes itself to entertaining visitors in summer, and leisure in winter.

Near the central part of the town and overlooked by the principal buildings and hotels, is a shallow valley, beneath which, deep in the bowels of the earth, is one of the most wonderful of Nature's laboratories. There she prepares solutions of various medicinal and mineral substances with a subtle power of combination which no chemistry has been able successfully to imitate, and sends the different solutions to the surface of the earth by channels which reach the light within a few rods of one another, yet discharge waters distinct in constituents, various in medicinal effects, and uniform in temperature.

We cannot wonder that, in an age which believed in a plurality of gods, mineral springs were regarded with mingled fear and veneration. We have very ancient accounts of such springs, which were valued for their natural and worshipped for their supernatural properties. Greek and Roman, and even Hebrew and Chaldaic writers, mention charmed fountains whose waters cured disease and almost restored the dead to life. The fabled fountain of eternal youth doubtless had its origin in the bubbling waters of some mineral spring, as well as in the fancy of the poet who first gave it a name. Even in the time of our Saviour, the Pool of Bethesda was famous, and was visited by invalids from all Palestine.

Saratoga County, near the center of which are the Springs, is bounded on the south and east by the Mohawk and Hudson rivers, along whose banks are a variety of picturesque drives through scenery of intrinsic beauty and interesting historic associations.

SARATOGA ILLUSTRATED.

Congress Hall

Is built on the site of the old and famous hotel of the same name which was burned in 1866, and occupies the larger part of the square bounded by Broadway, East Congress, Spring and Putnam Streets. Its situation is in the very center of the gay and fashionable hotel world of Saratoga, and is admirably arranged for seeing all the attractive phases of the "great watering-place" life. Its frontage on Broadway, the principal street of the town, is 416 feet, with a high promenade piazza 20 feet wide and 249 feet in length, commanding a view of the most brilliant portion of Saratoga. From the Broadway front two immense wings, 300 feet long, extend to Putnam Street, the northern wing, running along Spring Street and overlooking the celebrated Hathorn and Hamilton Springs on one side, and with the central wing which runs parallel with it, enclosing a very beautiful garden-plot. The southern front commands a full view of the famous Congress and Columbian Springs, and the beautiful Congress Park, owned and adorned by the Congress Spring Company. Ample piazzas extend around the back of the hotel, overlooking the grass and garden-plots of the interior court, affording cool and shady retreats in the afternoon, when entrancing music is discoursed by one of the best hotel bands in Saratoga.

Congress Hall is built in the most substantial manner of brick with brown-stone trimmings, and presents one of the most graceful architectural appearances in Saratoga. Its walls are 20 inches thick and hollow in the center, thus securing great strength and protection from heat of summer. The roof is a Mansard, with three pavilions, which afford wide and delightful views from the promenades on top. Interior fire-walls are provided to prevent the spread of fire, and Otis elevators afford easy access to all the floors of the house. The rooms are all large, high and well ventilated, and properly provided with annunciators, gas, etc. The halls, dining-rooms, parlors, and offices are of grand proportions, and are furnished with an elegance that bespeaks comfort and neatness in all its departments. The ventilation of the dining-room and kitchen has been much improved, and a Steam Heating Apparatus introduced on the main floor for use whenever changes in the temperature require it. Hot and cold

CONGRESS HALL, Saratoga Springs, N. Y.

H. S. CLEMENT Manager. CLEMENT & COX

RATES:—$3.00, $3.50 and $4.00 per day, according to location of rooms.

water have been carried to every floor, and a large number of baths and closets added for the convenience of guests.

There has also been a complete renovation of the furniture, and the rooms, halls, and parlors have been recarpeted, and 200 rooms refurnished throughout and the walls refinished. The public parlors have been refurnished with new Wilton carpets, and the reception rooms, office and dining-room renewed. The kitchen department has been thoroughly reorganized at a large expense, and will this year be made equal to the best. The office has been tiled and greatly improved. The laundry has been greatly improved and its facilities increased.

The rooms of Congress Hall are larger, and therefore afford pleasanter and more healthy apartments than any other hotel in Saratoga, and will accommodate over 1,000 guests in the most comfortable style. The beds are the easiest and best spring and hair mattresses to be found in this country, and ample presses, closets, etc., afford all desirable conveniences. The ball-room of the Congress is one of the finest in Northern New York, being most exquisitely frescoed and adorned with costly chandeliers and ornaments. It is in the block across Spring Street, but is connected with the north wing of the hotel by a light, graceful iron bridge suspended over the street, covered and protected, which, when illuminated on hop nights, is very picturesque.

Congress Hall is favored with a superior class of visitors, which annually includes the finest families of our metropolitan cities.

In 1878, Mr. W. H. Clement, of Cincinnati, Ohio, President of the Cincinnati and Southern R. R. Co., and Mr. John Cox, of New York, gentlemen of large means, purchased Congress Hall and have since added many improvements. They have placed it under its present efficient and popular management, which now includes Mr. H. S. Clement, who has attained distinction as a manager of first-class hotels and who was proprietor of Congress Hall in its palmiest days, when it stood without a rival in Saratoga.

The great success of Congress Hall is complete proof of the efficiency and popularity of the management. Owing to the very low purchase price of the hotel, the proprietors feel able to keep up the standard of style of its former glorious years and yet keep the prices at the lowest possible and present popular rates. Open from June 19th to October 1st.

THE CLARENDON, Saratoga Springs, N. Y.

AVERILL & GREGORY, Proprietors.

Rates, $2.50 to $4.00 per day, according to location of rooms.

SARATOGA ILLUSTRATED.

The Clarendon Hotel.

This elegant resort of Saratoga stands on Broadway, a short distance south of Congress Street, on one of the pleasantest sites in the village. Recent improvements have made this part of Broadway one of the most attractive portions of the great watering place. The Clarendon is one of the first-class hotels of Saratoga, and has always had the reputation of having a very fine class of guests. It has a quiet air of refinement about all its arrangements, and one feels quite at home in this cheerful and elegant hotel. It can accommodate about 500 guests. Over fifty thousand dollars have recently been expended in remodeling, modernizing, and equipping this hotel in the most improved manner. Among the improvements is a new Otis passenger elevator. The ample and beautifully shaded grounds afford delightful lounging places during the warm summer days. The *cuisine* of this hotel has always been noted for its excellence.

A good band discourses delightful music daily, morning and evening from the piazza overlooking the interior court, which is illuminated in the evening and presents a very picturesque appearance. All the surroundings of the house are pleasant, and there are no inside rooms.

The Clarendon is the only hotel in Saratoga which has a mineral spring within its own grounds. It partly incloses within its wings a beautiful park, ornamented with shade-trees, among which stands the tasteful pagoda covering the popular Washington Spring. This spring water is among the most valuable of the Saratoga waters. (See Analysis, page 68.) It is a tonic water which is highly prized by Saratoga residents, and popular with the visitors. Congress Spring Park is immediately opposite the Clarendon, and such of its guests as prefer Congress or Columbian waters to the springs within their own dooryard can easily reach them.

The Clarendon is a favorite with persons who seek surroundings that promote genuine comfort and afford the luxuries of an elegant summer home.

It has recently been purchased by Messrs. Averill and Gregory, who personally superintend the hotel. They are experienced and successful managers.

The Worden

Is situated on the corner of Broadway and Division Street, directly opposite the United States Hotel. It is one of the best constructed hotels in Saratoga, comfortably fitted up and admirably conducted by the proprietor, Mr. W. W. Worden. The Worden is the headquarters for tobogganists during the winter season, and is yearly becoming more popular with summer

residents and transient visitors, who appreciate comfort, quietness, good food, reasonable charges, never-failing courtesy, and attention. This hotel takes high rank among the Saratoga hostelries. It is conveniently located, being but two minutes' walk from the depot, has ample accommodations for 300 persons, and is open all the year round.

DRS. STRONG'S SANITARIUM, Saratoga Springs, N. Y.

Open all the year. Location delightful and central. Table and appointments first class. Bath department complete and elegant. Society genial and cultured. Summer resort of many eminent persons for rest and recreation as well as treatment. Among its patrons are Rev. Theo. L. Cuyler, D.D. (B'klyn); Rev. D. R. Kerr, D.D. (Richmond); Rev. Chas. F. Deems, D.D. (N.Y.); Rev. C. C. ("chaplain") McCabe, D.D.; Rev. Dr. Jno. Potts (Toronto); Bishops Foss and Bowman; Hon. F. C. Sessions (Columbus, O.); Rev. Homer Eaton, D.D. (M. E. Book Concern, N.Y.); Jas. McCreery (N.Y.); ex-Gov. Wells (Va.); Rev. Dr. McCosh (Pres. Princeton); T. Sterry Hunt, LL.D. (Cantab.); Judges Reynolds, Hand, Bliss, Drake; Med. Prof's Ross, Knapp, Miss Frances E. Willard, and many others equally well known.

Turkish, Russian, Roman, Electro-thermal Baths, Massage, Etc.

CHAPTER IV.
INSTITUTIONS AND BOARDING-HOUSES.

The institutions and boarding-houses of Saratoga afford excellent accommodations at moderate prices, and are decidedly homelike and healthful. Many of them have beautiful lawns for croquet and outdoor sports, and are very attractive in their external surroundings, while the prices for board are very moderate.

The institutions for the special treatment of diseases in Saratoga are few, but one or two are recognized by the medical fraternity as quite superior, and are certainly well supplied with medical appliances, and under competent management. We call attention especially to

Drs. Strongs' Sanitarium.

This excellent institution is pleasantly located on Circular Street, the most beautiful avenue in Saratoga, within five minutes' easy walk of the great hotels, Congress Spring Park, Hathorn, and the principal springs, and other sources of attraction. It is just retired enough for rest, and near enough to all the whirl.

The Sanitarium has the table, appointments, and elegance of a first-class hotel, steam heat, etc. Its bath department compares favorably with the best metropolitan establishments, and offers the only opportunity in Saratoga for obtaining Turkish, Russian, Roman, and Electro-thermal baths. Abundant facilities are afforded for recreation and amusement, comprising organ, pianos, parlor entertainments, fine croquet grounds, gymnasium, etc. A marked and very pleasant feature of the house is its genial cultured society and home-like sociability. It is open all the year for patients and guests, and is the summer resort of many eminent persons for rest and recreation.

Among its patrons are Rev. Theo. L. Cuyler, D.D. (B'klyn), Rev. D. R. Kerr, D.D. (Richmond), Rev. Chas. F. Deems, D.D. (N. Y.), Rev. R. D. Harper, D.D. (Phila.), Rev. C. C. ("Chaplain") McCabe, D.D., Rev. Dr. Jno. Potts, (Toronto); Bishops Foss and Bowman; Hon. F. C. Sessions (Columbus, O.), Rev. Homer Eaton, D.D. (Meth. Book Concern, N. Y.), Jas. McCreery (N. Y.); Ex-Gov. Wells (Va.); Presidents McCosh (Princeton),

Warren (Boston University) ; Judges Reynolds (Brooklyn), Drake (Washington), Hand (Penn.), Bliss (Mo.) ; Med. Profs. Ross (Chicago), Knapp (N. Y.), Ford (Ann Arbor) ; Hon. Geo. S. Batcheller, Asst. Sec. U. S. Treasury, and many others.

Saratoga Springs should have an institution managed by educated physicians, where professional advice, with able and constant medical supervision, can be obtained. Such is Drs. Strong's Sanitarium. A casual observer would not observe its medical character. There is no appearance of invalidism, and its prominent features are those of a first-class family hotel.

The proprietors have received a classical education, and are graduates of the Medical Department of the University of the City of New York. The institution is indorsed and largely patronize by the medical profession. Its ample halls, parlor, dining, bath and other public rooms are heated by steam, while its extensive piazzas and gymnasium afford opportunities for exercise.

In addition to the ordinary remedial agents available in general practice are such special appliances as Turkish, Russian, Roman, Electro-thermal, and every variety of hydropathic baths, Massage, Galvanic and Faradic Electricity, Vacuum Treatment, Movement Cure, Inhalation, Medicated Oxygen, Compressed and Rarefied Air, Health Lift, Calisthenics, Mineral Waters, etc., so that the institution is furnished with every appliance requisite for the treatment of Nervous, Lung, Female, and other chronic diseases.

The dry, uniform, and bracing climate, together with the cathartic, tonic, diuretic, alkaline, and alterative mineral waters, form attractions which bring invalids here at all seasons of the year. Physicians recognize the importance of the mineral waters in many courses of treatment. The danger from their indiscriminate use cannot be too strongly emphasized, as much of their efficacy and marvelous power over disease is due to their proper administration, and, if ignorantly used, they may become as potent agents for harm as they should be for good. Over twenty years' professional observation and experience eminently qualify the Drs. Strong to give advice in regard to them. The advantages of a well-regulated hygiene institution so completely equipped and under the able management of regularly educated physicians are obvious. Circulars sent on application.

SCHENECTADY.

Schenectady County, New York, 17 miles from Abany, 22 miles from Saratoga Springs, 281 miles from Buffalo. A quaint, old-fashioned Dutch town, in the Mohawk Valley. The site on which it is built is a tract purchased from the Indians by the agent of the Rensselaer estate. The settlement was commenced in 1661. It is situated on the Mohawk, and on the borders of one of the finest intervales in the State. In 1690 it contained eighty houses. On the 8th of February in that year, about three hundred French and Indians entered the palisades, which surrounded the city, at the unguarded portals, and fired the dwellings, and attacked the slumbering inmates. Most of the dwellings were destroyed, and the inhabitants who were not carried off, rushing from their beds to escape the savages, perished in the snow. Only a few reached Albany, the nearest shelter.

In 1795 Schenectady was made the headquarters of the "Western Navigation Company," organized to navigate the Mohawk River to Oneida Lake. It was incorporated as a city in 1776. Population, about 15,000. Besides a considerable amount of trade, which is now carried on here by means of the canal and the railways which center here, the people are largely engaged in various manufactures, among which are included machinery, cotton, carriages, agricultural implements, and various utensils, implements, etc. The engine houses and repair shops of the N. Y. Central Railroad Co. are very extensive, and one of the largest locomotive manufactories in the country is located here. This is a great market for broom corn, a staple product of the valley.

Union College, incorporated in 1795, was first erected in the city, but now graces an eminence on its eastern boundary, and commands a fine view for many miles up and down the Mohawk valley. The first college building was erected in 1814. It is largely endowed by grants from the State, and by private contributions. The college has attained a high reputation under the presidencies of Dr. Nott, Dr. Hickok, Dr. Potter, and its present president.

Aid is furnished from the State Fund, to students of limited means without reference to what profession they propose to follow. Through the liberality of E. C. Delavan, Esq., the "Wheatly Collection" of minerals and shells was secured for the college at a cost of $10,000. A department of civil engineering and analytical chemistry has been organized, affording ample facilities in this direction. Union College is the *alma mater* of Hon. W. H. Seward, and many other distinguished statesmen, and men of science and letters. The public schools are well conducted.

The Vale Cemetery Association was organized in 1858. The cemetery contains fifty acres, and is located in a beautiful vale on the border of the city. It is covered with native pines, and is tastefully laid out and ornamented.

Crossing the iron bridge that spans the Mohawk River at this point, we can see the University, as Union College is often called, on the right. The line now traverses those alluvial plains of Glenville which were called Maalwyck and Wolstina by the ancient Dutch colonists.

On the left is the fruitful Bouwland, and Hoffman's Ferry is approached by the Ionarenne Hills. The ferry was established in 1790 by Hermanns Vedder. Glenville was settled by the Dutch in 1665, and was on the manor of Sander Leendertse Glen.

HOFFMAN'S AND CRANE'S VILLAGE are the next two way-stations. At the former, a ferry was established in 1794 by Hermanns Vedder, whose ancestry had settled a century and a half before. It was called Vedder's Ferry until 1835; it was then purchased by John Hoffman, whose name it has since borne.

AMSTERDAM, Montgomery County, New York, 33 miles from Albany, 265 miles from Buffalo, an enterprising and prosperous city of more than 12,000 inhabitants, containing several large factories, and located in the most romantic scenery. It lies partly on an intervale stretching along the northern bank of the Mohawk River, and partly on the rolling upland which gradually rises for a distance of three miles, reaching an elevation of 500 feet. Three streams of considerable size flow through and about it. The soil in the valley is a deep rich alluvium; that on the hills is a fertile gravelly loam.

In operation here are oil factories, foundries, and agricultural works, a skate factory, a water-wheel manufactory, a burial-case manufactory, an extensive brewery, a steel-spring manufactory, and many others. The city also contains several churches, a female seminary, a bank, and a printing-office. A bridge crosses the Mohawk at this point. Considerable architectural taste is displayed in the construction of the residences. The next way-station is—

AKIN, preceding the historical region known as—

TRIBES' HILL, Montgomery County, New York, 39 miles from Albany, a small hamlet and district, deriving the name from the fact that the Indians were accustomed to assemble on this mound on important occasions, where they held their councils and listened to the eloquence of their chieftains. A suspension bridge crosses the Mohawk here, near Schoharie Creek where once stood Fort Hunter. In 1710 several hundred of the Palatinates, who had been previously located on the Hudson by the bounty of Queen Anne, migrated to this neighborhood. In 1780 Sir John Johnson, son of Sir William Johnson, accompanied by a band of Tories and five hundred Indians, made a descent upon Tribes' Hill, destroyed every house which had not a Tory occupant, killed many of the inhabitants, and carried others into captivity.

A second incursion was made by Johnson in October of the same year. The invaders destroyed nearly all the property they left untouched before. The house of Col. Fisher was boldly defended by himself and two brothers, both of whom were slain after one of them had killed seven Indians, with a hatchet, while defending the passage of the staircase with his single arm. The colonel was abandoned as dead, and the whole of his scalp torn from his head by the teeth of the infuriated Indian, but he recovered and survived this violence twenty-one years.

While these atrocities were going on, one of the neighbors escaped and aroused the country, and the Indians were attacked and defeated by Col. Dubois. Johnson and his men would have been captured had not General Robert Van Rensselaer, who commanded the militia, ordered the men to retire for the night, during which the enemy decamped. Johnson visited his inheritance no more. His vast estate was sequestered; his Dutch tenantry were displaced by settlers from New England. The British Governor, however, compensated him for his loss by a grant of $300,000 and a command in the army. Near Tribes' Hill are extensive stone quarries.

NEW YORK CENTRAL RAILROAD.

Five miles further on, we find ourselves alongside the platform at—

FONDA, Montgomery County, New York, 44 miles from Albany, the county seat of Montgomery County, and terminus of the Fonda, Johnstown & Gloversville Railroad. It is pleasantly located on the banks of the Mohawk, and derives its name from Douw Fonda, a Dutchman, who removed hither from Schenectady in 1751, and was subsequently murdered by the Indians, under Johnson, at the age of eighty-four, though he had been the early friend of this leader's father. Johnstown, three miles north of Fonda, was incorporated in 1808, and is now a thriving town. It lies on the southern border of the county.

This place was once the residence of the distinguished Sir William Johnson. This gentleman entered the wilderness as agent for his uncle, Sir Peter Warren, who had an extensive grant from Great Britain. He built a stone mansion here, surpassing in cost and grandeur every dwelling in the valley of the Mohawk. By his tact he won the confidence of the Indians, assuming their dress and learning to speak their language, and entering heartily into all their wild sports. He became agent for Great Britain, and was of great service in settling disputes with the Indians. In 1759, at his call, 2,000 Indian braves assembled, and were led by him to the head of Lake George, where he defeated the French under Dieskau.

For this Parliament voted him £5,000, and the King conferred a baronetcy upon him. He died in 1774, having spent forty years in the wilderness, which he declared were the happiest of his life. He is said to have been the father of a hundred children, and proud was the lofty chief to own that the blood of the great General flowed in the veins of those who were nominally his children. His title, estate, and Indian agency reverted to his son John. The latter espoused the royal cause during the Revolution, and retreated to Canada. The old manorial edifice, which still stands, attests its ancient grandeur.

Gloversville, four miles north of Johnstown, is noted for its extensive manufacture of gloves and mittens. It was incorporated in 1853, and contains a number of glove and mitten factories. Johnstown and Gloversville are connected here with the main line by the Fonda, Johnstown & Gloversville Railroad.

YOSTS, Montgomery County, New York, 49 miles from Albany, and **SPRAKER'S**, 52 miles from Albany, are on the way to—

NEW YORK CENTRAL RAILROAD.

PALATINE BRIDGE, Palatine, Montgomery County, New York, 55 miles from Albany. This place derives its name from the German Palatinates who settled here in 1713, and from the bridge which crosses the Mohawk, and separates it from Canajoharie. Passengers take the stage here for Sharon Springs, a place of considerable resort during the summer season. The ride from Canajoharie to the Springs, a distance of fourteen miles, is one of the most picturesque and beautiful to be found in this part of the country. The accommodations for visitors at the Springs will be found ample and satisfactory. In addition to the "Pavilion," one of the best hotels in the country, there are several other good houses where invalids, seeking a quiet resort and seclusion, can find comfortable quarters in private dwellings.

The mineral springs gush out of the bed of a small brook and from a steep woody slope. The curative properties of the waters were known to the inhabitants of the adjacent regions at the beginning of the present century. Their reputation was confined to the neighborhood until 1830, when their fame began to spread. These springs are now visited annually by hundreds from the large cities, seeking relaxation and enjoyment, as well as by invalids. Springs furnishing water of a character totally different are often found within a few rods, and sometimes a few feet, from one another. On the slope from which the streams flow are five different springs—chalybeate, white sulphur, blue sulphur, magnesia, and pure water. The white sulphur and the magnesia springs are held in the highest repute.

After Butler's raid on Fort Plain in 1780, when fifty-three houses were destroyed and upwards of seventy persons killed or captured, he was attacked by the garrison of Stone Arabia, a hamlet northeast of Palatine Bridge. After an action in which the attacking party were annihilated, Sir John Johnson led the British in retreat, and repelled the militia of the valley in a fight near St. Johnsville.

FORT PLAIN, Minden, Montgomery County, New York, 58 miles from Albany. A prosperous town containing numerous manufactories, including silk and the preparation of springs and axles. The Fort Plain Seminary and Female Collegiate Institute is chiefly under the patronage of the Methodist Episcopal denomination. The Academic building is a fine structure, situated upon a commanding eminence, overlooking the village, and is visible from the car window.

In 1780 the notorious Brandt and his Indians invaded the valley; on arriving at this place he found the women and children placed in the forts for safety, during the absence of their husbands on service. On the appearance of the enemy, these women, clad in their husbands' clothes, boldly stood forth upon the forts, and the red men, thinking them to be able warriors, declined the combat, and retreated to the shelter of the woods. Three miles distant, a stone church, built in 1770, still stands. The edifice was spared at Johnson's raid, as the principal contributors to it were in sympathy with him. Still it was fired upon, through pure wantonness, and the bullet-hole still remains for the inspection of the curious.

OTSEGO LAKE is one of the most beautiful sheets of water of all the chain of inland lakes in the central part of New York State, and affords fine fishing and sailing. It is quite celebrated for its bass, which are caught in large numbers.

COOPERSTOWN is situated at the south end of Otsego Lake, in a beautiful valley 1,200 feet above tidewater, and surrounded with the most charming country, rendered historic by the immortal pen of the novelist and poet Cooper, from whom the place derives its name.

Cooperstown contains two fine hotels, the Cooper House and Fenimore House. The former is open only in summer. A fine new steamer makes frequent excursions on Otsego Lake. Pleasure boats are to be obtained near the hotel, and the sailing, and excursions to the various nooks and pleasure-grounds around the lake, are delightful in the extreme.

ST. JOHNSVILLE, St. Johnsville, Montgomery County, New York, 64 miles from Albany, named from the ancient church of St. John, the site of the Revolutionary forts, House and Hill.

The first settlement was made in 1776, and suffered greatly during the Revolution. Two forts were erected here, which withstood every attack of the British and Indians in their murderous raids through this valley. The battle between Johnson's and Van Rensselaer's army was fought here in 1780. The village contains several extensive manufactories.

EAST CREEK, Manheim, Herkimer County, New York, is near the mouth of East Canada Creek, which is crossed by an iron bridge two hundred feet in length. We now pass along the Manheim intervales, with the Danube hills across the river. At Indian Castle, on the left, Sir William Johnson, who lived so long among the Indians, built a mission church in 1768, and the great Mohawk chiefs, Brandt and King Hendrick, and the American General, Herkimer, who was mortally wounded at Oriskany, resided in Danube, close by.

Ten miles from St. Johnsville is the busy town of—

LITTLE FALLS, Little Falls, Herkimer County, New York, 74 miles from Albany, a busy manufacturing and market town, romantically situated, in a deep valley or gorge of the mountain chain which extends through the State, from Pennsylvania to Lake Champlain, where it is connected to the Adirondack Mountains. The gorge is about three-quarters of a mile in width, and affords a passage to the Mohawk River, the Erie Canal, and the Central Railroad. The village, built against the sides of an abrupt acclivity, which rises four or five hundred feet, overlooks the Mohawk, which at this point descends forty-five feet in half a mile, forming a series of cascades and rapids, from which its name is derived. Geologists account for this remarkable chasm by supposing that long before the creation of man the whole valley west of this chain of mountains was submerged by an elevated lake; an overflow occurred at Little Falls, and by process of erosion a broad channel was cut, forming the present valley of the Mohawk.

In 1836 the valuable water privilege was turned to account by the erection of several manufactories upon the place. Woolen and cotton factories, paper mills, flour and grist mills, planing and saw mills, machine shops, foundries, and stores of every description, were soon in operation. Farm produce in large quantities is transported from the surrounding districts, especially butter and cheese, and is thence forwarded to the Eastern markets. Herkimer County is famous for its rich cheese. The Little Falls Academy and Union School indicate the interest felt in education, and the large number of churches marks the moral sentiments of the community. Population about 7,500.

About three miles below Little Falls still stands the residence of General Herkimer—a corruption of "Erghemar," his right name—who died from wounds received at the battle of Oriskany. It was built in 1763 of imported brick. His remains were interred on a knoll about one hundred and thirty yards from his house, and his grave is marked by a plain white tombstone.

NEW YORK CENTRAL RAILROAD.

HERKIMER, Herkimer, Herkimer County, New York, 81 miles from Albany. This is the county seat, situated on the bank of the Mohawk, near the West Canada Creek, and receives its name from General Herkimer. It was incorporated in 1807, and was formerly called "Stone Ridge." It is principally noted for its production of cheese, butter, and broom-corn. The earliest settlers were Palatinates, in 1722, refugees from the fury of Louis le Grand. A large paper-mill is in operation, making principally straw paper. A short distance from the present court-house stood Fort Dayton, erected just before the Revolution, which in those troublous times was a refuge for the defenseless people in that vicinity, when the fiendish Brandt hunted them for their scalps. Here connection is made with the Herkimer, Newport & Poland Railroad to Newport and Poland.

Two miles from Herkimer the cars stop at—

ILION, Herkimer County, New York, 83 miles from Albany, a beautiful village, having a population of 4,000, surrounded by sloping and wooded hills. Among its industries are the large factories of the Remington Company, producing firearms, sewing-machines, and agricultural implements. At least 750,000 breech-loading rifles have been made here, including 50,000 for the United States, 60,000 for Egypt, 10,000 for Rome, 3,000 for Japan, 42,000 for Denmark, 30,000 for Sweden, and 75,000 for Spain. During several months of the Franco-Prussian War, the Remington works were kept perpetually in operation, no less than 155,000 rifles being made and despatched to France. Several of the South American republics have been fitted out with firearms from this place. Immense quantities of agricultural implements have been made by the same company, which includes sewing-machines and cotton-gins among its productions. Eight hundred rifles can be made in one day at the factory if required. Both the railway and the Erie Canal pass through the village, greatly facilitating business.

FRANKFORT, Herkimer County, New York, 86 miles from Albany. Nearly a million pounds of excellent cheese are exported from this place each year. After speeding through a beautiful landscape region for twelve miles, the train glides through the suburbs of a city, and soon draws up in the station at—

UTICA.

Oneida County, New York, 95 miles from Albany, and 203 miles from Buffalo. It is the county seat of Oneida County, and contains about 40,000 inhabitants. Utica is a handsome and prosperous city, regularly built, and the second in size in Central New York. It was incorporated in 1832. It lies on the south bank of the Mohawk, on the eastern border of the county. The site of the city slopes from the river to an elevation of 150 feet. With Rome it shares the county seat of Oneida, each having its court-house, jail, and county officers. Besides the New York Central & Hudson River Railroad, which passes through its northern border, the Rome, Watertown & Ogdensburg Railroad, bringing in the travel from Watertown, Sackett's Harbor, Clayton, Ogdensburg, Ottawa, and points on St. Lawrence River and in Canada, and the Delaware, Lackawanna & Western Railroad, and the Utica, Chenango & Susquehanna Valley Railroad, contribute to the city's prosperity. Stages communicate with the surrounding country, which is rich in agricultural productions, and abounds in villages. The Erie Canal, the great waterway connecting the Hudson River with Lake Erie and the other great lakes, runs through Utica. It formerly connected here with the Chenango Canal, the latter running through the Oriskany and Chenango valleys to Norwich and Binghamton. This branch has since been abandoned.

Utica is largely engaged in manufacturing cotton and woolen goods, millstones, screws, musical instruments, telegraph apparatus, and a great variety of other articles. Two large steam woolen-mills and a steam cotton-mill give employment to at least 1,000 men. Several other manufactories afford occupation to fifty and sixty hands each. The Washingtonville Iron Works employs a large number of men. "Excelsior engines," intended especially for oil works, are manufactured here. Ornamental articles in iron are manufactured by two establishments. The city contains over 30 churches, a public library, and 7 banks with a combined capital of $2,000,000. There are 3 daily and 6 weekly newspapers.

The State Lunatic Asylum stands upon a fine farm of 130 acres, on the western border of the city. The building is a spacious and costly structure, with accommodations for 600 patients. The institution is admirably managed. Gardens, shops, and places for diversion are provided for those who are able to engage in manual labor; and well-chosen amusements and objects tending to arrest the attention and bring back the wandering mind, are supplied. Among other amusements, a monthly publication, "The Opal," is conducted by them. The statistics show that a large portion of the inmates have received essential benefit from the treatment and discipline of the institution.

The public schools of Utica are of an excellent character. The district libraries contain several thousand volumes. The new Free Academy building, erected at an expense of $81,500, is the finest academy in the State. The Female Seminary, destroyed by fire, has been rebuilt. The Academy of the Assumption, under the care of the Christian Brothers (R. C.), is an imposing edifice. The City Hall is a fine brick building, at the top of the hill, on Genesee Street, containing a large hall, council rooms, and city offices. The City Hospital, on Mohawk Street, is a fine building, as well in regard to internal arrangements as to external appearance.

The city water works cost $400,000. There is a strong and efficient fire department maintained. Utica derives much of its importance from being the market for rich and extensive rural districts, from which several railroads converge on this point.

At the time of the Revolution, Utica was a frontier trading-post, and the site of Fort Schuyler, built to guard the settlement against the French and Indians.

Connection is made here, by means of the Black River Division of the Rome, Watertown & Ogdensburg Railroad, with Trenton Falls, Lyons Falls, and the North Woods. Connection is also made with the Delaware, Lackawanna & Western Railroad for Richfield Springs, Norwich, and Binghamton.

Forest Hill Cemetery, a few miles south of Utica, is well laid out, and has many handsome monuments. Tourists will find it an interesting place to visit. Deerfield, just across the river from Utica, is mentioned by Bancroft as one of the centers of the Indian wars and massacres.

BIRD'S-EYE VIEW, TRENTON FALLS, N. Y.

NEW YORK CENTRAL RAILROAD.

TRENTON FALLS may be visited by taking the Rome, Watertown & Ogdensburg Railroad from Utica. They are about twenty miles distant. These falls, now a great place of resort, were scarcely known to tourists until 1822, when the first hotel was erected. Although the Falls appear small when compared with the Niagara, or the Genesee Falls at Rochester, the rugged wildness of the surrounding scenery, and the picturesque character of the valley and stream, render it a spot of extraordinary attraction.

The river forming the Trenton Falls is called West Canada Creek. There is no cataract at Trenton which in itself is pre-eminently grand or beautiful. It is more the position, form, and rapidity of the river which give the charm and make it considered by many as one of the most picturesque spots on the continent.

There are five cascades in the series, with a total fall of two hundred feet. The stream flows through a romantic ravine bordered by walls of Trenton limestone from 70 to 200 feet in height. The water is of a singular variety of brown hues,—from amber and topaz in the shallows to a dark umber in the deeper parts, "forming a rich effect when flecked with lines of foam and lighted by the sunshine."

There is ample accommodation for tourists in the immediate neighborhood, and in the village near by may be found a fine collection of fossils. Specimens are for sale at reasonable prices. There are few cabinets in the world which have not drawn upon this collection.

Three miles southwest of Utica is New Hartford, a fine growing village, containing several churches, cotton factories, a batting factory, flour-mill, tannery, and about 900 inhabitants. Clinton, eight miles southwest, is the seat of Hamilton College, incorporated in 1843. This institution is located upon a hill overlooking Oriskany Valley. The course of study embraces a collegiate and law department. A preparatory department is connected with the college. It has a library containing about 10,000 volumes, and a large cabinet.

The Clinton Liberal Institute, under Universalist control, is a flourishing school; it has a male and female department. Houghton Female Seminary (Presbyterian) is also located here. It is in the midst of fine natural scenery; and, enjoying the favor of the professors of Hamilton College, and communicating by steam cars with Utica, this institution possesses unusual advantages, and is deservedly popular.

RICHFIELD SPRINGS,

Otsego County, N. Y., 34 miles south of Utica, on Delaware, Lackawanna & Western Railroad. Hotels—Spring House, Hotel Earlington, Cary Cottage, Tunnicliffe Cottage, Canadarago House, Darrow House, Davenport, and others. Richfield Springs is situated on an elevated plateau 2,000 feet above the sea, with high hills on the north, east, and west, which offer a barrier to high winds and afford a climate at once invigorating and delightful. To the south, open gorges reveal a num-

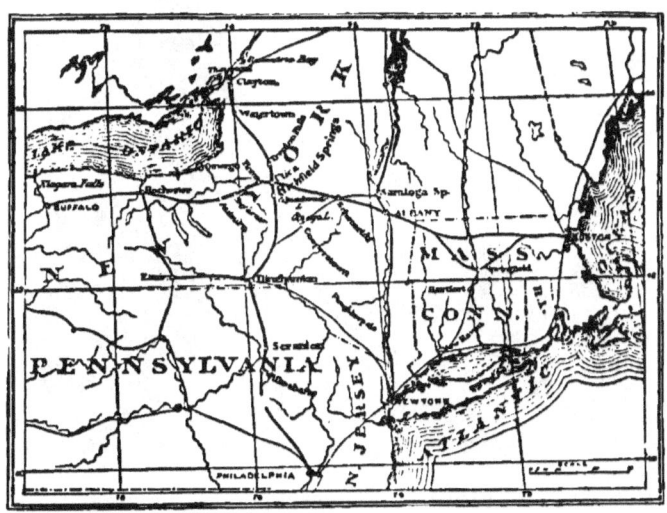

ber of beautiful lakes among the hills. These constitute a panorama of restful beauty, while they invite the strong to rambles on their shores, and fishing, boating, and bathing in their waters. The popularity of Richfield Springs as a resort is due to the invigorating climate, pure atmosphere, and the virtue of its mineral springs. The curative power of the strong sulphur springs in rheumatism and diseases of the blood has been abundantly demonstrated. Commodious bath-houses have been erected, and all the necessary appliances for hot sulphur baths and other methods of using the waters are supplied. Outdoor exercise is made possible and delightful to all by the well-kept highways and the charming drives in the neighborhood. The twelve-mile drive around Canadarago Lake is very beautiful. The lake is about three fourths of a mile south of the Springs, and is five miles long and about one and a half miles wide. It is one of the most beautiful little lakes of the State, and abounds in a variety of fine fish. The road is near the shore, but sufficiently high to give commanding views. The valley south of the lake affords an extended drive. Sunset Hill is an eminence

VIEW OF CANADARAGO LAKE AND RICHFIELD SPRINGS, N. Y.

near by, much frequented by reason of its ease of access and the views there obtained. Waiontha Observatory, on a mountain of the same name, two miles east of the Springs, affords charming and distant prospects, including views of the Adirondacks, and six beautiful lakes, one of which, six miles east from Richfield Springs, is the historic Otsego Lake, at whose foot is Cooperstown, famous as the home of J. Fenimore Cooper, America's great novelist. The whole region is full of points of interest to the lover of nature.

Several hotels and boarding-houses offer board at varying prices. The Spring House, owned and conducted by T. R. Proctor, and the Hotel Earlington, are the largest.

NEW YORK CENTRAL RAILROAD.

The traveler resuming his journey west from Utica over the New York Central & Hudson River Railroad passes through the hamlets of—

WHITESBORO, Whitestone, Oneida County, New York, 99 miles from Albany, a pleasant village, with streets finely shaded, and—

ORISKANY, Whitestone, Oneida County, New York, 102 miles from Albany, situated near the mouth of Oriskany Creek, and the scene of a disastrous battle fought in August, 1777, between General Herkimer and the Indians, the train arrives at the city of—

ROME, Oneida County, New York, 109 miles from Albany; 253 miles from New York. Fort Stanwix, which was besieged by the British in 1777, occupied a site which is now in the center of the city of Rome, and the battle of Oriskany was fought in the vicinity. Not a trace of the fort now remains. Here was also a mile of portage, which kept asunder the waters of the Mohawk and Wood Creek, and interrupted the navigation from Albany to the lakes. The Indians called it "De-o-wain-sta"—or "carrying-place for canoes." Over this interval all merchandise to and from the distant West had to be conveyed by men and ox-teams. Then, by way of Wood Creek and Oneida Lake, it reached Lake Ontario. In 1796 a canal was cut through this portage by the Western Canal Co., who deepened many of the shallows in the Mohawk, and constructed a lock at Little Falls, so that passage was afforded for boats of ten tons burthen. When going with the current, propulsion was easy; but on the return the tedious journey through the windings of the Mohawk was effected by sheer strength, with the aid of "setting-poles."

It is here that cheese was first made in factories, and that industry is still largely pursued. Other manufactures are—railroad iron, locomotives, and agricultural implements. The population of Rome is 12,000, and the city contains a handsome court house, 13 churches, a high school, 3 national banks, 2 savings banks, an academy, public library. Three newspapers are issued weekly. It is the junction of the New York Central, the Rome, Watertown & Ogdensburg, and the New York, Ontario & Western Railroads. The Erie Canal was begun in 1817 at this point, and in 1837 the Black River Canal was made from Rome to Lyons' Falls, connecting with navigable waters to the north. It ascends from Rome to the summit by seventy locks, occurring in a rise of 693 feet, whence it descends 386 feet in thirty-six locks. The canal is 35 miles long, and cost $3,225,000. Travelers going to Albany, New York, Boston, and the East take the New York Central R.R. at this place, and tourists from New York, Boston, Albany, Saratoga, etc., en route to Watertown, Ogdensburg, Thousand Islands, and northern New York, leave the New York Central R.R. at this point, and take the Rome, Watertown & Ogdensburg line. Sleeping-cars are run from New York to Cape Vincent, where connection is made with steamer for the Thousand Islands and Alexandria Bay.

The New York Central & Hudson River Railroad runs southwest from Rome, passing—

GREEN'S CORNERS, Rome, Oneida County, New York, 113 miles from Albany, a small station in the southwestern corner of the township, and—

VERONA, Verona, Oneida County, New York, 117 miles from Albany. East of the station are the Verona Springs, whose waters contain 720 grains of muriate of soda in each gallon, and are saturated with sulphuretted hydrogen gas, resembling the springs at Harrogate in England.

ONEIDA, Lenox, Madison County, New York, 122 miles from Albany. Built upon a portion of the territory of the Oneida Indians. The word signifies "The people of the stone." This tribe had a tradition that a certain stone followed them in their wanderings. This animated stone at length rested upon a lofty hill, upon which the Indians afterwards always held their councils. A boulder of gneiss, lying upon a farm at Stockbridge, was pointed out as the object of their veneration, and a few years since was removed to the entrance of Utica cemetery, where it still remains. The village is on Oneida Creek, and was incorporated in 1848. It has a population of 4,000, and is the center of a flourishing country trade. The Oneida Seminary is a well-conducted school.

On the banks of the creek, and about three miles from the village, a society called the "Oneida Community" is located upon a well-tilled farm of 390 acres. The Association, which includes both sexes, was organized by John H. Noyes, who originated their peculiar religious and social tenets in 1847. They do not marry, but live in common, and have a common property in all things, and affect to be guided in all their actions by inspiration. They are principally engaged in garden-

TOURISTS' IDEAL ROUTE,
NIAGARA TO THE SEA.
ROME, WATERTOWN & OGDENSBURG R. R.

Great Highway and Favorite Route for Fashionable Pleasure Travel.
Only All-Rail Route to Thousand Islands.

1889. NEW FAST TRAINS, AVOIDING STOPS. 1889.

WAGNER PALACE SLEEPING CARS.

NEW YORK AND PAUL SMITH'S, 15 Hours.
NEW YORK AND CLAYTON, 11 Hours.
NIAGARA FALLS AND CLAYTON, 9½ Hours.
NIAGARA FALLS, PORTLAND AND BAR HARBOR, MAINE.
Via Norwood, Fabyans, Crawford Notch, and all White Mountain Resorts.

WAGNER PALACE DRAWING-ROOM CARS.

NIAGARA FALLS AND CLAYTON.
ROCHESTER AND CLAYTON.
SYRACUSE AND CLAYTON.
ALBANY AND CLAYTON.
UTICA AND CLAYTON.

Direct and immediate connections are made at Clayton with powerful steamers for Alexandria Bay and all Thousand Island Resorts, also with Rich. & Ont. Nav. Co. Steamers for Montreal, Quebec and River Saguenay, passing all of the Thousand Islands and Rapids of the River St. Lawrence by daylight. For tickets, time-tables and further information apply to nearest ticket agent or correspond with General Passenger Agent, Oswego, N. Y.

ROUTES AND RATES FOR SUMMER TOURS.

A beautiful book of 200 pages, profusely illustrated, contains maps, cost of tours, list of hotels, and describes over 400 Combination Summer Tours via Thousand Islands and Rapids of the St. Lawrence River, Saguenay River, Gulf of St. Lawrence, Lake Champlain, Lake George, White Mountains, to Portland, Kennebunk, Boston, New York and all Mountain, Lake, River and Sea Shore Resorts in Canada, New York and New England. It is the best book given away. Send ten cents postage to General Passenger Agent, Oswego, N. Y., for a copy before deciding upon your summer trip.

THEO. BUTTERFIELD,
Gen'l Passenger Agent,
Oswego, N. Y.

E. S. BOWEN,
Acting Gen'l Manager.

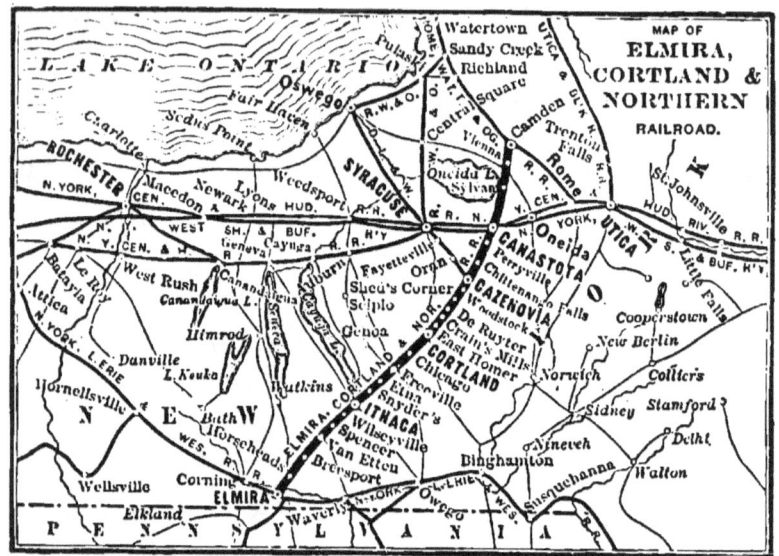

THE ELMIRA, CORTLAND AND NORTHERN ROUTE

As will be seen on above map, this line runs diagonally across New York State from Camden, where it intersects the Rome, Watertown, and Ogdensburg Railroad to Elmira, its junction with the Erie, Lehigh Valley, Pennsylvania, and Delaware and Lackawanna Railroads, crossing the New York Central and West Shore Railroads at Canastota, and following the beautiful, fertile valleys of the Chittenango, Tioughnioga, and Chemung. Six miles north of Canastota, at the east end of Oneida Lake, is Sylvan Beach, a beautiful and popular summer resort, noted for its magnificent beach of white sand, offering bathing facilities excelled only by Coney Island Beach. Twenty-five miles south is Cazenovia, on Cazenovia Lake, 1,200 feet above sea level, for many years a famous summer resort. The line crosses the Syracuse, Binghamton and New York Railroad at Cortland, a thriving manufacturing town of 10,000 inhabitants, noted for its immense wagon factories and wire cloth mills, and one of the State Normal schools. Twenty miles south, and fifty miles from Elmira, the line touches Ithaca, the seat of the magnificent Cornell University, with its 1,200 students, founded by Ezra Cornell, and best described by his words, "I would found an institution where any person can find instruction in any study!" North of the University is the wonderful Ithaca Gorge, one and a half miles long, containing seven or more waterfalls, the highest of which, Ithaca Fall, is 156 feet high, only 4 feet less than Niagara. Within ten miles of Ithaca are 150 waterfalls. These with the celebrated McGraw-Fiske Mansion, and the Cornell University, make Ithaca one of the most interesting places to the tourist. The line runs westerly from here through Spencer and Van Etten, climbing the mountain from Swartwood, at a grade of 125 feet to the mile, rising 1,400 feet in eight miles to Park Station, the summit. Thence it runs by easy grade to Elmira.

ing, nursery business, milling, and the manufacture of steel traps, sewing-silk, traveling-bags, cravats, and palm-leaf hats. The men are chiefly engaged upon the land, and the women in other profitable pursuits. They also publish a weekly paper called the "Circular."

There is a junction of the New York Central and the New York, Ontario & Western railroads at Oneida.

WAMPSVILLE, Lenox, Madison County, New York, 125 miles from Albany, is a small way-station. Two miles west we reach—

CANASTOTA, Lenox, Madison County, New York, 127 miles from Albany. This village contains several churches, a newspaper office, a bank, and a manufactory of astronomical and optical instruments. The microscopes and other instruments made here have acquired merited celebrity. The equatorial telescope of Hamilton College was made here. On a marsh near the village is a salt spring. Passengers for Oneida Lake, Cazenovia, Cortland, Ithaca, Elmira, and points near them, take the Elmira, Cortland & Northern Railroad at Canastota. This railroad runs from Canastota southwest through Madison, Cortland, Tompkins, and Chemung counties, New York State.

After passing the hamlet of—

CANASERAGA, Sullivan, Madison County, New York, 131 miles from Albany, we arrive at—

CHITTENANGO, Sullivan, Madison County, New York, 133 miles from Albany. This pretty village of about 1,000 inhabitants has several woolen and other factories. The settlement lies on the right bank of the Erie Canal, at the entrance to the narrow valley through which the Chittenango Creek, the outlet of Cazenovia Lake, makes its way to the great plain which extends from Syracuse to Rome. About a mile from the village, near the east bank of the stream, the famous sulphur springs of Chittenango are found. In their medicinal properties they closely resemble the celebrated White Sulphur Springs near Warrenton, Virginia. There is evidence that they possess considerable healing powers, especially in diseases of the skin, liver, stomach, and bowels. In cases where the patient has a tendency to pulmonary affection, the waters, like all that contain sulphuretted hydrogen gas, seem to have an injurious effect.

The scenery in the neighborhood of the springs is highly picturesque, and is best enjoyed from the hotel. The southern view is remarkably fine. The water, in its passage from the fountain-head to its appearance in the large basin, is made to pass through several artistic arrangements, which produce a pleasing effect; again, disappearing for some distance, it is seen next on the opposite side of the road, rising in several jets, and falling upon a rude heap of stones, which it has encased with a crystal covering resembling hoar-frost.

A little further south is a room for refreshments and recreation, and in a nook of the cliff, fifty feet above the fountain, reached by a winding path, is the gymnasium, shaded by birches, maples, and oaks. Across the creek, in the groves, are four pleasant cottages, belonging to the establishment, where families reside during the summer season. This is the narrowest part of the valley, and from an eminence on the opposite side are seen Cazenovia and Oneida lakes. About two miles above the spring the valley is suddenly terminated by a precipice, over which the Chittenango falls perpendicularly 140 feet into the deep gorge below—a scene of extraordinary beauty. It contains a woolen and other factories, tannery, and several churches, and the Yates Polytechnic Institute.

Chittenango can hardly be called a fashionable resort, but it is visited annually by many invalids, who use the medicinal waters with great benefit. Besides the hotels there are several cottages for summer residents, near the waters. From a hill in this vicinity is obtained a pleasing view of the Oneida and Cazenovia lakes and the intervening country. The Canaseraga Creek has a waterfall 130 feet high. The next two stations are—

KIRKVILLE, Manlius, Onondaga County, New York, 137 miles from Albany, and—

MANLIUS, Manlius, Onondaga County, New York, 140 miles from Albany. This latter village contains several mills and factories, several churches, and 1,000 inhabitants. It is situated on the border of Limestone Creek, where a branch of the river falls over a precipice 100 feet high, forming a fine cascade, and a pleasant summer resort. Near this place are sulphur and other mineral springs, but they have not yet attracted public attention. In the vicinity are three peculiar ponds, called the "Green Lakes," from the color of their waters. Passing—

DE WITT, a small way station, we are soon wending our way through the suburbs of the enterprising and prosperous city of—

SYRACUSE,

Onondaga County, New York, 148 miles from Albany, situated at the head of Onondaga Lake. It is the county seat of Onondaga County, and covers 8,500 acres. The population of the city has grown, since 1830, from 2,500 to nearly 100,000.

Syracuse is built mostly of brick, and has wide and well-paved streets; and from its central situation has attained considerable political and commercial eminence. There are one hundred and forty-four miles of streets within the municipal limits. From a very modest beginning, Syracuse has become one of the most important manufacturing centers in the country.

As a place of residence it is desirably located and possesses a delightful climate. There is a good system of rapid transit by means of horse cars and electric railways.

Schools of every grade, colleges, libraries, and reading-rooms abound. In addition to the excellent system of public and private schools, Syracuse boasts of a university of high standing among institutions of the kind. More than five hundred students are in attendance. There are three departments: the College of Fine Arts, the Medical College, and the College of Liberal Arts. A splendid library has been established in connection with the university, containing 13,000 volumes, exclusive of the Von Ranke library, recently donated, and placed in a handsome stone structure specially built to contain them.

The John Crouse College for Women is one of the greatest architectural ornaments in the city. Its utility is thoroughly appreciated. Theaters and other places of amusement are not wanting. Every religious denomination is well represented, and amply accommodated with buildings for devotional purposes, the total number of churches being sixty-two, with a seating capacity of thirty thousand.

Syracuse maintains a well-equipped fire department, an efficient police service, Board of Health, Public Works, and three companies of State militia; the armory stands within spacious grounds, and is large and substantial.

"As a manufacturing center," says the author of "Syracuse and its Surroundings," "it proves an advantageous and inviting field to capi-

NEW YORK CENTRAL RAILROAD.

tal in the establishment of new industries. In the manufacture of agricultural implements, mowing-machine parts, and knives, plows, power hammers, carriages, carts, wagons, and sleighs, Syracuse is not surpassed; while the steel works, rolling mills, blast-furnaces, tube, iron pipe, car-wheel, and sheet-iron works contribute to the city's prosperity. The cutlery, guns, hardware specialties, wagon and carriage springs, patented buckles, saddlery, hardware, and malleable iron goods manufactured here are used throughout the country.

"The vast sand beds of Oneida Lake furnish the material for making the manufacture of window and plate glass a profitable and growing industry. The building of steam engines, boilers, and the manufacture of stoves, furnaces, brick, tile, lime, cement, shoes, clothing, etc., are prominent features, while the products of her flour mills, canning factories, beer and ale breweries have achieved a wide reputation for their excellence."

Syracuse is celebrated for its salt-works, and stands upon ground somewhat more elevated than the marsh which is the source of its wealth. This marsh is rich in springs of brine, that yield salt in the proportion of 56 pounds from 35 gallons of brine. The existence of this brine is attributed to the constant dissolution of the saline crystals in the substrata. More than 500 acres are covered by solar works, or a surface of 8,403,840 square feet. The solar salt is much coarser than that produced by boiling. A grinding establishment improves it for dairy and table use. Works are erected at Liverpool and Geddes, as well as Syracuse and Salina. The annual amount produced collectively is about 8,000,000 bushels.

The railroad communications of Syracuse are extensive and important. The New York Central & Hudson River Railroad connects here with the Rome, Watertown & Ogdensburg Railroad, New York, West Shore & Buffalo Railway, Delaware, Lackawanna & Western Railroad, and the Syracuse, Ontario & New York Railway. The West Shore Railroad passes through on the north side of the canal, and has erected a handsome depot—one of the finest in the State.

The Erie Canal is an important accessory to the business facilities of Syracuse, and the Oswego Canal here unites with the Erie, of which it is a branch.

From Syracuse westward the New York Central & Hudson River Railroad has two routes. Through passengers take the main line, but travelers going to Auburn, Geneva, Seneca Lake, Watkins Glen,

Canandaigua, and other points on or connecting with the old division, change cars.

As the train draws out from Syracuse to continue its journey on the direct line, we have an excellent view of the innumerable salt sheds that line the shore of the lake, and see on every hand evidences of the enterprise and thrift which have made this city what it is. West of Syracuse the railway runs through—

AMBOY, Camillus, Onondaga County, New York, a small village.

WARNER'S, or **VAN BUREN CENTRE**, Van Buren, Onondaga County, New York, 157 miles from Albany.

JORDAN, Elbridge, Onondaga County, New York, 165 miles from Albany. This village is pleasantly situated on Skaneateles Outlet. Besides the railroad the Erie Canal passes through it. It contains five churches, two flour-mills, an extensive wheelbarrow and barrel factories. It also contains a capacious warehouse, many stores, and has about 1,500 inhabitants. The Erie Canal is fed from the outlet at this place.

WEEDSPORT, Brutus, Cayuga County, New York, 169 miles from Albany. It is on the Erie Canal, and contains a foundry, distillery, several flour-mills, several churches, and about 2,000 inhabitants. The Southern Central Division of the Lehigh Valley Railroad crosses the New York Central & Hudson River Railroad here.

PORT BYRON, Mentz, Cayuga County, New York, 172 miles from Albany. This place is located on the Owasco Outlet and the Erie Canal, and contains, besides several churches, a woolen factory, a flour-mill with ten run of stones, and other manufacturing establishments. After passing Port Byron the train traverses the great Montezuma marshes, and crosses the Seneca River near the Great Bend.

SAVANNAH, Savannah, Wayne County, New York, 180 miles from Albany; from Buffalo, 118. Named from the resemblance of 2,000 acres of low, marshy land, which produces abundance of long, coarse grass, to the Spanish savannas. The village is small, and contains about twenty dwellings.

CLYDE, Galen, Wayne County, New York, 186 miles from Albany. This village, on the Clyde River, received its present name in 1818. It contains ample church accommodation, banks, extensive distilleries,

NEW YORK CENTRAL RAILROAD.

steam flour-mills, furnaces, and shops, for the manufacture of agricultural implements, a large cooperage, brewery, malt-houses, tannery, and other manufactories, as well as extensive forwarding and commission establishments. Glass of an excellent quality is made here. Tobacco of good quality is raised in the vicinity. Extensive fields of peppermint are seen beside the railroad. The plant is grown for making the essence, and is said to be one of the most remunerative crops that can be cultivated. About one third of all the peppermint grown in the United States is raised in this neighborhood.

Seven miles beyond Clyde is—

LYONS, Lyons, Wayne County, New York, 193 miles from Albany, the county seat of Wayne County, and the junction of the New York Central and the Syracuse, Geneva & Corning railroads.

This town is situated at the conflux of Mud Creek and Canandaigua Outlet, and is one of the finest in the State, with a population of about 5,000. It is one of the oldest towns in Western New York, nearly midway between Syracuse and Rochester, and was settled in 1789. It contains many fine edifices, including a court house of tasteful cut stone, with a fine portico and dome. There are several churches, a union schoolhouse, banks, a variety of stores and manufactories of different kinds, including a furnace, machine-shop, and agricultural-implement shop, tile manufactory, brickyard, pottery, brewery, fanning-mill establishment, a saddle-tree factory, and a variety of others. Peppermint oil, apples, tobacco, cider, cherries, and grain are the principal exports. Ten thousand pounds of peppermint are annually distilled here. Railway connection is here made for Geneva, Seneca Lake, Ithaca, Watkins Glen, and points in Northern Pennsylvania. The stations on the branch of the New York Central Railroad running from Lyons to Geneva, are Thompson's, Cuddeback's, Mitchell's, Bennett's, and Geneva.

NEWARK, Arcadia, Wayne County, New York, 199 miles from Albany, is the next station west of Lyons. It is a thriving town, having about 3,000 inhabitants. The surrounding rich and fertile soil has made this a prosperous place and an important railroad and canal station. It contains several churches, furnaces, manufactories, and an improved plow factory. Spiritualism made its first "rap" near here, at Hydesville, a small place two miles distant, where it was first

NEW YORK CENTRAL RAILROAD.

heard by the noted "Fox Family," on the night of March 31, 1849. Connection is made here with the Sodus Bay Division of the Lehigh Valley Railroad, which extends from Gorham to Lake Ontario. Passing the small way-station of—

EAST PALMYRA, where the "Long Island Company" in 1791 purchased 5,500 acres of land for twenty-five cents per acre, we stop at—

PALMYRA, Palmyra, Wayne County, New York, 206 miles from Albany. This place has a population of more than 3,000. Its streets are broad and handsomely shaded. Within its limits are several churches, a union school having a large number of pupils, a bank and several considerable manufactories.

The parents of "Joseph Smith," the Mormon prophet, settled near here in 1819. Hunting for gold with his spade, Joseph, one day, according to his own account, "laid bare the golden plates of the Mormon Bible." He transcribed and published these as the "Book of Mormon." A convert mortgaged his farm to pay the printer. The tradition of the neighborhood says he was a "vagabond" and "scamp" from his youth. Marrying a respectable woman, he neglected his family, defrauded his friends and proselytes, but finally obtained his deserts at the hands of a mob in Nauvoo, Illinois.

After leaving Palmyra, the New York Central cars run parallel with the Erie Canal, through the village of Walworth, to—

MACEDON, Macedon, Wayne County, New York, 210 miles from Albany. Contains two churches, a grist and saw mill, furnace and machine shop.

FAIRPORT, Perinton, Monroe County, New York, 219 miles from Albany; from Buffalo, 72. Contains five churches, three flouring-mills, two saw-mills, a plaster-mill, two planing-mills, a saleratus establishment, machine-shop, and carriage shops. The train passes Penfield and Brighton, touches at East Rochester, and then enters the station at—

GENESEE FALLS, ROCHESTER, N. Y.

ROCHESTER,

Monroe County, New York, 7 miles from Lake Ontario, 67 miles from Buffalo, 229 miles from Albany, the fourth city of the Empire State in extent and population. Rochester, named after the original proprietor, Colonel Nathaniel Rochester, is a modern city on the Genesee River, seven miles south of its entrance into Lake Ontario, where it is crossed by the Erie Canal and the New York Central Railroad. In 1802 Messrs. Rochester, Fitzhugh, and Carroll purchased the so-called hundred-acre tract comprising the central part, on the west side of the river, of the present city of Rochester. The settlement was called Genesee Falls until its creation as a village, by an act of the legislature, in 1817, when it was called Rochesterville. Its present population is estimated at 130,000. The Genesee River lies west of the railroad depot, and the cars cross it going west towards Buffalo, just outside the depot, and immediately over the falls.

In the center of the city are the upper falls of the Genesee, a perpendicular cataract of 96 feet. Two other falls, of 83 and 26 feet, are a mile and a half below, the river running through a deep gorge in its limestone banks from 100 to 220 feet high. This great water power was the foundation of the prosperity and rapid growth of the city. Below the lower falls the river becomes navigable for all lake vessels.

The city—over five miles square—is regularly laid out with wide and handsome streets, of which many are lined with shade-trees. Main Street, on the east side, and Buffalo Street, on the west side of the river, form, by means of a stone bridge, one continuous street—the "Broadway" of the city—lined with handsome stores, hotels, public buildings, etc.

The suburbs are ornamented by numerous and elegant residences, surrounded by tasteful grounds and gardens. The waters of the Genesee River, flowing to the northward from the Alleghany Hills, in the southern part of the State and northern Pennsylvania, traverse the city and empty into Lake Ontario. Rochester stands in the midst of one of the finest wheat-growing regions in the world; hence it is that the available water power is of so much service in sustaining that branch of the city's commerce.

NEW YORK CENTRAL RAILROAD.

"With railroads converging from all directions: with Lake Ontario and the chain of great lakes opening communication with Canada and the West, and affording cheap transportation for merchandise and products of every description ; with the Erie Canal traversing the entire length and breadth of the State, connecting the Hudson River with Lake Erie ; with two lines of railroads running directly to the immense coal-fields of Pennsylvania,—the commercial facilities of Rochester are unexcelled."

Among the leading commercial interests of Rochester are ready-made clothing, boots and shoes, beer, flour, tobacco, nursery stock and seed-growing, iron-bridge building, manufacture of car-wheels, furniture, optical instruments, caskets, carriages, showcases, fine flannel, cotton goods, wood-working machinery, boilers, stoves, and furnaces, photographic supplies, dental supplies, artificial limbs, pianos, underwear, tents, ornamental iron, perfumery, lamps and lanterns, locomotive headlights, canned goods, glassware, bank locks, and agricultural implements. More than 4,000 acres are under cultivation for nursery purposes.

There are eleven beer and two ale breweries. In the flour industry, 20,000 bushels are ground and 4,000 barrels placed on the market daily. An immense trade is carried on in evaporated and dried fruits in Rochester and vicinity. In 1887, 30,000,000 pounds were prepared, worth $2,000,000. Between 25,000 and 30,000 persons are engaged in autumn and early winter every year in the preparation of fruits for domestic use.

Seven State banks and four savings banks are maintained in Rochester. The assessed value of real estate, on a basis of seventy-five per cent. of actual value, is $80,000,000.

Facilities for education in the city include the University, 31 public schools, a free academy, erected at the cost of $125,000, the Baptist Theological Seminary, the Reynolds Library, and a Law Library of 10,000 volumes.

Among the many benevolent societies are four orphan asylums, the Church Home, Home of the Friendless, the Industrial School, Home of Industry, and State Industrial School. The City and St. Mary's Hospitals provide for 500 patients.

The spiritual needs of the community are well provided for, there being 78 churches, representing Baptists, Christadelphians, the Church

NEW YORK CENTRAL RAILROAD.

of Christ, Congregationalists, Unitarians, Evangelicals, Friends, Hebrews, Lutherans, Methodist Episcopalians, Episcopalians, Free Methodists, Presbyterians, Covenanters, Reformers, Roman Catholics — who have a cathedral—Adventists, and Universalists. The Mount Hope and Holy Sepulchre cemeteries are large and well preserved, the grounds being beautifully ornamented.

Municipal and local affairs are creditably managed by public-spirited men. The Fire and Police Departments are efficient. Electricity is extensively used in lighting the thoroughfares. There are eleven street railway routes, some of which are to be run by cable and electrical storage systems.

Citizens and travelers in search of recreation can reach Lake Ontario within about 45 minutes. Conesus, Hemlock, Silver, Keuka, and Canandaigua lakes are all within easy distance.

Among the sights to be viewed by tourists when in and near Rochester are the University, City Hall, Theological Seminary, the Wilder Building, the Powers Building, the Upper Falls, and many of the manufactories connected with local and general trade.

Communications.. The Erie Canal crosses the Genesee by an aqueduct of cut stone, built at an expense of over $600,000. The Genesee Valley Canal is tributary to the Erie, and has its northern terminus here. It extends southerly, following up the general course of the Genesee Valley to Olean, on the Alleghany River, in Cattaraugus County. It is being extended from Olean to the coal regions of Pennsylvania.

Rochester is an important railroad center. Connections are made here with the Rome, Watertown & Ogdensburg Railroad running to Windsor Beach, Lake Ontario, and points east and west on Lake Ontario; with the New York, Lake Erie & Western R.R. for New York via Avon, Corning, and Elmira; with the Buffalo, Rochester & Pittsburg Railroad for Le Roy, Warsaw, Machias, Salamanca, and points in Pennsylvania; and with the Western New York and Pennsylvania for other places in New York and Pennsylvania; with Charlotte, by branch of the New York Central & Hudson River Railroad; and passengers for Brockport, Albion, Medina, Lockport, Suspension Bridge, and Niagara Falls, are carried over the Niagara Falls Division; and those for Buffalo, Cleveland, etc., continue on the main line of the New York Central R.R.

NEW YORK CENTRAL RAILROAD.

SYRACUSE TO ROCHESTER VIA AUBURN.
OLD ROUTE.

From Syracuse to Rochester the New York Central & Hudson River Railroad has two routes. The new route, described on page 90, follows the course of the Erie Canal, via Amboy, Warner's, Memphis, Jordan, Weedsport, etc., the distance between the starting-point and destination being 81 miles. The old route passes south through the lake country, a distance of 102 miles being traveled over between the two cities. This old route is termed the Auburn Division.

After leaving Syracuse, the next stations are Solway Works, Fairmount, Camillus, or Nine-mile Creek, and, amid the limestone highlands, Marcellus, containing paper and wool manufactories, Halfway, and—

SKANEATELES JUNCTION, where passengers for Skaneateles village and lake change cars. The lake is "one of the most charming bodies of water in Central New York." Bordered on the south by lofty hills, it is sixteen miles long, with an average width of one mile. Its waters are 860 feet above the sea, cool and clear, and well supplied with trout and other fish. The village of—

SKANEATELES, Skaneateles, Onondaga County, New York, 165 miles from Albany, is situated at the northern end and outlet of the lake and has many visitors in summer.

Skaneateles is about five miles distant from the station. It comprises a fine view, and is the seat of quite a large mercantile and mechanical business. Carriage manufacturing is carried on to a large extent, and has won a wide reputation for the place. Kellogg's Woolen Mill, near by, employs many hands. There are also flouring-mills, sawmills, machine-shops, etc.

Under the hills, at the south end of the lake, is Glen Haven village, a quiet summer resort reached by steamer. From eight to nine miles south-east of Skaneateles village is Amber, a romantically-situated hamlet at the foot of Otisco Lake, a placid and sequestered body of water four miles in length, in a deep valley bordered by hills 1,700 feet high.

From Skaneateles Junction, on our way to Rochester, the first station is Sennett, a small way-station, and five miles beyond is—

NEW YORK CENTRAL RAILROAD.

AUBURN, Cayuga County, New York, 174 miles from Albany, a handsome city of 25,000 inhabitants, and the capital of Cayuga County. It is picturesquely situated in the midst of a rich farming country, and occupies a portion of both sides of Owasco Outlet, which, having a descent of 120 feet, supplies abundance of water-power. Streets are wide, and well furnished with stores of all kinds. The site of the town is somewhat uneven, and the streets deviate from a rectangular plan. The principal public buildings and stores are on Genesee Street.

There are several extensive manufactories, including woolen goods, flour, paper, and machinery. Auburn Theological Seminary was founded in 1821 (Presbyterian), with a library of six thousand volumes; the building occupies a commanding site in the north part of the city. The Auburn State Prison is well known by its peculiar system of prison discipline; the building is a costly stone one, enclosed by a wall measuring 500 feet on each side, and about 30 feet high. The convicts sometimes exceed 800; they are employed in various manufactures, the proceeds of which are nearly sufficient to support the establishment.

The Cayuga Orphan Asylum is supported by State and county. The asylum for lunatic orphans occupies ten acres of ground. The cemetery, called Fort Hill, is located upon an eminence of historic interest. Tradition says that the eminence was the work of a race of beings who preceded the Indians in the habitation of this country, thought to be of the same family as the Aztecs of South America, and were called by their conquerors, the Indians, "Mound Builders." It was erected for a defense.

Auburn is also well known as the residence for nearly half a century of William Henry Seward, who was Secretary of State under President Lincoln through the troublous times of the civil war, 1861-5. Connection is made here with the Southern Central Division of the Lehigh Valley R.R., and Ithaca, Auburn & Western railroads.

AURELIUS Station is passed eleven miles west of Auburn.

CAYUGA, Aurelius, Cayuga County, New York, 185 miles from Albany, located upon Cayuga Lake, two miles south of the outlet. The lake is here crossed by a railroad bridge, a mile and fifty yards long and 22 feet in width, which cost $150,000. Steamboats run daily to Ithaca. Connection is made with Aurora and Ithaca by rail, and steamers also ply upon the lake between Cayuga and Ithaca.

NEW YORK CENTRAL RAILROAD.

SENECA FALLS, Seneca Falls, Seneca County, New York, 190 miles from Albany, a bustling and prosperous manufacturing town, with a population of over 8,000. It is situated upon the banks of Seneca River and the outlet of Seneca Lake. The river is about fourteen miles long, and has here a fall of fifty feet, which furnishes considerable water power. The Cayuga & Seneca Canal passes through the village. The principal articles produced are flour, cotton goods, machinery, paper, window sashes, and farming implements. It was in this township that Mrs. Amelia Bloomer first introduced the dress reform, and the style of dress that takes her name. The scene of Bayard Taylor's "Hannah Thurston" is laid in this vicinity.

To the north of Seneca Falls is Tyre, whose surface is divided between long drift-ridges and the low Montezuma marshes.

WATERLOO, Waterloo, Seneca County, New York, 193 miles from Albany; a prosperous manufacturing village, with a population of 4,000. The village has wide streets, shaded by large trees, and is a desirable place of residence. It has several important manufactories, including knitting-mills and shawl and carpet factories. A part of Waterloo is in each of the townships of Waterloo and Fayette. It is situated on the Seneca River, and is a station on the Seneca Canal. The public buildings include a beautiful court house and academy, Catholic and Protestant churches, a bank, public halls, and several hotels. There are a number of foundries, machine shops, flouring and grist mills. It is an important depot of lumber from the southwestern counties, and of coal from the Susquehanna and Blossburgh mines. Six miles beyond, the train passes along the foot of Seneca Lake.

GENEVA, Seneca, Ontario County, New York, 200 miles from Albany. This village is beautifully situated on the northern end of Seneca Lake, and is handsomely built on the western shore of the lake, the banks of which slope upward to the height of 160 feet, and join, at this elevation, the terraced gardens of many of the residences. The country about is fertile and picturesque. A short distance from this place is another monument of the "mound-builders."

Geneva enjoys a large local trade, the stores being ranged chiefly along the wide, main street beside the lake, and upon several bisecting streets. Many handsome houses, the property of affluent citizens, occupy higher ground out upon the lake, further to the south. A mile

SENECA LAKE
STEAM NAVIGATION CO., Limited.

TOURISTS POPULAR ROUTE
BETWEEN
WATKINS GLEN,
LONG POINT (where are located the Long Point Hotel and Pavilion),
GENEVA and NIAGARA FALLS.
SIX TRIPS DAILY DURING THE
EXCURSION SEASON.

Close connections at GENEVA with N. Y. C. & H. R. and L. V. R. Rs., at WATKINS with N. C. Ry.

MEALS ON STEAMERS.   FREE TRANSFER OF BAGGAGE.

W. B. DUNNING, General Manager,
GENEVA, N. Y.

JEFFERSON HOUSE, WATKINS GLEN, N. Y.
D. W. & G. W. LOVE, Proprietors.

Only fire-proof hotel in the place. It is newly refitted and refurnished and has running spring water. Free 'Bus to and from all trains and boats.

FIRST CLASS IN EVERY RESPECT.

SCUDDER'S
History of United States.

PRECEDED BY A NARRATIVE OF
THE DISCOVERY AND SETTLEMENT OF NORTH AMERICA,

And of the Events which led to the Independence of the 13 English Colonies.

By HORACE E. SCUDDER.

WITH MAPS AND ILLUSTRATIONS.   PRICE, ONE DOLLAR.

The leading characteristics of this excellent work are:

FIRST.—A Well Considered Text.

SECOND.—A New and Logical Division into Periods, with a Suggestive Method of Treatment.

THIRD.—The insertion of Topical Analyses for Review, as well as a full set of questions on Text and Maps.

FOURTH.—Accurate, Clear, and Distinct Maps, most carefully drawn and engraved, including Six Double Page and Six Single Page Colored Maps.

FIFTH.—Eighty Beautiful Illustrations by eminent artists. Also Superb Portraits of the following representative men: Columbus, the Discoverer; Penn the Founder; Franklin, the Philosopher; Washington the Patriot; Webster, the Statesman, Longfellow, the Poet; engraved by Closson, Johnson, and Kruell, with fifty other Portraits.

SIXTH.—Superior Mechanical Execution, and Low Price.

TEACHERS say: "It is the best equipped school book ever issued in the U. S." "Will both interest and profit our young folks." "The most useful and enjoyable school history." "Simple, accurate, interesting, and impartial."

TAINTOR BROTHERS & CO., Publishers, 18 Astor Place, New York.

and a half northwest of the village is a plot of ground called "Old Castle." It contains an Indian burying-ground, and in giving up the country the Indians stipulated that these few sacred acres should never be plowed. This pledge has not been violated. The Episcopal Church is a fine edifice, costing $25,000. Here, on a bluff overlooking the lake, is Hobart College, founded in 1823, and under the care of the Episcopalians. It has a medical department. The college property is valued at $166,000.

A powerful sulphur spring has recently been discovered at Geneva. Connection is made with the Fall Brook Coal Company's system of railroads, reaching Watkins, Penn Yan, Corning, and Williamsport. Here, too, tourists and others can leave for Ithaca via the Lehigh Valley Railroad. Steamboats ply daily between Geneva and Ithaca.

Passing Oaks Corners and Phelps, formerly Vienna, after a run of twelve miles, we arrive at—

CLIFTON SPRINGS, Manchester, Ontario County, New York, 212 miles from Albany. Here is a thriving village; several mineral springs here draw thousands of health and pleasure seekers to the town annually. Dr. Foster's Sanitarium, capable of accommodating two hundred and fifty guests, is a well-known and largely patronized institution. The doctor's skill and the virtues of the waters make these springs fountains of health. The water here abounds in the sulphates of lime and magnesia, and its use internally and externally is followed by the happiest results.

Continuing our journey, and passing the hamlets of Shortsville and Chapinville, the train stops at the beautiful village of—

CANANDAIGUA, Canandaigua, Ontario County, New York, 223 miles from Albany. This name is a corruption of "Gan-a-dar-gue," a chosen spot named by the Seneca Indians. The village is on the outlet of Canandaigua Lake, and is the county seat. Population about 6,000. It is distinguished for the picturesque beauty of its situation, and the elegance of its buildings. The view down Main Street, ending in the lake, has a peculiar charm. Besides the county buildings, it has several churches, a State arsenal, and an academy. There is here also a private asylum for the insane. In a room of the court house are the portraits of many of the most distinguished pioneers and most important men of the country.

NEW YORK CENTRAL RAILROAD.

Brigham Young once resided here; and at Fayette, in the adjoining county of Seneca, the first Mormon society was formed in 1830, three years after the pretended unearthing of the golden plates.

Besides its railroad connections with the N. Y. Central and the Northern Central railroads, it enjoys the use of two steamers on the lake plying between Canandaigua and the head of the lake, and stopping at the various charming resorts on the shores.

The lake that bears the name of the town is 15 miles long, 1 mile wide, 668 feet above tidewater, and 437 feet above Lake Ontario, into which it is emptied by the Clyde and Seneca rivers.

One mile east of Canandaigua, on a symmetrical hill, are the remains of the round fort which was held sacred by the Senecas as the place of their origin. Eight miles northwest is the fortress which was destroyed in 1687 by Hurons and several French regiments. The American army of General Sullivan destroyed the Senecas' town at Canandaigua in 1779, then proceeded on in a southwesterly direction, sacked and burned Honeoye and Conesus, drove the Indians before them at Conesus Lake, and destroyed Genesee Castle and town. This army was the means of razing at least forty Indian villages, and rendering useless 160,000 bushels of corn in the fields or granaries. A ride of ten miles through a fertile section of country, passing on our way Paddleford, Farmington, and West Farmington, brings us to—

VICTOR, Victor, Ontario County, New York, 233 miles from Albany, the site of an old battle-ground. In 1687 the Governor of Canada, with 1,600 soldiers and 400 Indians, met and defeated a hostile tribe, burned their village and several surrounding villages. The Senecas, in return, the following year, slaughtered one thousand of the conquerors, and took twenty-six prisoners, whom they tortured to death.

Between Victor and Rochester, a distance of eighteen miles, we pass Fisher's, Pittsford, Bryton, and East Rochester. Rochester, our destination by this route, is described on page 93.

NEW YORK CENTRAL RAILROAD.

ROCHESTER AND CHARLOTTE BRANCH.

The Rochester & Charlotte branch, Western Division of the New York Central & Hudson River Railroad, runs from Rochester depot to Ontario Beach. The stations en route are Center Park, Ames Street, Otis, Driving Park, Barnard's Crossing, Double Track Junction, Roberts' Dock, Yates' Dock, Charlotte—described on page 122 and the Rome, Watertown & Ogdensburg Railroad Crossing.

ONTARIO BEACH, Charlotte, 7 miles from Rochester, and the terminus of this branch, is an attractive summer resort. The surrounding country is as fertile as a garden, and a ride or walk in the vicinity presents scenes of beauty and varied color that none can fail to admire and enjoy. The village itself, with its well-shaded streets, tasteful houses, and public-spirited citizens, makes an ideal summer home.

Directly upon the shore of the lake, about a half-mile distant from the village, is the Hotel Ontario, erected in 1884. There are ample facilities for bowling, billiards, boating, fishing, dancing, and other amusements. The trains of the New York Central, after making a detour about the grounds, stop in front of the main entrance.

ROCHESTER TO BUFFALO AND NIAGARA FALLS.

Niagara Falls may be reached from Rochester by either the "Falls" Division or the Buffalo route. The distance from Rochester to Buffalo by the main line is sixty-nine miles. Passing in succession the stations and villages of Coldwater, Chili, Churchville, Bergen, and Byron, we reach—

BATAVIA, Batavia, Genesee County, New York, 32 miles from Rochester, 261 miles from Albany, which is delightfully situated in one of the richest and most fertile sections of the State. It is a town of 8,000 inhabitants, the capital of Genesee County, and is noted for its broad and handsome streets, beautiful shade-trees, and pleasant drives. Here is located the State institution for the blind, a ladies' seminary, and several manufactories. The surrounding district originally belonged to Massachusetts, and afterwards passed into the possession of Robert Morris and the Holland Land Company. This company opened roads, and disposed of their lands on liberal terms, until the county became well populated and prosperous. Batavia was founded in 1800. Here the first meeting to advocate the construction of the Erie Canal was held in 1809. The abduction of Morgan, the alleged betrayer of the secrets of Freemasonry, took place here. He came to Batavia to write and print his book. He made no secret of this work, and soon an excitement was raised, during which, on the pretense of taking him to Canandaigua for trial for money loaned him, he was carried off, none knew where. Some say he was executed at the mouth of Niagara River. The publication went on under one Miller. A civil war arose, men armed with clubs met to demolish the office, but a cannon in the hands of the citizens kept them off until the book was published, when violence ceased.

Connection is made at Batavia for all points on the Canandaigua, Batavia & Tonawanda branch, also the Batavia & Attica branch of the New York Central R.R., and the New York, Lake Erie & Western Railroad.

The first station on the branch road to Attica is—

ALEXANDER, eight miles from Batavia, which contains three churches.

ATTICA, in Wyoming County, 11 miles from Batavia, is situated on Tonawanda Creek. The Oak Orchard Acid Springs are situated about twelve miles northwest of Batavia, in the town of Alabama, on Oak Orchard Creek. These curious springs are nine in number, all located within a circle fifty rods in diameter; three of them issuing from a mound within ten feet from each other. In no two of them is the water alike. They are found, by analysis, to contain, besides other mineral substances, a quantity of free sulphuric acid. Large quantities of the water are bottled and sold for medicinal purposes.

Continuing on the main line to Buffalo from Batavia, we pass the village stations of West Batavia, Pembroke, Corfu, Crittenden, Wende, Looneyville, Grimesville, Forks, and East Buffalo, in running 35 miles through a fertile farming region.

NEW YORK CENTRAL RAILROAD.

BUFFALO,

Erie County, New York, 298 miles from Albany, a large and thriving city, the capital of Erie County, with a population of more than 200,000. It is located at the mouth of Buffalo River, at the foot of Lake Erie, and the head of Niagara River, which is here crossed by an iron bridge. The city has a water front of about five miles, running two and a half miles along the shore of the lake, and two miles along Niagara River. "The climate is pleasant and healthful; the streets are broad and generally lined with trees, and well paved, lighted, and supplied with sewers. There are many fine residences with attractive grounds, and numerous squares and public places. A combination of parks and pleasure-grounds has been laid out, extending over 500 acres. It comprises three sections, situated respectively in the northern, western, and eastern parts of the city, which, with the connecting boulevard, afford a drive of nearly ten miles."

Buffalo is the western terminus of the Erie Canal. From its geographical position it is at once the natural key to the commerce of the great lakes and the great Northwest, and also the artificial gate through which the boundless grain-fields of the West pour their treasures into Eastern markets. Next to New York city, Buffalo is the most important commercial city in the State. The French, who were its first visitors, named it "Bufllle"—English, Buffalo—from the wild oxen which they saw in great droves around. In 1813, during the war with Great Britain, this place suffered greatly; every house was destroyed, but one, which is still standing near the corner of Mohawk and Main streets. "The town was sacked and burned by the Royal Scots Regiment, on December 30, 1813. Fort Erie was captured in 1813 by the Americans, and again in 1814. After the heavy battles at Chippewa and Niagara Falls, the American army fell back to this point, and strengthened the defenses. The British army advanced to and besieged Fort Erie, and after a long cannonade made a determined night attack on several points. The assault on Towson's battery was repulsed by the 21st U. S regulars, after five successive charges, during which the British ranks were swept with canister." In 1815 buildings were again erected, and in 1825 Congress voted $80,000 for the sufferers. The principal influence in producing the rapid growth of the city was exerted by the construction of the Erie Canal, completed in October, 1825, which has its western terminus here. From the time when the quarrel between Buffalo and Black Rock, as to which should have the terminus, was decided in favor of Buffalo, to the present, it has been rapidly increasing in size and importance.

Buffalo Harbor, formed by the great Buffalo Creek, was, before the construction of the Erie Canal, obstructed by the washing in of sand from the lake; but by the energy and enterprise of the citizens a pier or breakwater was, after several failures, extended so far out into the lake as to control its "wash," and to enable the spring freshets in the creek to scour out the deposits, and maintain a deep and lasting channel. It was this success that decided the location, at this place, of the canal terminus. A continuous line of wharves extends along Buffalo Creek.

The Erie Basin, just north of Buffalo Creek, is protected by a breakwater from the lake storms; and the Ohio Basin, a little more than a mile up the creek, contains ten acres of sufficient depth to float the largest lake vessels. The Blackwell ship-canal extends more than a mile between Buffalo Creek and the lake, and is connected with the creek, the basins, and the Erie Canal, by numerous slips. At the end of the pier, which extends 1,500 feet into the lake, is a lighthouse, strongly built of stone and iron, and furnished with a first-class Fresnel dioptric light. The city is about sixty feet above the level of the lake, and the ground rises gradually as it recedes from the harbor. The more elevated portions afford fine views of the city, Niagara River, Lake Erie, and the Canada shore.

The business portion of the city is near the lake and river. Wharves, elevators, and extensive warehouses line the harbor; the largest of the latter is that of the Central Railroad, used exclusively for its own consignments. At the back of these immense buildings flows the Erie canal, with only narrow towpaths between its waters and the lofty warehouses. The number of vessels continually arriving and departing from this port is very great. Business is greatly facilitated by the elevators. There are twenty-two of these, which have an aggregate transfer power of 82,000 bushels per hour, and a warehouse capacity of 4,415,000 bushels. They were erected at a cost of $1,000,000. By the promptitude of their action fleets have been unloaded and enabled to leave the harbor in thirty-six hours after arrival. Great numbers of cattle from the West are shipped from Buffalo both by water and by rail.

Manufactures. The manufactures of Buffalo have already attained considerable magnitude. There are twenty establishments engaged in manufacturing iron, which employ 3,000 persons. The most important are those of the Union Iron Co., which has three blasting-furnaces, using 50,000 tons of iron ore and 50,000 tons of coal,—the Fletcher Furnace making upwards of 9,000 tons of pig-iron annually. Pratt & Co.'s iron and nail manufactory, turning out 40 tons per day; the Shephard Iron Works, Buffalo Steam-Engine and Iron Shipbuilding Works, and the Eagle Iron Works. The Niagara & Buffalo Steam Forge Works manufacture anchors and car-axles. There are ten flouring-mills that annually manufacture from 350,000 to 450,000 barrels. Among other manufactures are establishments for leather work, agricultural implements, distilled spirits, and cement.

Shipbuilding is also extensively carried on. There are, besides, eleven establishments for the refining of "petroleum," capable of producing 70,000 barrels per annum.

Public Buildings.—Among the principal public buildings is a large and handsome edifice at the corner of Seneca and Washington streets, in which is conducted the business of the post-office, the custom house, and the United States courts. It was constructed by the Federal Government at a cost of $140,000. The old and new court-houses, the former of which faces Lafayette Park on Main Street, are fine buildings. The United States Arsenal is in Batavia Street. There are also several admirably built markets in different parts of the city. The City Water Works Co. have constructed a reservoir on Niagara Street, eighty feet above the level of the lake, capable of containing nearly 14,000,000 gallons. Powerful engines are erected on the banks of the river to supply the reservoirs, the aggregate cost amounting to $500,000.

There are about one hundred churches in Buffalo, many of which are spacious and handsome. The Roman Catholic Cathedral of St. Joseph is built entirely of stone, in an elegant and expensive style. It is without galleries, and at the back of the altar is a tripartite window of stained glass, manufactured at Munich, representing the birth, crucifixion, and ascension of the Saviour. The Protestant Episcopal Church of St. Paul is an imposing edifice, and has a chime of bells which cost $15,000.

The principal cemetery is Forest Lawn, about three miles from the city. It is a spacious and well-chosen location, somewhat undulating in surface, and is tastefully laid out.

The public schools have a high reputation. In the highest department a complete academic course is taught, excepting the classics.

Institutions, etc.—The benevolent institutions include the Church Charity Foundation, the Buffalo and St. Vincent Orphan asylums, the City Hospital, a Marine Hospital, founded in 1833, the Hospital of the Sisters of Charity, the Boatmen's Friend Society, Association for the Relief of the Poor, Buffalo Industrial School, Martha Industrial School, the Firemen's Benevolent Association, the Benevolent Society of the Evangelical Lutheran St. John's Church, the Soldier's Rest, the Mutual Benefit Catholic Temperance Society, the Buffalo City Dispensary. There are many Masonic lodges, and lodges of the Order of Odd Fellows.

Besides these are the Medical Society of the County of Erie, the Buffalo Horticultural Society, and many other associations. The Young Men's Christian Association is a flourishing society, and has a fine building, with conveniently fitted rooms, containing a library of 10,000 volumes. The German Young Men's Association has 2,000 works, chiefly in German. The Medical College, on the corner of Main and Virginia streets, maintains the usual course of lectures. In the building of the Young Men's Association, besides their own rooms, are the rooms of the Society of Natural Sciences, the Buffalo Law Library, the Historical Society, and the Buffalo Fine Arts Gallery.

Connection is here made with the Lake Shore & Michigan Southern, and the Michigan Central Railroad for the West. A branch of the New York Central & Hudson River Railroad extends from Buffalo, along the Niagara River, to Niagara Falls, and thence to Lewiston.

The Buffalo Belt Line, connected with the New York Central & Hudson River Railroad, starts from Exchange Street in that city, and forms the belt by means of tracks having stations at Terrace, Georgia Street, Porter Avenue, Water Works, Ferry Street, Clinton Avenue, Black Rock, Amherst Street, Austin Street, Cross Cut Junction, Delaware Avenue, Villa Park, Main Street, Steele Street, Driving Park, Genesee Street, Broadway, William Street, and Seneca Street; thence to the starting-points.

NEW YORK CENTRAL RAILROAD.

ROCHESTER TO NIAGARA FALLS.

The trip over the Niagara Falls Division, the direct route from Rochester to Niagara, is made through a picturesque section of the State. Leaving the station at Rochester, the train runs west across the city, past the freight depot, crosses the Erie Canal, and traverses—

GATES, Gates, Monroe County, New York, 233 miles from Albany. The town of Gates adjoins Rochester on the west, and contains the suburban residences of some of the leading men of the city and State. Ex-Judge Addison Gardiner, of the Court of Appeals, and Gen. John H. Martindale, Attorney-General of the State, and other distinguished men, resided in this town. The business of the town is mainly agricultural, and from its gardens and orchards the markets of Rochester receive large supplies.

SPENCERPORT, Ogden, Monroe County, New York, 238 miles from Albany. This place derives its name from William Spencer, the pioneer settler. It is surrounded by a fine wheat-growing country, and contains four churches, a furnace, tannery, grist and saw-mills, and a population of 600.

ADAM'S BASIN, a canal village, is passed, and we reach—

BROCKPORT, Sweden, Monroe County, New York, 245 miles from Albany, "beautifully situated in the midst of a country teeming with abundant harvests, and inhabited by a prosperous and contented population;" the seat of a large normal school. The normal school building is built of red Medina sandstone, and is 400 feet long and four stories in height. Brockport is a busy town, and contains ample church and school accommodations. There are a number of mills and factories in Brockport, including shoe factories and manufactories of reapers, mowers and binders.

Crossing the Sandy Creek ravine, we arrive at Holley, near which are two sulphur and several salt springs. Still proceeding westward, we soon reach Murray, and then—

ALBION, Barré, Orleans County, New York, 259 miles from Albany, the capital of Orleans County, attractively laid out with wide streets, shaded by large trees, and containing many handsome residences. It contains a court house, erected in the center of the park, at a cost of $20,000. Albion is quite a busy and prosperous place.

NEW YORK CENTRAL RAILROAD.

The Tonawanda Swamp begins about five miles south of Albion; and the lake ridge, about three miles north, is about 165 feet above the lake, and marks its ancient shore-line. It is many leagues in length, and is from 100 to 300 feet wide at the top, along which runs the old highway. Eagle Harbor and Knowlesville are villages on the way to—

MEDINA, Ridgeway and Shelby, Orleans County, 268 miles from Albany. This village, on Orchard Creek, where it is crossed by the Erie Canal, contains several flouring-mills and stores, five churches, an academy, and a national bank. From quarries worked in the village is extracted the Medina sandstone, excellent for paving purposes. There are several salt springs in the vicinity. It has a population of 2,500.

MIDDLEPORT, Royalto, Niagara County, New York, 273 miles from Albany. This place contains five churches, fourteen stores, a furnace, steam stave-mill, one saw-mill, and two flouring-mills. Population, about 1,200.

GASPORT, Royalto, Niagara County, New York, 278 miles from Albany. Derives its name from a curious spring, which emits an inflammable hydrocarbon gas, or vapor. An enterprising storekeeper has succeeded in converting this vapor to a useful purpose by lighting his store with it. The place contains a church, an academy, and 300 inhabitants.

LOCKPORT, Lockport, Niagara County, New York, 284 miles from Albany, a city of nearly 20,000 inhabitants. At this point the railroad crosses the Erie Canal by a bridge 500 feet long and 60 feet in height. The canal falls 60 feet in a short distance and has five combined double locks. Its surplus water is distributed, through a hydraulic canal three fourths of a mile long, to the various manufactories of the city. This immense water power is the chief source of the city's prosperity.

Fine limestone and sandstone flaggings and building-materials are quarried here, affording employment to several hundred men. One stratum of the limestone is filled with fossils, and when polished presents a singular and beautiful appearance. It is used for ornamental purposes. Lockport has flouring-mills, saw-mills, iron foundries, cotton and woolen factories, a stave and shingle factory, a plow manufactory, a distillery, a plaster-mill and many stores.

LOCKPORT TO BUFFALO.

A branch of the New York Central & Hudson River Railroad runs between Lockport and Buffalo, a distance of 26 miles. The stations and villages on this line are West Lockport, Lockport Junction, Mapleton, Hall's Station, Sawyer's Creek, North Tonawanda, Tonawanda, North Buffalo, and three other stations within the limits of Buffalo city, before the Union Depot in that city is reached.

Small stations on the main line following Lockport are West Lockport, Lockport Junction, and Sanborn. We then come to—

SUSPENSION BRIDGE, a port of entry on the Niagara River, and described on page 113

CANANDAIGUA TO BUFFALO AND NIAGARA.

This line, the Canandaigua, Batavia & Tonawanda branch of the New York Central & Hudson River Railroad, runs west across an open farming country. Wheeler's, East Bloomfield, Miller's Corner, West Bloomfield, one and a half miles from the village of that name, Honeoye Falls, a busy manufacturing town on Honeoye Creek, and West Rush, are the stations thus far in their order.

Beyond West Rush the line crosses the Rochester Division of the Erie Railroad, the Genesee River, and the Genesee Valley Canal. There are stopping-places at the Genesee Valley Canal and Buffalo, Rochester & Pittsburg junctions, and at Caledonia the Attica Division of the Erie Railroad is approached and it runs parallel with the present route to Batavia. At—

LE ROY, Genesee County, New York, a village on Oatka Creek, is Ingham University, a school for young ladies, and the Staunton Conservatory, a massive stone building, containing a large collection of minerals and South American curiosities, with a collection of paintings.

Before arriving at Batavia, described on page 101, we pass Stafford; and the stations between Batavia and Niagara Falls are Pierson's, East Pembroke, Richville, Falkirk, Akron, East Clarence, Clarence Centre, Transit, Getzville, Tonawanda, and North Tonawanda.

NIAGARA FALLS.

Niagara County, New York, 305 miles from Albany, 21 miles from Buffalo. The Falls of Niagara, the grandest specimen of nature's handiwork on the continent, are equally magnificent at all seasons and under all circumstances. Whether viewed by sunlight, or moonlight, or the dazzling glare of electricity, their wonderful proportions are always sublime. The whirling floods, the unvarying thunderous roar, the vast sheets of spray and mist that are caught in their liquid depths by sunbeams, and formed into radiant rainbows, as if homage was paid by the skies to creation's greatest cataract.

The Niagara River, extending from Lake Erie to Lake Ontario, a distance of thirty miles, has a total fall of 334 feet ; the greater part of the descent is confined to a distance of seven or eight miles, within which space are the grandest rapids and falls in the world. The rapids are so strong two miles above the falls as to entirely prevent navigation. There are three distinct cataracts. The Horseshoe Fall, so called from its crescent shape, is by far the largest, and is in the direct course of the river ; it is 2,000 feet wide and 154 feet high.

The American Fall is 669 feet wide, and the Central Fall 243 feet, each having a fall of 163 feet. The two latter are separate from each other, and from the former, by Goat Island.

The aggregate width of descending water is thus 2,900 feet, and the flow is unceasing and nearly uniform in amount throughout the year. The amount of water discharged is computed to be 100,000,000 tons per hour. More water passes in these fearful torrents in seven seconds than is conveyed through Croton Aqueduct in twenty-four hours. At the Horseshoe Fall the concussion of the falling waters with those in the depths below occasions a spray that veils the cataract two thirds up its height.

Above this impenetrable foam, to the height of fifty feet above the fall, a cloud of light spray rises, which, when the sun shines upon it in the proper direction, displays magnificent solar rainbows.

Charles Dickens describes his first impression of Niagara Falls in the following characteristic style :

"I hardly know how I got down, but I was soon at the bottom, and climbing over some broken rocks, deafened by the noise, half blinded by the spray, and wet to the skin. We were at the foot of the American Falls. I could see an immense torrent of water tearing headlong down from some great height, but had no idea of shape or situation, or anything but vague immensity. When we were seated in the little ferry-boat and were crossing the swollen river immediately before both cataracts, I began to feel what it was; but I was in a measure stunned, and unable to comprehend the vastness of the scene. It was not until I came on Table Rock and looked—Great Heaven! on what a fall of bright green water!—that it came upon me in its full might and majesty. Then, when I felt how near to my Creator I was standing, the first effect and the enduring one—instant and lasting—of the tremendous spectacle, was Peace. Peace of mind, tranquillity, calm recollections of the dead, great thoughts of eternal rest and happiness; nothing of gloom and terror. Niagara was at once stamped upon my heart, an image of beauty, to remain there changeless and indelible until its pulses cease to beat forever."

No just or adequate impression can be conveyed by language of the grandeur and sublimity of Niagara. The artist's pencil alone can give a faint conception of the scene, but even this is inadequate to express intelligently the charm of perpetual changing which absorbs the spectator.

GOAT ISLAND is midway between the American and Canada shores, in the midst of these boiling waters, and divides the American and Horseshoe Falls. It is separated from Bath by a narrow stream, and the latter island is connected with the American shore by a wooden bridge, 700 feet long, over the wildest part of the rapids. It is said the first white person who ventured to cross the rapids at Goat Island was Israel Putnam, in 1755.

On the shore of the island, and beneath the smaller of the American Falls, is the Cave of the Winds, a cavern formed by the decay of the softer substratum rock, whilst the hard superincumbent limestone still forms the roof. In front of the cave the center fall descends, 240 feet in width, and compresses the air to such a degree that a fearful din continually reigns within the watery cavern, which is heightened by the foaming spray, which rushes along the stony floor, mounts up the darkened sides, spreads over the roof, and thence descends in continued

VIEW FROM PROSPECT POINT, NIAGARA FALLS.

drenching showers. Luna Island and the Three Sisters should be visited, as each has peculiar attractions.

The first white visitor looked upon the falls in 1640. The Cat Indians, who dwelt near it, endeavored to propitiate the spirit of its waters by annually sacrificing a human victim at its shrine. The most beautiful Indian maiden was selected for this honor. In the presence of a great assemblage she was placed in a white canoe, with the finest fruits and flowers, and the fragile bark, pushed out into the stream, carried her over this awful portal to eternity.

The Niagara River, below these stupendous falls, rushes through a deep chasm of 200 feet in height. Three miles below the falls is the Whirlpool. Just here the scenery is wild and somber, and the banks of the river are steep. It is caused by the abrupt turn of the river at this point, the waters of which rush with such violence against the cliff on the Canadian side as to occasion a severe reaction and rotary motion, drawing everything that flows down the river within the vortex; below the Whirlpool is another series of rapids. The most comprehensive view of the falls is obtained from the Canada side, where the descending water of the three falls can be seen at the same time. The river is crossed just below the falls by a magnificent suspension bridge for carriages and foot passengers. A ferry at the foot of the American Falls also transports foot passengers over the raging river.

In 1885 the Legislature of the State of New York passed a law providing for the purchase of the property around Niagara Falls, and the establishment of the Niagara Park, owned and controlled by the State of New York through a State Commission. Thus the greatest of American wonders is to be preserved for the free enjoyment of the American people and tourists who visit the grandest and most sublime waterfall of the known world. No charge for admission to any part of the Park is permitted, and all obstructions to an uninterrupted view of these marvels of nature are removed. The grounds are being suitably arranged and beautified.

The railroad connections at Niagara Falls are as follows, viz.:

To the West via Suspension Bridge and Canada, by the Michigan Central R.R., Grand Trunk Railway, and via Buffalo, by the Lake Shore & Michigan Southern R.R., and New York, Chicago & St. Louis R.R. (Nickel Plate), Buffalo, New York & Philadelphia R.R., and the Buffalo & Pittsburg R.R.

NIAGARA FALLS.

NEW YORK CENTRAL RAILROAD.

To the East via Rome, Watertown & Ogdensburg R.R., New York Central & Hudson River R.R., New York, West Shore & Buffalo R.R., Delaware, Lackawanna & Western R.R., Lehigh Valley R.R., New York, Lake Erie & Western R.R.

The steamboat connections are via Lewiston, N. Y., with the steamers of the Richelieu & Ontario Steam Navigation Co. to Toronto, and through Lake Ontario and down the St. Lawrence River to Montreal and Quebec. Passengers have the choice to go to points in eastern Canada from Toronto by the Grand Trunk Railway, or by Richelieu and Ontario Navigation Co.'s steamers, on the tickets of the steamer line.

From Buffalo steamers run westward through Lakes Erie, Huron, Michigan and Superior.

SUSPENSION BRIDGE, Niagara County, New York, 303 miles from Albany, an incorporated village of 2,000 inhabitants, situated on Niagara River, two miles below the cataract, of which it commands a fine view. The International Suspension Bridge crosses the river at this point, and connects the Canada railways with those of the States. The length of the bridge is 800 feet; height above the water, 230 feet; width, 24 feet; supported by four wire cables $9\frac{1}{4}$ inches in diameter, and has a sustaining capacity of 12,400 tons. The towers are 88 feet on the American side, and 78 on the Canadian. Its total weight is 800 tons, and its cost $400,000. There are two floors, the upper for the railroad track, and the lower for wagons. It was commenced in 1854, John A. Roebling, of Trenton, New Jersey, being the engineer. The east end of the bridge commands a fine view of the river above up to the Falls, and of the rapids under and below the bridge, for three-quarters of a mile to the Whirlpool. The water of these rapids runs at the rate of 25 miles per hour, with breakers dashing from 10 to 20 feet in height. When seen from the shore, they present one of the grandest sights of the kind seen in the world, and the tourist has not seen all of Niagara until he has stood on the shore, 150 rods below the bridge. Deveaux College is a charitable institution under Episcopal management, and was established by the munificence of Hon. Samuel Deveaux, who bequeathed property amounting to upward of $200,000 in value for that purpose. The building was erected in 1855–56. The village contains several hotels, of which the Monteagle is the largest and best.

The Great International RAILWAY SUSPENSION BRIDGE Over the Niagara River
In Full View of Niagara Falls,
Connecting THE ERIE RAILWAY AND GREAT WESTERN RAILWAY OF CANADA.

NEW YORK CENTRAL RAILROAD.

PROSPECT PARK, twelve acres in extent, adjoins the American Fall, with a frontage of several hundred feet along the gorge. Descent to the water's edge can be made by means of an inclined railway. It may be useful to know what it is necessary to pay in the way of fees etc., during a visit to the sights in this vicinity:—

Goat Island—Guide and suit to go through "Cave of the Winds"	$1 00
Prospect Park—Down and up the inclined railway (each way)	10
Prospect Park—Round trip on "Maid of the Mist," including rubber suit	50
New Bridge—Niagara Falls to Canada and return—each person (carriage 25 cents)	25
Museum—On Canada side near the Falls	50
Under Horseshoe Falls Canada side—guide and suit	1 00
Burning Springs	50
Old Suspension Bridge—over and return	25
Whirlpool Rapids and Park—inclined railway, Canada side	50
Whirlpool Rapids and Park—Elevator, American side	50
Whirlpool—Stairs, American side	50
Whirlpool—Inclined railway, Canada side	50
Niagara Falls to Suspension Bridge, street car, over old bridge, in Whirlpool Rapids Park (Canada side), return same way	55
If each is paid separately	85
Niagara Falls to Suspension Bridge, street car, walk to Buttery's Whirlpool Rapids, elevator, return same way	40
If each is paid separately	60
Niagara Falls to Suspension Bridge, street car, transfer from Suspension Bridge to old Whirlpool (American side), and return	55
If each is paid separately	85
Hack hire—regular rate, per hour	1 50
Hack hire to take in all places of interest for party of four (4) or more in each hack, each	1 00

No charge is made for entrance to the park.
The small steamer "Maid of the Mist" makes regular trips to the foot of the Falls, affording advantageous views of the cataract.

NEW YORK CENTRAL RAILROAD.

BUFFALO TO NIAGARA FALLS, SUSPENSION BRIDGE, AND LEWISTON.

One of the routes traversed by the New York Central & Hudson River Railroad is from Union Depot, Buffalo, to Lewiston, via Tonawanda. After leaving the depot, and passing Buffalo Terrace, Ferry Street, Black River, and North Buffalo we reach—

TONAWANDA, Tonawanda, Erie County, New York, 11 miles from Buffalo. This place is at the confluence of the Niagara River and Tonawanda Creek, and lies partly in Niagara County. The Canandaigua & Niagara Falls branch of the Central Railroad terminates here, as does also the branch extending to Lockport. The village contains several churches, a number of manufacturing establishments, also an iron foundry and machine works, saw-mills, shingle-mills, a planing-mill, and a population exceeding 2,000. It has a good harbor, and store-room for 250,000 bushels. Much lumber received from Canada is sawed and reshipped.

Beyond **NORTH TONAWANDA**, and **GRATURCK**, on the same line, is—

LA SALLE, Niagara, Niagara County, New York, 5 miles above Niagara Falls. At this port was built, two centuries ago, the first vessel that ever navigated the waters of Lake Erie; she was sixty tons burden. Salvos were fired at its launch, and a *Te Deum* was sung.

Niagara Falls and Suspension Bridge are described on page 110.

LEWISTON, Lewiston, Niagara County, New York, 7 miles from Niagara Falls, at the north base of the mountain range through which, according to Lyell, the Niagara has cut its way during the past thirty-five thousand years. This village is at the head of the navigation of Lake Ontario. It contains four churches and about 1,200 inhabitants. The R., W. & O. R. R. connects here with the New York Central & Hudson River Railroad. During the summer steamboats ply daily between Lewiston and ports on Lake Ontario and the St. Lawrence River, reaching Montreal in twenty-seven hours. It is a place of active trade. Besides the county buildings, it contains an academy and numerous stores. In 1812 the tavern at Lewiston was conducted by Mr. and Mrs. Hastler, the former of whom is said to have been "Sergeant Hollister," and his wife the "Betty Flannagan" of Cooper's

"Spy." River View, two miles from Lewiston, is at the summit, where a fine view of the Niagara River and the Canadian shore may be obtained. Opposite may be seen the splendid monument erected to the memory of the gallant General Brock, who was killed at Queenston in the war of 1812. A fine suspension bridge, 60 feet in height, and having a span of 1,045 feet, was built from Lewiston to Queenston in 1850, but this was subsequently capsized during a heavy gale and has been replaced.

The Tuscarora Reservation is three miles east of this place, and still gives inhabitation and sustenance to several hundreds of the tribe. The Tuscaroras were driven by hostile tribes from their home in North Carolina in 1712 and migrated to New York, where they joined the Iroquois confederation, afterward known as the Six Nations.

ROME, WATERTOWN & OGDENSBURG RAILROAD.

THE ROME, WATERTOWN & OGDENSBURG RAILROAD

is the chief connecting railway between Western and Central New York and Northern New York and Canada. Beginning at its western terminus, Niagara Falls, it runs northwesterly to Suspension Bridge and Lewiston, and thence easterly along the southern shore of Lake Ontario to Charlotte, Windsor Beach, Oswego, Richland, Watertown, The Thousand Islands, Ogdensburg, and Massena Springs, opening up a rich and beautiful country along the shore of Lake Ontario and northern New York. With its various branches it touches many important cities and towns, including Niagara Falls, Rochester, Oswego, Syracuse, Rome, Utica, Watertown, Ogdensburg, and many other large towns, and forms an important line connecting Niagara Falls and the West with Northern New York, Montreal, the Adirondacks, and the Green and White Mountain regions, and Canada.

At Suspension Bridge, railroad connections are made with the Michigan Central and Grand Trunk Railways for Canada, Detroit, Chicago, and the West, and with the New York Central Railroad for Buffalo and points west via Lake Shore & Michigan Southern R. R.; also with the New York, Lake Erie & Western R. R.

At Lewiston, N. Y., it connects with steamers on Lake Ontario for Toronto and other points on the Lake Ontario and the St. Lawrence River, and with the New York Central R. R.

From Charlotte, N. Y., a branch of the R. W. & O. R. R. runs to Rochester, where it connects with the New York Central and the Rochester & Pittsburgh railroads, and New York, Lake Erie & Western for points south. Steamers run to points on Lake Ontario.

At Sterling Junction it connects with the Southern Central Division of the Lehigh Valley Railway for Auburn, Elmira, Mauch Chunk, New York, and Philadelphia; at Wallington with the Sodus Bay and Southern Division of the Pennsylvania Railroad for Clifton Springs, Penn Yan, Watkins, Elmira, and points south.

At Oswego it connects with its Phœnix Line, running to Syracuse via Fulton and Phœnix, and also with the Delaware, Lackawanna & Western Railroad, leading to Syracuse, Binghamton, Scranton, and New York City, and with the Ontario & Western Railroad, leading southeast through New York State to New York City.

From Richland Junction a branch runs through Pulaski to Central

ROME, WATERTOWN & OGDENSBURG RAILROAD.

Square, where it connects with the New York, Ontario & Western R. R., and to Syracuse, connecting with the New York Central, the New York, West Shore & Buffalo, the Delaware, Lackawanna & Western, and the Syracuse & Ontario Railways for points east, west, and south.

Another branch leads from Richland Junction to Rome, N. Y., where it connects with the New York Central & Hudson River R. R. It runs north, through the fertile regions of Oneida, Jefferson, and St. Lawrence counties, to Watertown, Cape Vincent, Ogdensburg, and Norwood, and forms the direct line with the New York Central & Hudson River R. R., from New York and Albany to Thousand Islands, St. Lawrence River, and Lake Ontario.

From Watertown, N. Y., branches diverge to Sackett's Harbor and Cape Vincent on Lake Ontario, and to Carthage, Harrisville, and the Oswegatchie fishing grounds near the North Woods.

At Cape Vincent a fine steamer connects with the railroad for Thousand Islands and Alexandria Bay, whence steamers run down the St. Lawrence River to Montreal and Quebec.

The northern connections of the Rome, Watertown & Ogdensburg Railroad are at Ogdensburg and Norwood, on the Ogdensburg & Lake Champlain Railway, with which it connects for northern New York, Adirondacks, Lake Champlain, Montreal, Quebec, St. Albans, Burlington, and other towns in Vermont, White Mountains, Boston, Portland, and other points in New England, and at Massena Springs, where it connects with the Grand Trunk Railway for Montreal and Quebec.

At Ogdensburg it connects by steamer with Prescott, Canada, where connection is made with the Grand Trunk Railway, the St. Lawrence and Ottawa Division of the Canadian Pacific Railway for Ottawa City, the capital of the Dominion of Canada, and with steamers for the route of the St. Lawrence through Lachine Rapids to Montreal, Quebec, and the provinces eastward.

It will thus be seen that the Rome, Watertown & Ogdensburg is a very important line of railway. It runs through the fertile and productive portions of the Empire State, and is the great route to the most famous and interesting resorts of the United States. The railway is equipped with elegant palace and sleeping coaches and fine passenger cars, and has an excellent train service. Competent management, and courteous attention from employees, and thorough equipment have made the road popular and brought it to the front rank of railways.

ROME, WATERTOWN & OGDENSBURG RAILROAD.

ROME, WATERTOWN & OGDENSBURG RAILROAD.

	PAGES
NIAGARA FALLS TO MASSENA SPRINGS	115–136
LEWISTON JUNCTION TO LEWISTON	121
ROCHESTER, WINDSOR BEACH, AND ONTARIO BEACH	122
SYRACUSE TO PULASKI	126, 127
RICHLAND TO ROME	127
WATERTOWN JUNCTION TO CAPE VINCENT	129–131
DE KALB JUNCTION TO OGDENSBURG	134
SYRACUSE TO OSWEGO	125
UTICA (TO CLAYTON 109 MILES) TO OGDENSBURG	138–152
CARTHAGE, WATERTOWN, AND SACKETT'S HARBOR	131–133
CLAYTON TO THERESA JUNCTION	144

CONNECTIONS.

All Rome, Watertown & Ogdensburg Railroad trains run solid to and from New York Central & Hudson River Railroad Station at Niagara Falls via Suspension Bridge Station.

At NIAGARA FALLS, with N. Y. C. & H. R. R. R.; West Shore R. R.; Michigan Central R. R.; N. Y., L. E. & W. R. R.

At SUSPENSION BRIDGE, with N. Y. C. & H. R. R. R.; Michigan Central R. R.; Grand Trunk R'y (Gt. Western Div.); N. Y., L. E. & W. R. R.; West Shore R. R.

At WINDSOR BEACH, with Rochester Line, R., W. & O. R. R.

At ROCHESTER, with N. Y. C. & H. R. R. R.; West Shore R. R.; B., R. & P. R. R.; N. Y., L. E. & W. R. R.; W., N. Y. & P. R. R.

At WALLINGTON, with Penn. R. R. (Sodus Bay & So. Div.).

At STERLING, with Lehigh Valley R. R. (So. Cent. Div.).

At OSWEGO, with N. Y., O. & W. R'y; D., L. & W. R. R., also PHŒNIX LINE; R., W. & O. R. R. to Syracuse.

At CENTRAL SQUARE, with N. Y., O. & W. R'y.

At SYRACUSE, with N. Y. C. & H. R. R. R.; West Shore R. R.; D., L. & W. R. R.; S., O. & N. Y. R'y.

At ROME, with N. Y. C. & H. R. R. R., and N. Y., O. & W. R'y.

ROME, WATERTOWN & OGDENSBURG RAILROAD.

At CAPE VINCENT, with St. Lawrence River Steamboat Co. for Kingston, connecting at Kingston with Grand Trunk R'y and Kingston & Pembroke R'y; also with steamer to Alexandria Bay and Thousand Island resorts.

At UTICA, with N. Y. C. & H. R. R. R.; West Shore R. R.; D., L. & W. R. R.; N. Y., O. & W. R'y.

At SACKETT'S HARBOR, during summer season only, with steamer for Henderson Harbor.

At CLAYTON, with palace steamer "St. Lawrence" for Alexandria Bay, Thousand Island Park, Round Island Park, Westminster Park, etc.; also with steamboat for Gananoque, connecting at Gananoque with Thousand Islands R'y for Grand Trunk R'y Junction without transfer.

At CLAYTON, with Richelieu & Ontario Navigation Co.'s Royal Mail Line Steamers for Montreal, Quebec, and River Saguenay, passing all of the Thousand Islands and Rapids of River St. Lawrence by daylight. Trains run to steamboat dock at Clayton. Connection is also made with this line at Alexandria Bay, Brockville, and Prescott.

At MORRISTOWN, with ferry for Brockville.

At BROCKVILLE, with Grand Trunk R'y; also Canadian Pacific R'y for Toronto, Montreal, Ottawa, and points on the Upper Ottawa River.

At OGDENSBURG, with Central Vermont R. R. (O. & L. C. Div.); also with ferry to Prescott.

At PRESCOTT, with Grand Trunk R'y; also with Canadian Pacific R'y for Ottawa.

At NORWOOD, with Central Vermont R. R. (O. & L. C. Div.) and connections for Paul Smith's, and Adirondack Mountain resorts; Fabyan's, and all White Mountain resorts; Portland, Bar Harbor, and the sea-coast resorts of Maine, St. Andrew's, N. B., and all Eastern resorts.

At MASSENA SPRINGS, with Massena Springs & Ft. Covington R'y.

R. W. & O. R. R. New Fast Trains will be run during Season of 1889, avoiding stops, and making Quick Time, from Utica, from Syracuse, from Rochester, from Niagara Falls and from Suspension Bridge to Clayton, at which point immediate connection is made with Palace Steamer "St. Lawrence," for all Thousand Island Resorts.

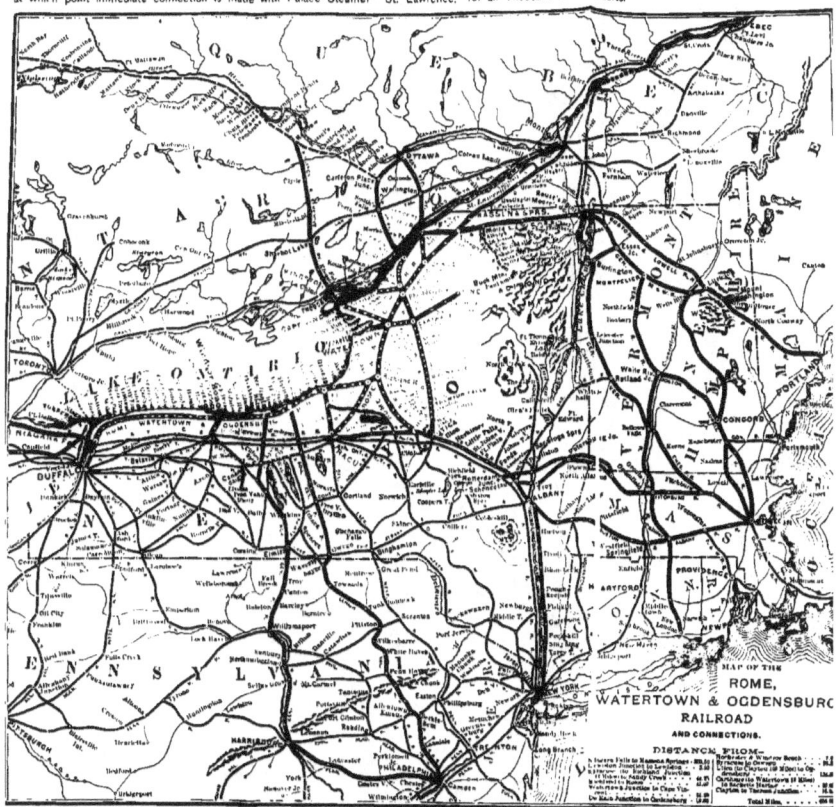

EXCURSION TICKETS AT REDUCED RATES WILL BE ON SALE AT ALL STATIONS

DRAWING ROOM CARS ON DAY TRAINS.   SLEEPING CARS ON NIGHT TRAINS.

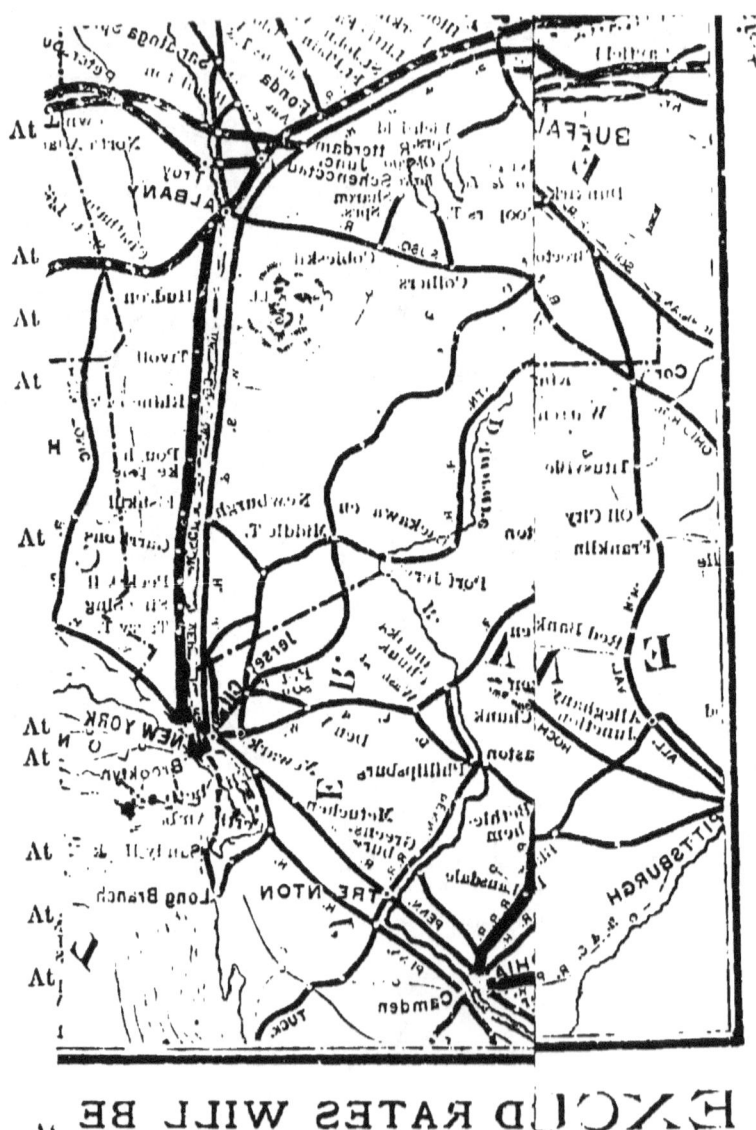

ROME, WATERTOWN AND OGDENSBURG RAILROAD.

NIAGARA FALLS LINE.

With Niagara Falls—described on page 110, as a starting-point on the line, the first station eastward is Suspension Bridge—described on page 113.

All through trains of the Rome, Watertown & Ogdensburg Railroad, both east-bound and west-bound, allow ample time for passengers to view the Falls.

The **NIAGARA RIVER**, through which the waters of all the great lakes, except Ontario, and all their tributaries—the whole draining an area of at least 150,000 square miles—flow on their way to the sea, falls 336 feet in its course of 36 miles. The descent from Lake Erie to the Falls of Niagara, a distance of 22 miles, is 15 feet. At the verge of the cataract, **GOAT ISLAND**, formerly called Iris Island, parts the channel into two courses, the larger of which, with an average width of 2,000 feet, plunges down 165 feet at the **HORSESHOE FALL**. The other, known as the **AMERICAN FALL**, is 800 feet wide, with a plunge of 159 feet. It is estimated that 100,000,000 tons of water pass over the falls every hour.

The channel of the river turns abruptly about three miles below the Falls. The famous **WHIRLPOOL** is formed here, the surging waters being enclosed by cliffs 350 feet high. The depth of the channel at this point is about 400 feet.

After passing Suspension Bridge we are treated to a delightful panorama picture of wild and picturesque scenery. The summit of the mountain is reached at **RIVER VIEW** station, whence is obtained an unobstructed prospect of the river and the Canadian shore.

LEWISTON is seven miles below the Falls. On the Canadian side, directly opposite, is Queenston. After leaving Lewiston, the road skirts Lake Ontario, passing through what is considered to be one of the finest farming sections of the State. Passing the stations and villages of Hay-

ROME, WATERTOWN & OGDENSBURG RAILROAD.

wards, Ransomville and Wilson, we reach, after a thirty-five minutes' run, the station and hamlet of—

NEWFANE, where stages are waiting to convey intending visitors to Olcott, a favorite boating and fishing resort on Lake Ontario. Between Newfane and the next station of interest are Hess Road, Somerset, County Line, Lyndonville, and Carlyon.

WATERPORT, forty-five minutes from Newfane, is a pleasant little village, largely engaged in flouring, and the manufacture of plows and other agricultural implements. Thence, along the same route, we pass Carlton, East Carlton, Kendall, East Kendall, Hamlin, East Hamlin, Parma, and Greece, whence, twelve minutes later, we reach—

CHARLOTTE, Monroe County, New York, 82 miles from Suspension Bridge, and about 7 miles north of Rochester. In the vicinity are several watering-places, including Windsor Beach and Ontario Beach, both popular and pleasant summer resorts. Charlotte is the port of Rochester on Lake Ontario.

ROCHESTER LINE.

For purposes of easy reference, the branches of the Rome, Watertown & Ogdensburg Railroad will be described as nearly as possible in the order in which they occur, commencing from the western terminus of the Niagara Falls line, and running eastward from Niagara Falls to Massena Springs. The first of these is termed the Rochester Line, seven miles in length, running southward from Windsor Beach, on the Niagara Falls line, to State Street Station, Rochester city. The intermediate stations are Rifle Range and Brinker Place, Rochester.

Tourists and others traveling by this line from Rochester can continue, after reaching Windsor Beach Station, in a westerly direction to Suspension Bridge and Niagara Falls, or in an easterly direction, to Oswego, Watertown, Cape Vincent, Philadelphia, Clayton, Morristown, Ogdensburg, Norwood, and Massena Springs. The R., W. & O. R. R. service of trains on this route is regular and frequent.

Running eastward from Windsor Beach are the stations—

SEA BREEZE, a well-known and attractive summer resort, near Irondequoit Bay, Pierce's, Webster, Union Hill, Lakeside, Ontario, and Sodus.

IRONDEQUOIT BAY, LAKE ONTARIO.

ROME, WATERTOWN & OGDENSBURG RAILROAD.

At Wallington, 32 miles east of Charlotte, and 113 miles from Buffalo, the Sodus Bay & Southern Division of the Pennsylvania Railroad connects for Sodus Point, a noted summer resort on the lake, and about three miles distant. Sodus Point is delightfully situated on Lake Ontario and the west shore of Sodus Bay. The fishing is excellent, there being abundance of bass and pickerel. The boating privileges are also satisfactory.

On the east shore of Sodus Bay is a well-known summer home, "The Bluffs," accessible from Alton station, two miles past Wallington. Five miles beyond this last-named station is—

ROSE, from which Lake Bluff is reached by carriage from Port Glasco, and steamer to destination. Ten minutes' journey from Rose brings us to—

WOLCOTT, a stopping-station for those bent on piscatorial pursuits. There is excellent pike, pickerel, and black-bass fishing in Port Bay throughout the year. The next station is Red Creek, and five miles to the eastward is—

STERLING, where the Southern Central Division of the Lehigh Valley Railroad connects for Fair Haven on Lake Ontario, and Auburn, Sayre, Mauch Chunk, and all points in the Lehigh Valley region. Following Sterling on the route eastward are Sterling Valley, Hannibal, Wheeler's, and Furniss. Then, after a run of five miles from Furniss, we come to—

OSWEGO, Oswego County, New York, population 25,000, 151 miles from Suspension Bridge. Hotels—Doolittle House and Lake Shore Hotel. The charming city of Oswego is upon the shore of Lake Ontario, and almost heading the famous Thousand Islands of the lovely St. Lawrence River. It has the natural advantages of both lake and river. The pure air, excellent drainage, and other natural advantages contribute to make Oswego the third healthiest city in the United States. The city is built on ground sloping to the Oswego River on either side.

The streets are 100 feet wide, and laid out in right angles, making blocks 200 by 400 feet, and affording frequent opportunity for public parks, of which there are two large ones and several of lesser size. The streets in the residence part of the city are really magnificent

OSWEGO HARBOR, FROM ROME, WATERTOWN AND OGDENSBURG RAILROAD BRIDGE.

avenues, bordered by grand old trees, and presenting a delightful vista of shade, with a glimpse of both lake and river.

Along the lake shore west for three miles is a wide and cultivated road for carriage and bridle, with all of nature's grandeur of beach and bluff.

The Oswego Yacht Club has a fleet of yachts, sailboats and steam yachts, which, with the excellent sailing and fishing which Lake Ontario affords, contributes to the fascinating pleasure of the summer sportsman. The Oswego Canoe Club has a fleet of canoes.

The city has 10 grain elevators, 17 churches, 2 daily and 2 weekly newspapers, an opera house, a public library of 20,000 volumes, and important manufacturing interests. The foreign commerce aggregates $8,000,000 annually.

The principal buildings are the United States Custom House and Post Office, built of Cleveland limestone, and the City Hall, a very ornate building of Onondaga limestone.

The old and historic fortification, Fort Ontario, stands on the right bank of the river, in the middle of a high plateau commanding the town, the harbor, and its approaches.

The principal hotels are the Lake Shore House (capacity 150), and the Doolittle House (capacity 250). The former is ably managed by Mr. James G. Bennett, and is the property of the Rome, Watertown & Ogdensburg Railroad Company. The station and general offices of that company occupy a part of the hotel block. Tourists will find this house very pleasant and convenient to railroads.

The Doolittle House is first-class in all respects. Under this house is located the famous "Deep Rock" mineral spring, celebrated for the health-giving properties of its waters.

Oswego is the diverging point of the Phœnix Line of the Rome, Watertown & Ogdensburg R. R., which forms a direct line from Oswego to Syracuse; of the New York, Ontario & Western Railway, and the Oswego and Syracuse Division of the Delaware, Lackawanna & Western Railroad, leading to Syracuse, Binghamton, Scranton, and New York. Beyond Central Square the New York, Ontario & Western Railway continues southward, skirting the eastern shore of Oneida Lake, passing North Bay and Fish Creek—popular summer resorts—and finally terminating at New York.

The Delaware, Lackawanna & Western Railroad affords a direct route from Oswego to Binghamton, Scranton, and New York.

PHŒNIX LINE.

The branch of the Rome, Watertown & Ogdensburg Railroad, which runs from Oswego southward, 37 miles to Syracuse, is called the Phœnix Line. The intermediate stations are Bridge Street in Oswego City and—

FULTON, Oswego County, New York, a thriving town of about 5,000 inhabitants, situated on the east side of the Oswego River. On the west side of the Oswego River is Oswego Falls. Both these towns are largely engaged in manufacturing industries, and the combined population of the two towns is about 7,000. Trains stop at Cayuga Street and at Oswego Falls in Fulton.

PHŒNIX, Oswego County, New York, the next station southward, is a pretty village, containing about 2,000 inhabitants, and is located on the boundary line between Oswego and Onondaga counties. The Oswego Canal passes through the place.

THREE RIVER POINT, the next station, is in the midst of attractive natural scenery; the confluence of the Oneida, Seneca, and Oswego rivers presenting a view at once striking and beautiful.

WOODARD, Onondaga County, New York, is the junction point of the Phœnix line with the Syracuse Division of the Rome, Watertown & Ogdensburg Railroad. Three miles south of Woodard Junction is Liverpool, described on page 126, and seven miles south of Woodard is the city of Syracuse, see page 88.

Resuming the journey on the main line of the Rome, Watertown and Ogdensburg Railroad, eastward from Oswego, we pass through the agricultural town of—

SCRIBA, Oswego County, New York, and then arrive at—

NEW HAVEN, Oswego County, New York, a pretty village of five hundred inhabitants, eleven miles east of Oswego, and one and a half miles south of Lake Ontario. There are fine opportunities for black-bass fishing in the lake off New Haven.

MEXICO, Oswego County, New York, is a beautiful village of about 500 people. Mexico Point and Port Ontario on Lake Ontario are about four miles from Mexico station. They are much frequented as resorts,

ROME, WATERTOWN & OGDENSBURG RAILROAD.

and offer, among other attractions, excellent bass fishing. These points may also be reached by private conveyance from—

SAND HILL, Oswego County, New York, the first station east of Mexico, and five miles from it.

PULASKI, Richland, Oswego County, New York, 105 miles from Ogdensburg, a flourishing village of 2,000 inhabitants on Salmon River, a half-shire town of Oswego County. It has several churches, an academy, court house, newspaper offices, banks, and several manufactories.

RICHLAND JUNCTION, Oswego County, New York, 29 miles east of Oswego, is at the junction of the main line of the Rome, Watertown & Ogdensburg Railroad, with two of its important branches—one running from the south and west from Syracuse, and one from the south and east from Rome. It is the converging point of the R., W. & O. system. These two branches form a V, with its apex at Richland. Richland Junction is 100 miles from Ogdensburg, 42 miles from Rome, 180 miles from Suspension Bridge, 41 miles from Syracuse, and 29 miles from Oswego.

In describing the Syracuse branch we begin at Syracuse (see page 88), and follow the line northeastward to Richland. The first town, north and four miles from Syracuse, is—

LIVERPOOL, Salina, Onondaga County, New York, 37 miles from Richland. This is a flourishing village of 2,000 inhabitants, on the east bank of Onondaga Lake. It contains extensive salt works and other industries, a union school, and several churches. It was first settled in 1795 by John Danforth and his three sons, from Worcester, Mass. Three miles north of Liverpool is—

WOODARD, Onondaga County, New York, at the junction of the Syracuse Division with the Phœnix Line to Oswego.

CLAY, Clay, Onondaga County, New York, 31 miles from Richland. A hamlet upon Seneca River, with about 300 people. A very fertile country surrounds this village.

BREWERTON, Cicero, Onondaga County, New York, 27 miles from Richland. A flourishing village of 500 inhabitants, on the outlet of Oneida Lake. Fort Brewerton, one of the line of English forts between Oswego and Mohawk Valley, was situated on the south shore of Oneida Outlet, opposite the present village of Brewerton. Frenchman's Island and South Bay are places of resort for pleasure-seekers.

CENTRAL SQUARE, Hastings, Oswego County, New York, 24 miles from Richland. An important village of 500 people in the south part of the town of Hastings, where the R., W. & O. R. R. crosses the N. Y., Ontario & Western.

HASTINGS, Oswego County, New York, is 18 miles from Richland Junction, and has a village population of about 300 people.

PARISH, Oswego County, New York, is a flourishing village of about 500 inhabitants. It is 15 miles southwest from Richland.

Between Parish and Richland Junction the railroad passes through the small villages of Holmesville, Union Square, 11 miles from Richland, and the large town of Pulaski, described on page 126.

Starting from Rome (see page 83) on the New York Central Railroad, the eastern branch of the V of the Rome, Watertown & Ogdensburg Railroad extends in a northwesterly direction through the village of Taberg, 7 miles from Rome, thence to—

McCONNELLSVILLE, Oneida County, New York, 13 miles northwest of Rome, a small village, largely engaged in the manufacturing of chairs. It also does a large corn-packing business.

CAMDEN, Oneida County, New York, is a flourishing village, widely known for its chair factories and corn-packing establishments.

WILLIAMSTOWN, Oswego County, New York. Eight miles from this place is Redfield Square, where there is excellent trouting and good boarding accommodations.

KASOAG, Oswego County, New York, is a small station.

ALBION, Oswego County, New York, is a small village. Only six miles from it are Salmon River Falls, which are 110 feet high, and well worth seeing.

Passengers from Rome and intermediate stations on this section, and from Syracuse and intermediate stations on the opposite side of the V, can, on arriving at Richland Junction, continue on to Watertown, Cape Vincent, Philadelphia, De Kalb Junction, Ogdensburg, Norwood, or Massena Springs.

ROME, WATERTOWN & OGDENSBURG RAILROAD.

Ten minutes from the time we leave Richland Junction we pass Sandy Creek. Five miles beyond is Mannsville, and two miles farther on is Pierrepont Manor. Then, after a rapid journey of six miles, we arrive at—

ADAMS, Jefferson County, New York, 82 miles from Ogdensburg, an incorporated village of 1,500 inhabitants, on North Sandy Creek, containing several churches, two banks, a seminary, printing-offices, and several manufactories. From here stages run daily to Henderson Harbor, a resort on Lake Ontario noted for fine fishing and its handsome cottages, where many wealthy people spend their summers. From Adams the railroad runs north through Adams Center, Rice's, and—

WATERTOWN, Jefferson County, New York, 68 miles from Ogdensburg. Hotels—Woodruff, Kirby, Globe, Crowner, Harris, and City. An important city of 13,000 inhabitants, beautifully situated on Black River. Its railroad connections are with the several branches of the Rome, Watertown & Ogdensburg Railroad. The Cape Vincent Branch of the latter unites here with the main line. The city is in the midst of a very rich agricultural community, and has derived much of its wealth from the extensive dairying business carried on in Jefferson County. The city was incorporated in May, 1869, and is noted for the enterprise, wealth, and culture of its inhabitants. The county seat of Jefferson County is in this city, and the County Court House on Arsenal Street is a fine brick and stone building, containing the offices of the clerk and other county officers. It is handsomely laid out, and contains many elegant and costly residences and two good hotels.

The city has ten banks, three newspaper offices, two or three insurance companies, and a variety of manufactures, embracing sewing-machines, paper, flour, pearl barley, portable engines, tools, machines, pumps, carriages, harnesses, tinware, etc. The Black River, with its falls here, furnishes abundant water-power, which is largely utilized. The city has 12 or 15 churches, an academy, and a Young Men's Christian Association, which maintains a reading-room and literary entertainment. Black River is crossed in the city by 3 carriage and 2 railroad bridges. One of the carriage bridges is a beautiful wire suspension bridge, with iron girders, which, with the falls of the river, presents an interesting and picturesque view to the traveler visiting the

BRIDGE AND FALLS AT WATERTOWN, N. Y.

ROME, WATERTOWN & OGDENSBURG RAILROAD.

city. The city is supplied with water from Black River through a reservoir 200 feet above the level of the town, which also supplies a beautiful fountain in the public square. The city is underlaid by the Black River limestone, and on both sides of the river there are extensive caves which may be explored at will. Numerous fossils peculiar to this limestone formation are found here, and this whole region is very interesting to the scientist, who would enjoy exploring its cavernous rocks and selecting fossilites, and to the tourist who appreciates the wonders of nature as seen in its marvelous geological formations.

The Cape Vincent Division of the R., W. & O. R. R. runs from Watertown Junction westward through the hamlets of Brownville (500

R., W. AND O. R. R. STATION, HOTEL AND DOCK. CAPE VINCENT.

population), Limerick, Chaumont, Three-mile Bay (500 population), Rosiere, carrying the tourist in 45 minutes to—

CAPE VINCENT, Jefferson County, New York, 20 miles from Watertown. Population, 1,500. Hotels—St. Lawrence, Rathbun, and Cape Vincent. Here the magnificent chain of great fresh-water lakes, Superior, Michigan, Huron, Erie, and Ontario, which stretch

ROME, WATERTOWN & OGDENSBURG RAILROAD.

city
voir
ful
Rive
whic
ston
to tl
ing
as s

T
Wat

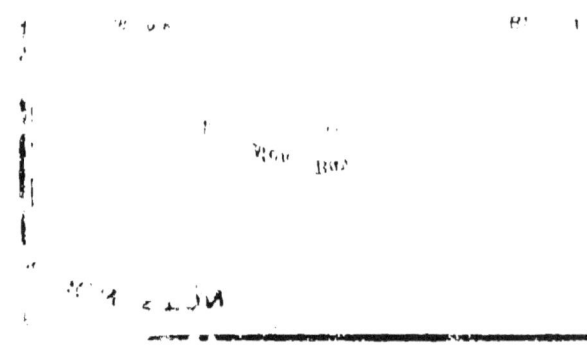

I
pop
Ros
C
Wa
and
lake

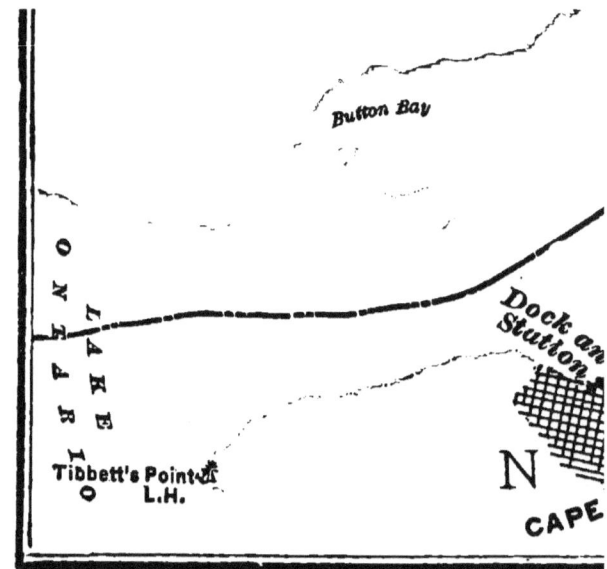

ROME, WATERTOWN & OGDENSBURG RAILROAD

along the Western continent for 1,500 miles, forming the most marvelous chain of inland waters in the world, discharge their emerald waters from Ontario into the grand and beautiful St. Lawrence, and are carried through its channels a thousand miles eastward to the boundless Atlantic. Here numerous steamboats and vessels receive or discharge their valuable freights of lumber and other products gathered from the shores of Lake Ontario and St. Lawrence. Here thousands of tourists embark for the delightful tour of the Lake and the St. Lawrence River with its manifold islands and beauties.

Cape Vincent village is a pretty town of considerable commercial importance, and has several churches and stores. It is an important shipping point, due to its favorable situation at the junction of Lake Ontario and the St. Lawrence. It has attractions as a summer residence, and many prominent people spend their summers here to enjoy the cool, refreshing breezes that sweep the great inland sea for two hundred miles. The steamer Maud is also on hand to convey passengers to Wolfe Island or to the picturesque city of Kingston, Canada, a voyage of about nine miles. Travelers going to Alexandria Bay and the Thousand Island Park are conveyed from the wharf alongside the depot, on the steamer J. F. Maynard. This boat connects with R., W. & O. R. R. trains, making two round trips daily between Cape Vincent and Alexandria Bay, touching at all points, and in a delightful sail of two hours on the majestic St. Lawrence are brought to these famous resorts. In its course down the river the J. F. Maynard passes many of the most beautiful private islands of the river, and it may be safely asserted that no other steamboat tour of its length in the land embodies such a constant and varied succession of lovely vistas as are here presented. Connections are made at Alexandria Bay with the Richelieu & Ontario Navigation Co.'s steamers, for resorts further down the river, through Lachine Rapids, to Montreal and Quebec.

Undoubtedly the best bass and muscalonge fishing in the world will be found in the vicinity of Wolfe Island, just off Cape Vincent, the largest of the Thousand Islands, being thirty miles long and from seven to ten wide. The steamer Maud will land passengers at Marysville, a small village on the island opposite Kingston. At the west end of Simcoe Island, directly off the lighthouse, is deep water, which affords excellent bass fishing during July and August. At the head of Wolfe Island lies Horseshoe Island. Between the two are many

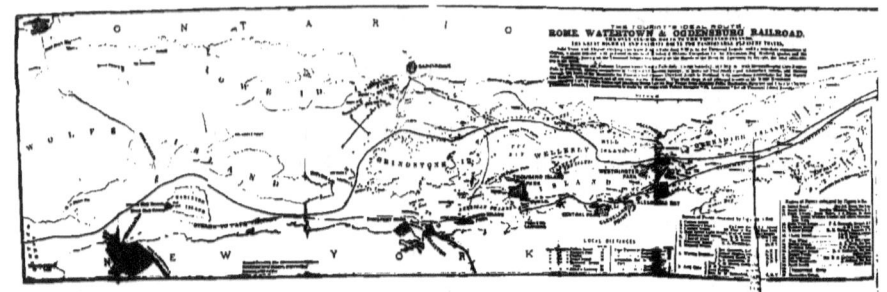

ST. LAWRENCE RIVER.

ROME, WATERTOWN & OGDENSBURG RAILROAD.

rocky shoals where early fly-fishing for bass cannot be equalled on the St. Lawrence. The many bays along the island east of Marysville afford abundant opportunity for sport in trolling for pickerel, pike, muscalonge, and other "gamey" fish.

CARTHAGE, WATERTOWN & SACKETT'S HARBOR LINE.

A line of the Rome, Watertown & Ogdensburg Railroad, nearly 30 miles in length, runs from Sackett's Harbor to Carthage, through Watertown Junction, thence forming, in its eastward course, one side of an equilateral triangle made complete by a section of the Niagara Falls line and a section of Utica line, converging at Philadelphia.

SACKETT'S HARBOR.—Houndsfield, Jefferson County, New York, 103½ miles from Utica, is a town full of historic interest, situated upon the eastern end of Lake Ontario, and the terminus of this branch of the railroad. Population, 800. It was named from Augustus Sackett, the first settler of the village, and was incorporated in 1814, and was made a "collection district" in 1805, and in the war of 1812 with Great Britain was the seat of vast military operations. In July, 1812, a formidable British fleet of five frigates made an attack on the fortifications at Sackett's Harbor. The bombardment was extended over a considerable period, ending in the repulse of the attacking force. It is said that one shot from the garrison killed and wounded at least thirty men on the Royal George. Two months later, a fleet of ten vessels, fairly well equipped for active service, left the Harbor, but were eventually compelled to return under fire of a British naval force.

Then began active shipbuilding operations, the Americans working hard at Sackett's Harbor, the British at Kingston. In May, 1813, Sir James Yeo, the British commander, made an attack on the position, bringing one thousand men, six ships of war, and nearly one hundred guns. This time the garrison became panic-stricken, and half a million dollars' worth of property and a man-of-war were destroyed by fire during the flight of the militia. They slowly rallied, however, encouraged by the regular forces, and compelled a withdrawal of the British invaders.

During the year following four forts were completed, with command of eighty-four guns. Six thousand New York militia were located in fortified quarters.

ROME, WATERTOWN & OGDENSBURG RAILROAD.

In the fall of 1814 the American commander sailed from the harbor to Kingston with eight fighting vessels, and blockaded the British ports. Several weeks later the British commander launched another ship, carrying 112 guns and a crew of 1,000 men. The appearance of this re-enforcement caused a retreat of the blockaders, the British in turn proclaiming a blockade at Sackett's Harbor. While acting on the defensive, the men in harbor were kept busy building two more ships; but before these were ready peace was proclaimed and work abandoned.

Col. Brady was stationed here and had command of Madison Barracks, built in 1816 to 1819. He collected and buried in one grave the remains of several brave men who fell in the war of 1812 to 1815. At Sackett's Harbor the railroad connects with a steamer to and from Henderson Harbor.

The first station after leaving Sackett's Harbor for the eastern terminus of the line is **ALVERSON'S**, three miles distant. From there we have a run of half an hour to Watertown, described on page 128.

BLACK RIVER, Rutland, Jefferson County, New York, 85¼ miles from Utica, on Black River, from which it is named, and containing about 200 inhabitants. The village is partly in the town of Rutland and partly in Le Ray. In the town of Rutland is a remarkable valley, known as the Rutland Hollow, which extends through the town upon the lower terrace of the plateau, parallel to Black River. It appears like the bed of an ancient river, deeply excavated in the limestone, and was probably formed by abrasion.

FELT'S MILLS is a village of about 300 inhabitants, on Black River. There is considerable trade done here in lumber. A tannery has also been working for some years.

GREAT BEND is the last station before reaching—

CARTHAGE, Wilna, Jefferson County, New York, 74 miles from Utica. Carthage is finely situated on Black River, at the lower terminus of the Black River Canal Improvement. It contains several churches, banks, a newspaper office and various manufactories, and a population of 2,500. It was formerly called Long Falls, but was incorporated as Carthage in 1841. A bridge across Black River was erected here in 1813. It is now a State bridge, and has been rebuilt with iron.

The Morristown Division runs from Carthage to Morristown on the St. Lawrence, thence along the south shore of the river to Ogdensburg.

ROME, WATERTOWN & OGDENSBURG RAILROAD.

CARTHAGE TO HARRISVILLE.

The Oswegatchie fishing grounds are reached by way of Harrisville. A line has been built in a northeasterly direction, forming part of the Rome, Watertown & Ogdensburg railway system, from Carthage, having stations at Clearwater, Natural Bridge, Diana, and Harrisville, and terminus at Fuie.

Joseph Bonaparte, brother of the First Napoleon, built a house and residence near the Natural Bridge in 1829. For the accommodation of his guests he caused a small house to be erected on Lake Bonaparte, near Diana, on the way to Harrisville.

From Watertown to De Kalb Junction on the Niagara Falls Line of the R. W. & O. R. R. the intermediate stations are Sandford's Corners and—

EVAN'S MILLS, Jefferson County, New York, a pleasant village of 500 inhabitants. Three miles from here is the Le Ray mansion, built in 1809, where President Madison was once hospitably entertained.

PHILADELPHIA, Jefferson County, New York, 59 miles from Ogdensburg. A village of 500 inhabitants, on Indian River, where the main line of the Rome, Watertown & Ogdensburg R. R. crosses its Eastern Division, and where passengers for Lowville and places in Lewis County, Trenton Falls, Clayton, Morristown, and Sackett's Harbor change cars. Iron ore is found in considerable quantities in the upper part of the town. The Shurtliffe mines are the principal ones. From Philadelphia the road runs north through Antwerp, a village of about 1,000 people, and Keene's, to

GOUVERNEUR, St. Lawrence County, New York, 36 miles from Ogdensburg. Hotels—Van Buren House, Fuller House. This is a flourishing village of 3,000 inhabitants on the Oswegatchie River. It has many fine residences and extensive manufacturing interests, a bank, several churches, an academy, formerly the Gouverneur Wesleyan Seminary, two or three newspaper offices, and carries on a large local trade. It has a beautiful rural cemetery on the south bank of the Oswegatchie River, opposite the village, and has also a fine fair ground. In the township are extensive and valuable iron mines and other minerals. At Natural Dam, a mile below the village, is an immense lumber mill. A stage line runs from Gouverneur to the western part of the Adirondack Mountain region, about fifteen or twenty miles distant.

From Gouverneur the railroad runs through Richville to—

DE KALB JUNCTION, St. Lawrence County, New York, 19 miles from Ogdensburg, where it unites with the Potsdam Branch running from Norwood on the Ogdensburg & Lake Champlain R. R. De Kalb Junction is a small village on the Oswegatchie River, deriving its chief importance from its railway connections. The Ogdensburg branch of R., W. & O. R. R. diverges from the main line here to Ogdensburg.

Towns on the R., W. & O. R. R. north of De Kalb Junction are here described.

CANTON, St. Lawrence County, New York, 17 miles from Norwood. Hotel—Hodskin House. Canton is a very pretty town of about 2,500 population. It is the county seat of St. Lawrence County, and contains the county court house, the St. Lawrence Academy, a fine union graded school, a bank, a newspaper office, and numerous stores and manufactories. It is on Grass River, which furnishes water-power to the various manufactories of leather, iron castings, machinery, flour, lumber, etc., which are located here. A stage line runs from Canton to the Adirondack woods. A small steam yacht runs in summer from the village to a picnic grove five miles distant.

POTSDAM, St. Lawrence County, New York, 7 miles from Norwood. Hotels—Albion House, Matheson House. This beautiful and prosperous town of about 4,000 inhabitants is situated on Raquette River, in the midst of a rich farming district. The river here is broken by islands and rapids, and furnishes abundant water-power, which is utilized by numerous manufactories of lumber and articles produced from wood. The village contains a national bank, a newspaper office, numerous stores, and handsome residences. The Potsdam State Normal and Training School, one of the most prosperous of the several State normal schools, is located here. From Potsdam a stage runs 21 miles to the Forest House at the foot of the Adirondacks, where guides and boats can be procured for a trip through the fishing and hunting grounds of the famous North Woods.

NORWOOD, St. Lawrence County, New York, 383 miles from Boston, 287 miles from Niagara Falls. Hotel—Whitney Hotel. This village of 2,000 inhabitants is at the junction of the Rome, Watertown

& Ogdensburg Railroad with the Ogdensburg & Lake Champlain Railway. Travelers going to Malone, Adirondacks, Lake Champlain, Montreal, Vermont, White Mountains, Boston, and points in New England take the Ogdensburg & Champlain Railroad at this point. The R., W. & O. R. R. now runs from Norwood to Massena Springs on the Raquette River.

MASSENA SPRINGS, St. Lawrence Co., N. Y. Hotel—Hatfield. This village takes its name and derives its chief importance from the celebrated springs located in it. It is on the Raquette River and on the Rome, Watertown & Ogdensburg Railroad, about six miles from Norwood and six miles from Brasher Falls on the Ogdensburg & Lake Champlain Railroad. From Ogdensburg a line of steamboats runs during the season to the village in connection with the steamers from Lake Ontario, St. Lawrence River, Niagara Falls, the Thousand Islands, and Alexandria Bay. By taking these boats at Ogdensburg, the traveler can have a splendid sail on the St. Lawrence, passing through the Gallup and the Du Platte Rapids. The springs are about five miles from the celebrated Long Sault Rapids. The climate is very healthful.

We append the analysis of the Massena waters by Prof. Ferd. F Mayer, of the New York College of Pharmacy:

At the temperature of 60° F. the specific gravity is 1.0817, that of water 1.000. The following exhibit shows the solid and gaseous ingredients:

	A in one Litre. (**A.**)	B—in one Gallon. (**B.**)
Chloride of Sodium	1.36795 Grammes,	79.792 Grains
Chloride of Potassium	0.00871 "	0.508 "
Chloride of Magnesium	0.51308 "	29.927 "
Bromide of Magnesium	0.01155 "	0.673 "
Bicarbonate of Lime	0.08319 "	4.852 "
Bicarbonate of Iron	0.00838 "	0.488 "
Sulphate of Lime	1.04116 "	60.931 "
Sulphate of Soda	0.06003 "	3.500 "
Phosphate of Soda	0.02203 "	1.320 "
Hyposulphate of Soda	0.07210 "	4.205 "
Sulphate of Sodium	0.02410 "	1.405 "
Silicate of Soda and organic compounds	0.19160 "	11.176 "

3.40448 Grammes 198.678 Grains.
Sulphuretted (a free.............0.0155 Grammes } 22.373 c. c.
Hydrogen) b half comb....0.0175
Per Gallon, 5.307 Cubic Inches.

Professor Mayer, in the course of his analysis, ascertained the fact that the waters of the Massena Springs are almost identical with those

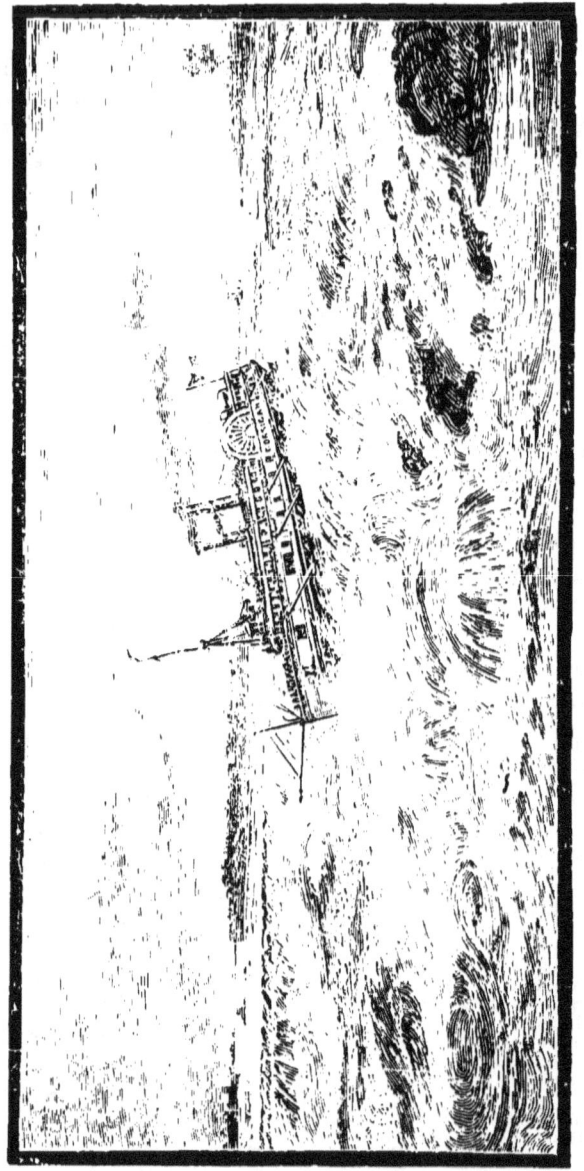

RUNNING THE LACHINE RAPIDS, ST. LAWRENCE RIVER.

of the celebrated Spa at Baden in Austria, and also that at Eilsen, in Germany. The water issues in a copious stream from the fountain near the edge of the river bank. It is perfectly clear, cold, and sparkling; it emits an odor of sulphuretted hydrogen gas which is a little unpleasant at first, but, after drinking it for a few days, persons prefer it to ordinary drinking-water.

THE NORTHERN ADIRONDACK RAILROAD.

This enterprising line now offers to the public a speedy and elegant means of reaching much of the best hunting and fishing territory in the Adirondacks. It extends from Moira on the Ogdensburg & Lake Champlain Division of the Central Vermont Railroad southward into the Adirondack wilderness.

The greater part of the splendid forest lands through which this road extends belongs to the company, and are now set apart as a perpetual preserve for game and fish, open to the patrons of the line.

The Northern Adirondack Railroad is to be extended southward to Raquette Pond. This is the tourist route to Paul Smith's.

"**PAUL SMITH'S**," the principal gateway and distributing-point to all resorts in the Adirondack Mountains, is now reached from New York city quickly and directly by the New York Central & Hudson River R. R., Rome, Watertown & Ogdensburg R. R., via Norwood, Moira, and the Northern Adirondack R. R., the fast line and most comfortable route to the Adirondacks. Commencing Sunday, June 30th, Wagner palace sleeping-cars leave Grand Central Station, New York, 6 P. M. daily, except Saturday; leave Albany, 10.30 P. M.; leave Utica, 12.45 A. M.; arrive Norwood, 6 A. M.; Moira, 7.12 A. M.; Paul Smith's Station, 8.32 A. M., where lunch is served; arrive Paul Smith's Hotel, 9.30 A. M.—in time for a sumptuous breakfast. The time by this new fast line from New York to Paul Smith's Station is only fourteen hours; to Paul Smith's Hotel, fifteen hours. This is the only through-car route and the only standard-gauge route.

Returning, stage leaves Paul Smith's Hotel daily, except Sunday, at 2.10 P. M. Sleeping-cars leave Paul Smith's Station, 3.30 P. M.; leave Norwood, 6.10 P. M.; arrive Utica, 10.55 P. M.; Albany, 1.55 A. M.; Grand Central Station, New York, 6.45 A. M.

From Niagara Falls, Suspension Bridge, Rochester, and other points

ROME, WATERTOWN & OGDENSBURG RAILROAD.

on Rome, Watertown & Ogdensburg R. R., take White Mountains Express, which leaves Niagara Falls, 8.10 P. M.; Suspension Bridge, 8.30 P. M., and carries through sleeping-cars to and from Moira via Norwood. Excursion tickets at reduced rates are on sale at all ticket offices in New York, Buffalo, Niagara Falls, Rochester, Syracuse, and at principal ticket offices of Rome, Watertown & Ogdensburg R. R., and its connecting lines. Be sure your tickets read via Rome, Watertown & Ogdensburg R. R. to Norwood, thence via Moira and Northern Adirondack R. R.

Paul Smith's Hotel is pleasantly situated on the Lower St. Regis Lake, in the heart of the Adirondack Mountains, 2,000 feet above tidewater, amidst a dense growth of pine and balsam forest, and in the immediate vicinity of the best fishing and hunting grounds to be found in the Adirondacks. The house, which is one of the largest hotels north of Saratoga, is situated 100 feet from and 30 feet above the lake, and has accommodations, with its cottages, for 350 guests. Rooms are large and well ventilated, single and *en suite*, two to ten communicating. The hotel is elegantly furnished throughout, and supplied with all modern improvements. The dining-hall and service will be kept up to the usual high standard of excellence, and the table supplied with the delicacies of the season. The richest milk and cream from the proprietor's herd of select Alderneys is one of the principal features of fare; also fresh vegetables from the hotel garden.

Lower St. Regis Lake is one of the many beautiful bodies of water that are found in the Adirondacks, and is about one mile in width by one and a half in length. Its shores are high or gently sloping, and well wooded. High hills seclude and protect it from strong winds, making it unusually safe and pleasant for boating and fishing. It is connected by navigable streams with several other pretty lakes, giving it unsurpassed advantages for delightful excursions, etc.

Good fishing is to be had in Lower St. Regis and the brooks emptying into it. Also, in the many lakes and ponds in its vicinity. Waters are stocked yearly with brook and lake trout from the Adirondack State Hatchery.

Of the climate and its wonderful benefits to those afflicted with pulmonary and lung diseases, enough has already been written to make mention of it unnecessary.

An extensive addition has been built this spring, containing forty

SPARTAN PASS — RAINBOW FALLS.
CHATEAUGAY, N. Y.

ROME, WATERTOWN & OGDENSBURG RAILROAD.

elegant sleeping-rooms large parlor, ladies' billiard-room, and a dance-hall. Also, general improvements on the premises and grounds, offering increased advantages for the amusement and comfort of guests.

A first-class livery is connected with the house, where carriages and horses can be had at all hours, also saddle-horses. Many beautiful drives over good roads can be taken from here.

Telegraph and post-offices (daily mail) in the house, also telephone connection with all principal resorts in the Adirondacks. Amusements, boating, shooting, fishing, hunting, driving, billiards, bowling, lawn tennis, etc. Brook-trout fishing is best in May and June; fly-fishing in July, August, and to September 15th. Deer can be killed from August 15th to November 1st. Hounding deer is permitted between September 1st and October 5th.

A general store in the hotel contains all necessaries for supplying camping parties, excepting tents and blankets, at reasonable prices, including fishing-tackle, ammunition, etc.

The through sleeping-car service via the fast line, New York Central & Hudson River R. R., Rome, Watertown & Ogdensburg R. R. via Norwood, Moira & Northern Adirondack R. R., between New York and Paul Smith's Station, where stages connect for Paul Smith's Hotel, seven miles distant, makes this resort so accessible to people of New York and the South, that it is destined to be more popular than ever.

ROME, WATERTOWN & OGDENSBURG RAILROAD.
EASTERN DIVISION.

The Eastern Division of the Rome, Watertown & Ogdensburg Railroad runs from Utica through the valley of the Black River in a northwesterly direction to Sackett's Harbor on Lake Ontario, and Clayton, Alexandria Bay, Morristown, and Ogdensburg on the St. Lawrence River. It passes through a rich farming region, which is diversified with romantic and picturesque scenery, and forms the most direct route from New York, Philadelphia, and points south and east of Utica to the wonderful Trenton Falls, Thousand Islands, Ogdensburg, and points on the St. Lawrence River. It runs through Trenton, Boonville, Remsen, Alder Creek and Lowville—favorite points of departure for the Fulton chain of lakes, John Brown's Tract, and Adirondack region—and is the shortest and quickest route from Utica to Clayton,

HIGH FALLS, TRENTON FALLS, N. Y.

ROME, WATERTOWN & OGDENSBURG RAILROAD.

Alexandria Bay, and Brockville and Prescott, Canada—favorite points for connecting with the steamers of the Royal Mail Line that navigate Lake Ontario and the St. Lawrence River from Toronto to Montreal and Quebec—and the quickest route to the famous Thousand Islands. Wagner palace and sleeping cars are run through from New York to Clayton without change.

After leaving Utica the first station on this route is—

MARCY, Marcy, Oneida County, New York, 5½ miles from Utica. This is a small post village in the town of Marcy, named from Gov. William L. Marcy when the township was formed from Deerfield in 1832. The township is a rolling, fertile intervale, rising into a table-land about 300 to 500 feet above the valley.

STITTVILLE, Trenton, Oneida County, New York, 10 miles from Utica. A post-village on the line of Trenton township, containing a church, cotton factory, and about 300 inhabitants.

HOLLAND PATENT, Trenton, Oneida County, New York, 12 miles from Utica. This is a post village of about 500 inhabitants in the west part of the township of Trenton, and named in honor of Henry, Lord Holland, a former owner of 20,000 acres of land, principally in the township of Trenton. The Holland Land Company purchased in 1801, in this vicinity, and in the western part of New York State, some 77,000 acres of land. Gerritt Boon, the agent of this company, was one of the early settlers of the town, and from him the town of Boonville was named.

TRENTON, Trenton, Oneida County, N. Y., 16 miles from Utica. This beautiful village is at the junction of Cincinnati and Steuben creeks. It contains four or five churches and about 500 inhabitants. It was originally incorporated under the name of "Oldenbarneveldt," but in 1864 was organized at Trenton. This village is only 1¾ miles from the famous Trenton Falls.

TRENTON FALLS, Trenton, Oneida County, N. Y., 18 miles from Utica. Trenton Falls Village contains about 400 inhabitants, and derives its chief importance from being near the celebrated falls from which it derives its name.

Trenton Falls consist of a series of six waterfalls on the West Canada Creek, which plunges through a deep gorge cut through the

PART OF "HIGH FALLS," TRENTON FALLS, N. Y.

Trenton limestone from 70 to 300 feet in depth, forming a ravine of peculiar wildness and indescribable beauty. The volume of water pouring over the falls is not large, but plunging over precipitous heights, and rushing down long rapids in fleecy, foaming madness through the deep chasm, presents a scene that has for years charmed the admirer of the wild and weird, combined with the grand and sub lime in nature. The Indian name of the stream is Kany-a-hoo-rs, signifying "leaping or slanting water," which with Ka-na-ta, "dark brown water," has passed with its originators into the forgotten past; but this "child of a thousand rapid running rills" flows on forever, charming the tourist from all parts of the world, amid its forest bowers and rocky grottos. The Indian name of the village was One-ti-a-dah-que, signifying "in the bone." It is not our purpose to give an extended detailed sketch of this remarkable place, but would refer the reader for such to a handbook on Trenton Falls, published by Mr. M. Moore, proprietor of Moore's Hotel, Trenton Falls, the son-in-law of the Rev. John Sherman, the white pioneer of the place, and proprietor of the first public hotel for visitors, erected here in 1822. Since this beautiful resort was first brought to public notice, great improvements have been effected to make the tour of the falls more easily accomplished. Tons of overhanging and projecting rocks have been removed, staircases constructed, and paths opened, and hotel accommodations provided. Moore's Hotel is the largest and best, and is near the proper entrance to the scenery of the falls. A few steps from its piazzas bring the tourist to the path leading to the falls, and introduce him to the panorama of delightful views that develop as he makes the tour. The Moore Hotel is open from June to September, but convenient accommodations may be obtained near by for those who desire to visit the falls at other seasons of the year.

PROSPECT, Trenton, Oneida County, N. Y., 18¼ miles from Utica. Hotel—Perkins House. On West Canada Creek, above Trenton Falls, is a post village of about 400 inhabitants, several churches, and an extensive saw-mill and tannery. Above Prospect are some of the most beautiful portions of these famous falls, and it will be found a convenient place from which to make the complete tour of this charming vicinity. There are many beautiful views near here. The Perkins House, the best hotel, is a neat brick building, well fitted up, and kept in very good style. There is a livery connected with the house.

SHERMAN FALLS. TRENTON FALLS, N. Y.

REMSEN, Remsen, Oneida County, N. Y., 21 miles from Utica. A village of about 700 inhabitants, first settled in 1794. In 1808 several Welsh immigrants settled in this place, who were soon followed by more natives of Wales, and the town of Remsen contains more Welshmen and descendants born in America than any other town in N. Y. State. The Welsh number more than one half of the inhabitants of the town, and of 12 churches 10 hold services in the Welsh language.

EAST STEUBEN, Steuben, Oneida Co., N. Y., 25 miles from Utica. A flag station in east part of town of Steuben. The township of Steuben is sparsely settled, and was named in honor of Baron Steuben, to whom the State of New York, in 1786, gave 16,000 acres of land known as Steuben's Patent.

ALDER CREEK, Boonville, Oneida County, New York, $28\frac{1}{2}$ miles from Utica. A station for the village of Alder Creek, one mile east. This village is quite a favorite point of departure for tourists to the Adirondack region.

BOONVILLE, Boonville, Oneida County, New York, $34\frac{3}{4}$ miles from Utica. Hotel—Hurlbert House. This town was named from Gerritt Boon, agent of the Holland Land Co. It is an important village of 1,600 inhabitants, in the northwest part of the township of same name, and contains several churches, banks, a printing-office, and several manufactories. It is on the summit level of the Black River Canal, and contains most of the navigable feeder which supplies this summit. This village is one of the great starting-points of visitors to the Adirondack region, and large numbers of tourists fit out every summer from Boonville for the tour through the North Woods. The Hurlbert House is the favorite hotel, and parties can arrange in advance for accommodations and guides, by addressing the proprietor, who will furnish particulars to tourists and visitors on application.

LEYDEN, Leyden, Lewis County, New York, $38\frac{1}{4}$ miles from Utica. A flag station in town of same name.

PORT LEYDEN, Leyden, Lewis County, New York, $41\frac{1}{2}$ miles from Utica. Port Leyden is the chief village of the town, having about 1,000 inhabitants. The village lies partly in the town of Greig. Iron ore is found near the village, but attempts to manufacture it into pigs have thus far been unsuccessful on account of the sulphur in the ore.

ROME, WATERTOWN & OGDENSBURG RAILROAD.

LYONS FALLS, West Turin, Lewis County, New York, 44½ miles from Utica. Lyons Falls is a small village near which are the High Falls of the Black River, which plunge over a gneiss rock 63 feet in height, and form a wild, picturesque scene, much visited by lovers of the romantic and weird phases of nature. The township of West Turin rises from the intervale along the Black River, by successive terraces, to the hills on the west about 1,000 feet above the valley of the river. Dairying is the principal occupation of the farmers, and there are several cheese factories in the township.

GLENDALE, Martinsburgh, Lewis County, New York, 51 miles from Utica. A small village on the railroad, containing two hotels and a few houses. Another small village of the same name is about three fourths of a mile distant.

MARTINSBURGH, Martinsburgh, Lewis County, New York, 54¼ miles from Utica. Quite an important village of 500 inhabitants, with an academy, several churches, a printing-office, with several stores and mills. Named from General Walter Martin. The town is largely engaged in dairying. Whetstone Gulf, near the south border of the town, is a deep ravine, 3 miles long, which has scenery of great beauty. Chimney Point, 2 miles west of Martinsburgh, is another ravine, worn by Roaring Brook into the Utica slate underlying the town, from 200 to 250 feet deep. The Chimney is a pyramidal mass of slate, left by the wearing action of the two streams that here unite, one falling in a beautiful cascade. Above this point the stream is bordered by precipitous walls, and the ravine is finally obstructed by a cascade preventing further ascent. These localities are well worthy of a visit by the tourist who loves to see the marvelous works of nature.

LOWVILLE, Lowville, Lewis County, New York, 58¼ miles from Utica. Hotel—Kellogg House. This is one of the prettiest villages in northern New York, and has a population of about 2,500. It abounds in well-shaded streets, handsome residences, fine drives, and excellent hotels. It is the county seat of Lewis County, and is the seat of Lowville Academy, an institution of high educational standing, which has been long established, and maintains a separate male and female department. Lowville is the principal village of Lewis County, and contains 2 banks, 2 newspaper offices, several churches, two or three large hotels, and a number of manufactories of various kinds, embracing scythe, snath, sash and blind factories, a foundry and other varieties. The leading hotel is the Kellogg House, which is one of the largest in northern New York. It is built of brick and is furnished in good style, and its table is excellent. An omnibus runs to and from the railroad station to meet trains, and a first-class livery is connected with the house. The Kellogg House is a proper headquarters for parties visiting the celebrated North Woods, or Adirondack Region. Guides and all the appurtenances required can be obtained in Lowville.

About Lowville are many beautiful drives. The wonderful curiosities of Whetstone Gulf and Chimney Point, alluded to in descriptions of Martinsburgh, are only a few miles from this village.

Hough's History describes the former as follows: "The chasm, extending about three miles, is bordered by precipitous banks 200 to 300 feet in height. The stream is quite irregular in its course, presenting sharp angles and sudden turns, which afford at every step new points of interest, and a constant succession of magnificent views. The walls approach nearer as we ascend the stream, until they may be reached by the outstretched arms, and the torrent is compressed into a deep, narrow chasm, which forbids further progress without difficulty and danger."

Chimney Point has acquired the name from a vast triangular pyramid of slate rock formed by the junction of two gulfs. To the left of this, as seen from the banks above, a stream of moderate size falls in a beautiful cascade about 60 feet high, breaking into a sheet of foam upon the rough bed down which it glides. The finest views are presented from the banks, but such as prefer to descend will find themselves amply rewarded by the pleasing variety of scenery which the locality presents.

CASTOR LAND, Denmark, Lewis County, New York, $68\frac{1}{2}$ miles from Utica, is a village in the east corner of the township of Denmark, opposite the Black River bridge, below the junction of Beaver and Black rivers.

DEER RIVER, Denmark, Lewis County, New York, 70 miles from Utica. A village of about 40 houses, on the river of same name. Copenhagen, a village of about 700 inhabitants, lies about 3 miles west of the station. Dairying is the chief business of the town.

This brings us to **CARTHAGE**, described on page 132.

ROME, WATERTOWN & OGDENSBURG RAILROAD

STERLINGVILLE, Philadelphia, Jefferson County, New York, 83¼ miles from Utica.

PHILADELPHIA, Philadelphia, Jefferson County, New York, 86½ miles from Utica. This village of about 500 inhabitants is at the junction of the Eastern Division with the main line of the Rome, Watertown & Ogdensburg R. R., running to De Kalb Junction, Ogdensburg, and Norwood, on the Ogdensburg & Lake Champlain Division of the Central Vermont R. R. Passengers for Gouverneur, Canton, Potsdam, Norwood, and Massena Springs should change to main line here, although parties going to Massena Springs may continue on to Ogdensburg and take the steamer there for Massena. Passing Shurtliffs, a flag station, we reach—

THERESA JUNCTION, Theresa, Jefferson County, New York, 92¼ miles from Utica, the junction of the Clayton Branch with the Morristown Division, which runs to Morristown and Ogdensburg.

From Theresa Junction to Clayton is 16 miles. The Clayton Branch runs west through Stroughs, Orleans Corners, a small village, to—

LAFARGEVILLE, Orleans, Jefferson County, New York, 101 miles from Utica, containing an academy and several houses.

CLAYTON, Clayton, Jefferson County, New York, 108 miles from Utica. Hotels—Hubbard House, Walton House, and New Windsor Hotel. This village, with a population of 1,700, is on the southeast bank of the St. Lawrence River, at the mouth of French's Creek, by which name it was formerly called. Clayton contains four churches, an academy, a number of stores, and is an important river and shipping town. The R., W. & O. R. R. connects here, without transfer, for Alexandria Bay and other points. The St. Lawrence Steamboat Express carries a solid train, making direct and immediate connections with the principal resorts and summer homes in the entire Thousand Island region. The Royal Mail Line of steamers for Montreal and Niagara Falls touch at this point also. Clayton is the base of supplies for the cottage people all along the river. It is quite accessible to most of the popular resorts in the Thousand Island region.

THOUSAND ISLANDS, ST. LAWRENCE RIVER.

Thousand Islands, River St. Lawrence.

THE NEW WINDSOR,
CLAYTON, N. Y.

THIS Hotel has been newly re-built and furnished throughout; is located centrally, with magnificent river frontage, within fifty feet of the St. Lawrence, affording beautiful views of the River and Islands from its verandas. Is guarded against fire, and is supplied with hot and cold water. Tourists and pleasure seekers will find this a first-class Hotel. Delightful scenery, pure air, good boats, fishing-tackle, and experienced oarsmen always in attendance.

FISH PACKED AND SHIPPED FOR PARTIES WHEN DESIRED.

W. P. HAWES, Manager.

Thousand Islands, River St. Lawrence.

ISAAK WALTON HOUSE.

THE LARGEST AND FINEST HOUSE AT CLAYTON, N. Y.

Has fine view of the St. Lawrence, and is the oldest fishing resort on the river. Good boats, fishing-tackle, and experienced oarsmen always in readiness. Steam yachts provided when desired.

For terms and circulars, address

S. D. JOHNSTON, Proprietor,
CLAYTON, N. Y.

THOUSAND ISLANDS,
RIVER ST. LAWRENCE.

HUBBARD HOUSE,

CLAYTON, N. Y.

Lovers of Delightful Scenery, Pure Air, and Excellent Fishing

Will find every facility afforded them at this House.

GOOD BOATS, FISHING TACKLE, AND EXPERIENCED OARSMEN

Will always be in attendance,

AND FISH PACKED AND SHIPPED FOR PARTIES WHEN DESIRED.

The Table is supplied daily with fresh VEGETABLES and MILK from the Hubbard House Farm.

J. T. HUBBARD, - - Proprietor.

THE THOUSAND ISLANDS.

The region covered by the name "The Thousand Islands" is a portion of the St. Lawrence River extending some 30 miles from Cape Vincent, N. Y., to Alexandria Bay. The noble St. Lawrence is here studded with islands of various shapes and sizes, giving rise to the name of the "Thousand Islands," and forming one of the most beautiful and picturesque portions of American scenery. The broad St. Lawrence, expanded here to the width of a large lake, studded with these thousands of rocky, wooded islands with their myriad rocks, inlets, and promontories, and washed by the beautiful, clear, marine-colored waters of this mighty river, presents to the appreciative lover of nature one of the most charming and fascinating resorts that the world affords. It is doubtful if, among all the places of popular summer resort in this country, any one of them has within the late few years sprung into such favorite prominence as has the River St. Lawrence, along that section embracing the Thousand Islands.

In the old Indian days this beautiful extent of the river went by the name of Manatoana, or Garden of the Great Spirit; and indeed, when the islands were covered with thick forests, and the wild deer swam from isle to isle, and each little lily-padded bay, nestling in among the hills and bluffs of the islands, teemed with waterfowl that were never disturbed by the report of a gun, it seemed appropriate that the Indian, in his half-poetic mood, should dedicate this beautiful region to his Supreme Deity. It was emphatically a wilderness garden ; and to-day, although Alexandria Bay exhibits many phases of active life, the Thousand Islands are not in the least tinctured with the common appearance of ordinary watering-places. There are hundreds, thousands of places, rugged, wild, and solitary, among which a boat can glide, while its occupant lies gloriously at ease; little bays, almost landlocked, amid the resinous odors of hemlock and pine, where Nature charms with resistless fascination, and solitude holds its captive spellbound. Such scenes as these may be found in that beautiful, placid Lake of the Isle, lying amid the piney hills of Wellesley's Island, reflecting their rugged crests in its glassy surface.

Soon after leaving Cape Vincent, the steamer touches at **CARLE-**

TON ISLAND, ten miles down the river, and several miles from Alexandria Bay, where several pretty club houses and cottages, owned by residents of Rome, Utica, and Ithaca, are seen. Bluff Island, in the Canadian channel, rises abruptly 80 feet above a depth of 100 feet of water at its feet, and affords a magnificent view of the islands of both channels of the river.

The reader should note the huge stone chimneys which stand out boldly against the sky, upon the bluff at this place. They mark the site of old Fort Frontenac, built here, during the Revolutionary war, by British engineers, and which is still well preserved, as it must be for centuries to come, its trenches being cut in the solid rock. The scenery from this point to the neighborhood of Clayton, where a stop is made, is very attractive; several handsome cottages are seen upon Prospect Park, a short distance below, and immediately opposite are the notable summer homes of ex-Lieut.-Governor Alvord and Mr. Chas. G. Emery of New York. The latter is an expensive place.

"**ROUND ISLAND PARK** occupies the entire island from which it takes its name. **ROUND ISLAND** is situated in the American channel of the river St. Lawrence, one and a half miles below Clayton, and one-fourth of a mile from the south shore of the river. The island is about one mile long and 1,400 feet wide, and takes its name from its shape, which is nearly oval. It is undoubtedly the gem of the Thousand Islands, and with its elegantly appointed first-class hotel, now in its ninth season and greatly enlarged, the many beautiful cottages along the shore, splendid drives, beautiful grounds, luxuriant foliage, substantial docks, and peerless water front, there is no doubt that it will verify the confident prediction of the originators of the enterprise, and be the favorite resort among the Thousand Islands.

"The great charm of Round Island Park is its freedom from repressive conventionalities. Guests at the hotel and cottages vie in the general effort to promote the enjoyment of all. Flannels are in order at all times, and yet there is an abundant opportunity for the display of costumes at the hops, which occur almost nightly at the hotel, an excellent orchestra being maintained throughout the season."

PROSPECT PARK. Prospect Park is a projecting point of mainland, one mile above Clayton, formerly known as Bartlett's Point. Its peculiar configuration gives it advantages which are not possessed by any other park on the St. Lawrence River. "Projecting into the water, it commands an unbroken view, in either direction, of the river and its scenery. It rises as a bluff in one place to the height of 85 feet, and at another spot attains an altitude of 100 feet above the water. The view from this bluff on a clear day is enchanting in its loveliness. To the westward, Lake Ontario, 17 miles distant, and Carleton Island, may be seen in pale outline; looking down the river, Alexandria Bay and the miniature world of parks, hotels, and island homes are within the range of vision; to the north the spires of Gananoque, and farther west those of Kingston, stand in sharp relief against the cloudless sky.

"Turning from all this, a glance southward captivates the beholder with the beauty of the landscape, gentle slopes, wooded hills and fruitful fields indicating thrift and intelligent husbandry, spread out before him. The glow of sunset is the finishing touch which Nature gives to this delightful picture. The visitor at the Park will soon make this elevated spot his favorite haunt."

THOUSAND ISLAND PARK, 3 miles below Round Island, is an extensive tract at the head of Wellesley's Island, which forms the contracted American channel leading to Alexandria Bay. Several hundred summer homes are ranged along the water front and hidden amid the dense groves, which afford shade and seclusion. The Thousand Island Park Hotel, which occupies a commanding site, is one of the largest on the river. A system of educational and religious meetings, somewhat similar to that in vogue at Chautauqua, serves to attract a large number of visitors to this place, an extensive tabernacle having been built for the purpose. A picturesque lighthouse marks the American channel, which continues for 7 miles to Alexandria Bay.

WELLESLEY'S ISLAND is one of the more prominent islands, and extends from a point five miles below Clayton to a point a little below Alexandria Bay, and is nine miles long, with an average width of one and one-half miles. On the lower part, directly opposite and half a mile from the village of Alexandria Bay, is located Westminster Park, comprising 500 acres of land, and now in the hands of an association which is rapidly improving it and disposing of lots. From the summits of this island, which are reached by easy slopes either in car-

THOUSAND ISLAND PARK.

riages or on foot, the whole group of the Thousand Islands, extending along the river for a distance of twenty miles, is brought into full view.

MARY ISLAND is about 1,600 feet in length, oval-shaped, and of about the same elevation as the adjacent portion of Wellesley's Island. A narrow passage, used by the fishing-boats, separates it from the eastern extremity of Wellesley's Island. A short rustic bridge connects the two islands.

BONNIE CASTLE is a charming island, formerly the country seat of the late J. G. Holland.

Before reaching Alexandria Bay, Central Park, a popular resort on the American shore, is seen.

LOCAL DISTANCES.

FROM CAPE VINCENT.		FROM ALEXANDRIA BAY.	
To Carlton Island...............	2 miles.	To Westminster Park..........	1 mile.
" Prospect Park...............	13 "	" Rochfort...............	3 miles.
" Clayton...............	14 "	" Central Park...............	2 "
" Round Island...............	16 "	" Carlton Island...............	24 "
" Thousand Island Park......	18 "	" Prospect Park...............	13 "
" Fisher's Landing............	20 "	" Thousand Island Park......	8 "
" Alexandria Bay............	26 "	" Fisher's Landing............	6 "
" Kingston...............	10 "	" Ogdensburg...............	32 "
" Gananoque...............	15 "	" Montreal...............	140 "

ALEXANDRIA BAY, Jefferson County, New York. Hotels—Thousand Island House, Crossman's. Alexandria Bay is on the southeast shore of the St. Lawrence River, 30 miles from Cape Vincent, 12 miles from Clayton, and 32 miles from Ogdensburg. It has been regarded as the leading tourist point among the islands, having been noted as a resort for anglers for many years. Here, as at other points along the river already referred to, excellent boats, manned by professional fishermen, will enable visitors to enjoy the exciting sport of trolling for the large fish in which these waters abound. At Alexandria Bay, the large passenger steamers of the Richelieu and Ontario Navigation Company stop and take on board the tourists destined for the voyage of twelve hours down the rapids of the St. Lawrence River to Montreal and beyond. Passengers going to the White Mountains via Rouse's Point, over the O. & L. C. R. R., also take these boats as far as Ogdensburg.

The Thousand Island House commands many of the grandest views

BONNIE CASTLE, THOUSAND ISLANDS.

ROME, WATERTOWN & OGDENSBURG RAILROAD.

of the river in both directions. The hotel will accommodate about 500 guests. Those who stop here will find the rest, comfort, and attention which they seek in going from city to country, and every facility will be afforded them for seeing and enjoying the rare scenery and varied amusements of the river and islands. Families and parties can be accommodated with desirable suites of rooms at reasonable prices, with private dining-rooms if desired. Invalids can have fire in their rooms when wanted, and whatever else the hotel can provide in the way of special comforts and attention.

There are numerous country seats and cottages scattered upon the various islands of this famous region, and presenting an indescribable charm to one of the loveliest of Nature's pictures.

Of this favored locality an able writer has said : " The air is light, dry, and mellow, and is adapted to the constitution of almost every one, producing a kind of peace-with-all-the-world feeling, and endowing one with a new and wondrous activity. Fogs rarely occur here, and you can remain day and night out of doors without peril to health. Neither is the night atmosphere damp and heavy, as it is near the seashore and at many of the inland resorts; it is generally with tardy steps that one withdraws indoors at meal-time or for the night. Many a time have we, after retiring to our bed, opened the blinds and windows of our room so as to obtain one more view of Nature in her evening dress, before closing our eyes for the night. Our room commanded a prolonged view of the river. A delicate breeze would be rippling the waters, which, through the mingled light of moon and stars, looked like countless spangles of silver. The islands across the channel threw their black shadows upon the scene, from out the darkness of which peered here and there the light of some islander, who, like ourselves, was loath to go to bed. Then a strain of music would be heard coming from some happy craft, far enough away to prevent all discord, and permit only the harmony to reach our ears. And then, with such soothing strains filling our souls, with all serene without, Nature's sweet restorer, Sleep, would steal away our senses."

The Rome, Watertown & Ogdensburg R. R., after reaching Clayton, makes direct and immediate connection for Alexandria Bay and other points, without transfer, at steamboat dock. Passengers by the Rome, Watertown & Ogdensburg R. R. leave New York at Grand Central Depot on the 6 P. M. train of the New York Central & Hudson River

LINLITHGOW. THOUSAND ISLANDS.

ROME, WATERTOWN & OGDENSBURG RAILROAD.

R. R. on through Wagner sleeping-car, and arrive at Clayton at 5.45 A. M. next day, and Alexandria Bay at 6.55 A. M.

Ogdensburg is the terminus of the R., W. & O. R. R., connecting with the Lake Champlain Division of the Central Vermont R. R., for Vermont and the East.

One of the Canadian mail line of steamers leaves Toronto at 10 o'clock every morning, except Sunday, for Montreal, stopping at Kingston, Clayton, Alexandria Bay, Brockville, Prescott, and ports beyond. These boats leave Alexandria Bay at 8 A. M. and arrive at Montreal at 6 P. M.

By the same line, travelers and tourists may take a sleeping-car at night from New York Central depot, breakfast at Watertown, continue by rail to Cape Vincent, then run, without transfer, to Alexandria Bay for dinner. Trains leaving the Grand Central station, New York, in the morning, reach Thousand Islands late in the evening.

From Theresa Junction the route to Morristown and Ogdensburg is through—

THERESA VILLAGE, Theresa, Jefferson County, New York, $94\frac{3}{4}$ miles from Utica. A village of about 1,000 inhabitants, near High Falls of the Indian River, where the river falls in rapids about 85 feet within one fourth of a mile.

REDWOOD, Alexandria, Jefferson County, New York, 101 miles from Utica. Hotel—American. This village contains about 800 inhabitants, and is six miles from Alexandria Bay, to which stages run on arrival of the passenger trains on this railroad. The scenery around Redwood is picturesque, and abounds in numerous lakes, which afford excellent fishing for pike, pickerel, lake trout, and various kinds of bass. The "American" is an excellent hotel.

ROSSIE, Rossie, St. Lawrence County, New York, $108\frac{1}{4}$ miles from Utica. A small village of 200 inhabitants, at the head of navigation on the Indian River. The township is rich in minerals, such as graphite, heavy spar, calcite, zircon, phlogopite, celestine, spirelle, carbonate of iron, arsenical pyrites, etc.

HAMMOND, Hammond, St. Lawrence County, New York, $112\frac{1}{4}$ miles from Utica. This village is in the midst of a fertile agricultural region.

GLIMPSES OF NOBBY ISLAND, THOUSAND ISLANDS.

ROME, WATERTOWN & OGDENSBURG RAILROAD.

BRIER HILL, Morristown, St. Lawrence County, New York, 118 miles from Utica. Quite an important business center in the town of Morristown, a little west of the central part of the town.

MORRISTOWN, Morristown, St. Lawrence County, New York, $123\frac{1}{4}$ miles from Utica. Morristown is an important village on the east bank of the St. Lawrence River. It contains about 500 inhabitants, and is opposite Brockville, Canada, with which it is connected by steamers, and at which point connection is made with the St. Lawrence River steamers, the Canadian Pacific Railroad, and the Grand Trunk Railroad for Ottawa and various parts of Canada. Steamers also run from Morristown to Ogdensburg, Alexandria Bay, the Thousand Islands, and other points on the St. Lawrence River. Morristown Park, one mile from Morristown, is a delightful resort on the river shore, with an elegant hotel called the Terrace House. Trains stop directly in front of this hotel. The Rome, Watertown & Ogdensburg Railroad extends from Morristown along the east bank of the St. Lawrence River to Ogdensburg, where connection is made with the Ogdensburg & Lake Champlain Division of the Central Vermont R. R., and by steam ferry with Prescott, Canada, the Montreal and Quebec steamers, and the Grand Trunk Railway.

OGDENSBURG, Oswegatchie, St. Lawrence County, New York; population, 12,000; 406 miles from Boston, 285 miles from Niagara Falls. Hotels — Seymour House, Windsor House. The city of Ogdensburg is on the St. Lawrence River, at the termini of the Ogdensburg & Lake Champlain and the Rome, Watertown & Ogdensburg Railways. It is on a hillside and plateau just at the mouth of the Oswegatchie River, which drives the machinery of several factories, large dams having been built for the purpose. Ogdensburg is a United States port of entry and delivery, and has a custom-house and post-office built of Ohio sandstone, at a cost of about $250,000. Among the several churches may be mentioned the First Presbyterian, a handsome structure of stone. Along the east bank of the Oswegatchie are fine private residences, many of which are surrounded by handsome gardens and ornamental grounds. The city is supplied with water on the Holly System by a corporate company. The main street is lined with handsome stores. There are three banks, three daily newspapers, and several manufactories.

CITY OF MONTREAL.

ROME, WATERTOWN & OGDENSBURG RAILROAD.

From the wharf of the passenger station may be seen, on the opposite side of the St. Lawrence, the stone windmill where the last scene of the Mackenzie Rebellion of 1838 was enacted. There a little band of brave though mistaken "patriots" held out for nearly a week against several times their number of royal troops and militia. Ogdensburg was one of the points selected for a base of operations during the Fenian invasion of Canada in 1866.

At Ogdensburg connections are made with Ogdensburg & Lake Champlain Railroad; also with ferry for Prescott. At Prescott, with Grand Trunk Railway; also with Canadian Pacific Railway for Ottawa.

ST. LAWRENCE HALL,

MONTREAL.
HENRY HOGAN, - - - Proprietor.

For the past thirty years this HOTEL familiarly known as the "ST. LAWRENCE" has been a household word to all Travelers on the Continent of North America, and has been patronized by all the ROYAL and NOBLE Personages who have visited the City of Montreal.

This HOTEL, including the entire block which is admirably situated, being in the very heart of the city and contiguous to the General Post Office, Public Buildings and other places of Interest and of Business, has recently been acquired by Mr. Henry Hogan, the former proprietor, who has handsomely and appropriately decorated and renovated the interior, and completely refitted the whole of the apartments with new furniture, comprising 100 new rooms making the present number of apartments 250, A new and elegant Passenger Elevator has also been added, and the Halls and Public Rooms are lighted by the Electric and Incandescent Lights, making it the most attractively lighted Hotel in the Dominion.

The HOTEL is managed by Mr. Samuel Montgomery under the immediate personal supervision of Mr. Hogan, than whom no one is better qualified to conduct an hostelry of such magnitude as the ST. LAWRENCE HALL, and than whom no one has gained a better reputation as an obliging, generous and considerate host.

Hotel Coaches are in attendance on Arrival of all Trains and Steamers.
All Baggage Checks should be given to the Porters in Attendance.

Gentlemen and Ladies'

TAILOR,

259 St. James Street,

MONTREAL, CANADA.

———•••———

GENTLEMEN'S CLOTHING

TO ORDER ON SHORT NOTICE.

Ladies' Suits, Coats, Riding Habits,

ETC.,

FROM EXCLUSIVE STYLES AND PATTERNS,

TO ORDER ON SHORT NOTICE TO

Accommodate Transient Travel.

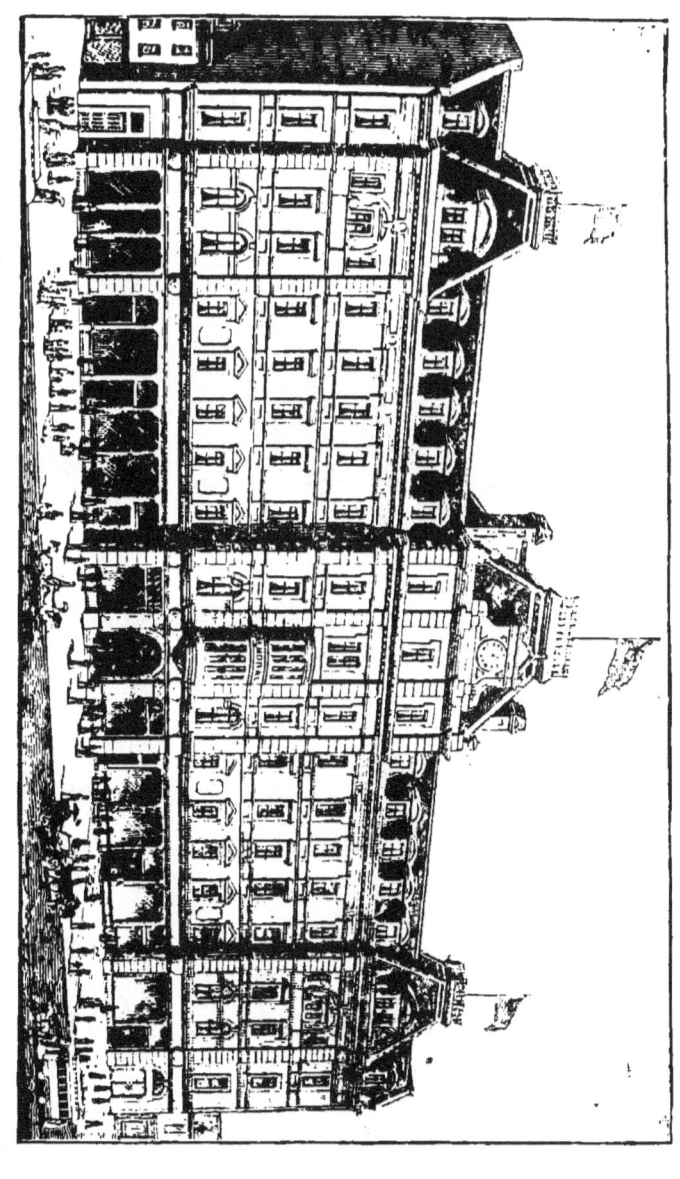

THE BALMORAL HOTEL, NOTRE DAME ST., MONTREAL, CANADA.

ERECTED IN 1885 AND 1886.

The most central and elegantly furnished hotel in Montreal. Accommodations for 400 guests. Nothing known to modern hotel builders that would add to the comfort or convenience of guests has been left undone

S. V. WOODRUFF, Manager.

THE
YOST WRITING MACHINE.

TYPE-BARS WITH ABSOLUTE AND PERMANENT ALIGNMENT.

No Ribbon.   Direct Printing.   Unlimited Speed.
Simple.   Noiseless.   Portable.

MUIR, HAWLEY & MAYO CO.,

SALES AGENTS,

343 BROADWAY, NEW YORK.

The NEW YORK TRIBUNE

has prepared an excellent volume on all the different open air exercises and amusements in vogue in America, 500 large pages, 150 illustrations. Price, $1.00 per copy.

Every one who goes into the country in the Summer would derive far more amusement from his stay among the hills, waters, and forests, from having one of these books for reference, and the benefit is great to every one who rides horseback, sails, rows, plays tennis, shoots, or swims; to say nothing of taking part in the multitude of other amusements described at length in the book. Many a gallant and successful yacht has been built from lines laid down in this work. Many a man and woman have learned to ride horseback from its teachings. And readers of all ages and conditions have testified heartily to the great benefit this book has been to them. The topics are all treated by men who know what they are talking about. There are chapters on Archery, Horsemanship, all kinds of Ball, Tennis, Fishing, Trapping, Yachting, Boating, Canoeing (with rules for building boats large and small), Swimming, Shooting, Bicycling, Photography, Winter Sports, etc., etc., etc. The distressing accidents of Summer can all be avoided by following the rules of this book. Price, $1.00 per copy.

THE TRIBUNE.

It is no trouble to change the address of the TRIBUNE to readers in the country. Terms are:

	1 year.	6 mos.	3 mos.	1 mo.
Daily, 7 days a week,	$10 00	$5 00	$2 50	$1 00
Daily, without Sunday,	8 00	4 00	2 00	90
Sunday Tribune, .	2 00	1 00	50	——

THE TRIBUNE, NEW YORK.

BUSINESS OR PLEASURE

THE GREAT SCENIC ROUTE

OF AMERICA.

A continuous Panorama of magnificent scenery from the Seaboard to the Lakes.

THE MAGNIFICENT PULLMAN SERVICE VIA THE

ERIE RAILROAD

AND ITS CONNECTIONS IS UNSURPASSED BY ANY ROUTE

TO AND FROM THE WEST.

THROUGH SERVICE TO

CLEVELAND, CHICAGO, CINCINNATI, AND ST. LOUIS.

If on a business trip, take the ERIE.
If on a pleasure trip, take the ERIE.
Under any circumstances, take the ERIE,
AND YOU WILL TRAVEL OVER A RAILROAD UNEQUALED IN FACILITIES FOR COMFORT AND SAFETY.

CHAUTAUQUA LAKE

is on the Main Line of the ERIE RAILROAD. Express Trains between New York, Boston, and Cleveland, Chicago, Cincinnati, St. Louis etc., land passengers at **Jamestown** and **Lakewood.** Pullman Buffet service. No extra charge for fast time.

L. P. FARMER, Gen. Pass. Agent.

GEO. De HAVEN, Ass't Gen. Pass. Agent.

HUDSON RIVER BY DAYLIGHT.

DAY LINE STEAMERS,

"NEW YORK" AND "ALBANY,"

Leave Brooklyn, by Annex, 8 A. M., New York, Vestry St., Pier 39, N. R. (adjoining Jersey City Ferry), 8.40 A. M., and foot 22d St., N. R., 9 A. M., landing at Yonkers, West Point, Newburgh, Poughkeepsie, Rhinebeck, Catskill, and Hudson. Returning, leave Albany, 8.30 A. M., from foot of Hamilton St., arriving in New York at 5.30 P. M.

CHOICE OF TWO ROUTES
TO THE
RESORTS OF THE CATSKILLS.

CONNECTIONS:

WEST POINT—With Stages for Cranston's and West Point Hotels, and with down boat at 2.50.
NEWBURGH—With down boat at 2.15.
POUGHKEEPSIE—With down boat 1.20.
RHINEBECK—With Ferry for Rondout, and Ulster and Delaware R. R for *Catskill Mountain Resorts*, and Wallkill Valley R. R for **Lake Mohonk**.
CATSKILL—With Catskill Mountain R. R.
HUDSON—With Boston and Albany R. R., for Chatham, Pittsfield, North Adams, Lebanon Springs, etc.
ALBANY—With through trains for Utica, Alexandria Bay, Geneva, Niagara Falls, Buffalo, Watertown, Thousand Islands and Western points. Special trains from the Steamers' Wharf to and from Saratoga. Through tickets sold to all points.

DINING SALOON ON THE MAIN DECK.

Meals served on the European Plan.

AN ELEGANT ORCHESTRA ON EACH STEAMER.

Tickets reading via New York Central and Hudson River R. R., or West Shore, between Albany and New York, are available on these Steamers.

For Beauty, Grandeur, and Healthfulness, no Region in the World compares with

LAKE GEORGE

AND THE

Adirondack Mountains

ELIZABETHTOWN,
KEENE VALLEY, LAKE PLACID,
SARANAC, CHATEAUGAY, LOON,
AND ST. REGIS LAKES.

THE ONLY DIRECT LINE TO THIS SUMMER PARADISE
IS THE

DELAWARE AND HUDSON R. R.

The "FAVORITE TOURIST ROUTE" to

Saratoga,   Round Lake,
Ausable Chasm,   Sharon Springs,
Lake Champlain,   Howes Cave,
Cooperstown,

And the celebrated GRAVITY RAILROAD between Honesdale and Carbondale.

THE SHORTEST AND MOST COMFORTABLE ROUTE BETWEEN

NEW YORK AND MONTREAL.

Rail Tickets are good for passage on the Lake Champlain Steamers. The new route to Paul Smith's and Saranac Lake via the D. & H. and the Chateaugay Railroads from Plattsburg is 67 miles shorter than via any other line. Only one hour's stage ride to the famous Lake Placid.
Enclose Six Cents in stamps for illustrated descriptive book of the line to

H. G. YOUNG,   J. W. BURDICK,
General Manager,   *General Passenger Agent,*

ALBANY, N. Y.

PEOPLE'S EVENING LINE
BETWEEN
NEW YORK AND ALBANY.

During the Season of Navigation, the Steamers

DREW or DEAN RICHMOND,

Capt. **S. J. ROE.**   Electric Lights in Every Room.   *Capt.* **THOS. POST,**

WILL LEAVE NEW YORK FOR ALBANY,

Daily, Sundays excepted, at 6 P. M., from Pier 41 (Old No.) North River, Foot of Canal Street.

Connecting with trains for SARATOGA, LAKE GEORGE, LAKE CHAMPLAIN, the ADIRONDACKS and Summer Resorts of the NORTH, EAST AND WEST.

Saratoga Office, 361 Broadway.

LEAVE ALBANY.

Every week day at 8 P. M., or on arrival of trains from NORTH, EAST and WEST, connecting at New York with ALL EARLY TRAINS for the SOUTH. Meals on the European Plan.

FOR TICKETS IN NEW YORK

Apply at Company's Office (Pier 41 North River); and at all principal Hotels and Ticket Offices in New York, and on board the Steamers. R. R. Office throughout the country.

Tickets sold and baggage checked to all points WEST via N. Y. C. & H. R. R., N. Y. & W. S., D. & H. C. Co , Fitchburg, Cent'l Vt., B. & A., and O. & L. C. Railroads, etc.

W. W. EVERETT,   J. H. ALLAIRE,   M. B. WATERS,
  President.   *Gen'l T. Agent.*   *Gen Pass Agent.*

DRINK THE GENUINE
EXCELSIOR WATER
OF SARATOGA.

CURES DYSPEPSIA, HEADACHES, CONSTIPATION, ETC.

Sold on Draught and in Bottles by First-class Druggists and Hotels.

TRADE MARK

The Genuine **EXCELSIOR WATER** is sold on Draught only through the Trade Mark. Ask your druggist for it, and be sure you get the "**EXCELSIOR**" drawn through the Trade Mark as shown in the annexed sketch. Avoid Artificial and Recharged Waters.

The "Excelsior" Water is unequalled as a cathartic and diuretic, and is used with great success in treating diseases of the Liver and Kidneys. See below letters from two of our best known medical men.

From Fordyce Barker, M. D., of New York.

I make great use of the various mineral waters in my practice, and I regard the "Excelsior" Spring Water of Saratoga as the best saline and alkaline laxative of this class. Sparkling with Carbonic Acid Gas, it is to most persons very agreeable to the taste, and prompt in action as a gentle Diuretic and Cathartic.
FORDYCE BARKER, M. D.

From Alfred L. Loomis, M. D., of New York.

During my whole professional life I have been accustomed to use freely the Water of Congress and Empire Springs. About six months since, accidentally, I was furnished with a few bottles of the "Excelsior" Spring Water, and found it so much more agreeable to the taste and pleasant in its effects than either Congress or Empire Water, that I have since used it myself, and recommend it to patients requiring a gentle Cathartic and Diuretic.   A. L. LOOMIS, M. D.

THE BOTTLED "EXCELSIOR" WATER
is unexcelled, and retains all its properties unimpaired for years.

Address **FRANK W. LAWRENCE,**
Proprietor Excelsior and Union Springs,
SARATOGA SPRINGS, N. Y.

DRS. STRONG'S SANITARIUM,
SARATOGA SPRINGS, N. Y.

POPULAR SUMMER RESORT. **Open all the year.** Receives patients or boarders, permanent or transient. Location central, quiet, shady, and within three minutes' walk of the large hotels, principal springs, Congress Park, and other sources of attraction. Fine Lawn, Tennis and Croquet Grounds. Desirable rooms, extensive piazzas, ample grounds. **Table and appointments First-Class.** Heated by steam. The bath department is complete and elegant, affording **Turkish, Russian, Roman, and Electro-thermal Baths and Massage.**

Genial, cultured society and a pleasant home are always found here. It is the resort of many eminent persons for rest and recreation. Among its patrons and references are Rev. THEO. L. CUYLER, D.D. (Brooklyn ; Rev. D. R. KERR, D.D. (Richmond); Rev. CHAS. F. DEEMS, D.D. (N. Y.); Rev. R. D. HARPER, D.D. (Philadelphia) ; Rev. C. C. "Chaplain" McCABE (Chicago); Rev. Dr. JNO. POTTS (Ottawa); Bishops Foss and BOWMAN; Hon. F. C. SESSIONS (Columbus. O.); J. M. PHILLIPS (M. E. Book Concern, N. Y.); JAS. McCREERY (N. Y.); ex-Gov. WELLS (Va.); Presidents McCosh (Princeton), WARREN (Boston Univ.); Judges REYNOLDS (Brooklyn), DRAKE (Washington), HAND (Penn.), BLISS (Mo.); Med. Profs. Ross (Chicago), KNAPP (N. Y.), FORD (Ann Arbor), and many others equally known.

During the entire year the Sanitarium is made specially attractive to its guests by frequent entertainments of varied character. There is no appearance of invalidism. The remedial and hotel interests in no way interfere, patients receiving at all times every care and attention. The proprietors are "regular" physicians, graduates of the Medical Department, University of the City of New York. The Sanitarium is one of the most complete in its appointments in the country, and is endorsed and largely patronized by the medical profession. Besides the ordinary remedial agents available in general practice, such special appliances are used as Massage, Turkish, Russian, Roman, Electro-thermal, Hydropathic Baths ; Galvanic and Faradic Electricity, Pneumatic Cabinet, Vacuum Treatment, Movement Cure, Compressed Air, Oxygen and Medicated Inhalations, Health Lift, Calisthenics, and the Mineral Waters. *SEND FOR CIRCULAR.*

SARATOGA
GEYSER WATER!

THE LEADING WATER OF SARATOGA.

FOR DYSPEPSIA it is unrivaled. It contains more Soda and Magnesia combined than any other Saratoga water.

FOR KIDNEY DISEASES it, beyond dispute, excels all other waters. It contains a *much larger quantity of Lithia* than any of the so-called Lithia waters.

AS A CATHARTIC, when taken rather warm before breakfast, it is *mild yet thorough*. It is not a harsh water.

BEWARE OF MANUFACTURED WATER.

Ask for SARATOGA Geyser.

For sale by the Glass, fresh from the Bottle, at our office, 3 and 4 Congress Park Place, Saratoga Springs, N. Y. Address

GEYSER SPRING CO.,
SARATOGA SPRINGS, N. Y.

TOURISTS' IDEAL ROUTE,
NIAGARA TO THE SEA.
ROME, WATERTOWN & OGDENSBURG R. R.

Great Highway and Favorite Route for Fashionable Pleasure Travel.
Only All-Rail Route to Thousand Islands.

1889. NEW FAST TRAINS, AVOIDING STOPS. 1889.

WAGNER PALACE SLEEPING CARS.

NEW YORK AND PAUL SMITH'S, 15 Hours.
NEW YORK AND CLAYTON, 11 Hours.
NIAGARA FALLS AND CLAYTON, 9½ Hours.
NIAGARA FALLS, PORTLAND AND BAR HARBOR, MAINE.
Via Norwood, Fabyans, Crawford Notch, and all White Mountain Resorts.

WAGNER PALACE DRAWING-ROOM CARS.

NIAGARA FALLS AND CLAYTON.
ROCHESTER AND CLAYTON.
SYRACUSE AND CLAYTON.
ALBANY AND CLAYTON.
UTICA AND CLAYTON.

Direct and immediate connections are made at Clayton with powerful steamers for Alexandria Bay and all Thousand Island Resorts, also with Rich. & Ont. Nav. Co. Steamers for Montreal, Quebec and River Saguenay, passing all of the Thousand Islands and Rapids of the River St. Lawrence by daylight. For tickets, time-tables and further information apply to nearest ticket agent or correspond with General Passenger Agent, Oswego, N. Y.

ROUTES AND RATES FOR SUMMER TOURS.

A beautiful book of 200 pages, profusely illustrated, contains maps, cost of tours, list of hotels, and describes over 400 Combination Summer Tours via Thousand Islands and Rapids of the St. Lawrence River, Saguenay River, Gulf of St. Lawrence, Lake Champlain, Lake George, White Mountains, to Portland, Kennebunk, Boston, New York and all Mountain, Lake, River and Sea Shore Resorts in Canada, New York and New England. It is the best book given away. Send ten cents postage to General Passenger Agent, Oswego, N. Y., for a copy before deciding upon your summer trip.

THEO. BUTTERFIELD,
Gen'l Passenger Agent,
OSWEGO, N. Y.

E. S. BOWEN,
Acting Gen'l Manager.

SARATOGA VICHY WATER.

Most Delicious of Saratoga Waters.

ASSISTS DIGESTION.

CORRECTS ACIDITY OF THE STOMACH.

REGULATES THE KIDNEYS.

A FINE TABLE WATER.

It mixes well with Syrup, Wines, or Milk.

For Sale by the Glass, fresh from the Bottle, at our Office,

351 Broadway, Saratoga Springs, N. Y.

ADDRESS

SARATOGA VICHY SPRING CO.

SARATOGA SPRINGS, N. Y.

Ocean Grove Hygienic Institute,

OCEAN GROVE, NEW JERSEY.

A Seaside Sanitarium, where patients may be treated or have operations performed, either by their family physician or surgeon, or supervised by him, with suitable surroundings and appliances at the seaside in summer or winter. For such purposes, rooms, nurses, and attendants will be furnished members of the regular profession, or they may with confidence send patients, suffering from any receivable condition, with prescription for a course of treatment; directions will be followed, and results reported. We are careful to avoid all appearances of a hospital, while we secure every attention to our patients. I refer by special permission to D. HAYES AGNEW, M.D., and WM. HUNT, M.D., of the University of Pennsylvania; J. M. DACOSTA, M.D., of Jefferson Medical College, J. E. GARRETSON, M.D., of Medico Chirurgical College, Philadelphia; Rev. E. H. STOKES, D.D., Rev. A. E. BALLARD, Rev. JOS. H. THORNLEY, of Ocean Grove; Rev. G. W. MILLER, D.D., and Rev. GEO. LANSING TAYLOR, D.D., Brooklyn; Rev. C. P. MASDEN, D.D., New York City.

Our Methods embrace—**1st, Rest :**—In the midst of Pine Groves, three hundred yards from the sea. **2d, Exercise :**—Calisthenics—Gymnastics—Riding—Driving—Boating—Bathing—Massage and Electricity. **3d, Diet:**—Selected when necessary; unrestricted in ordinary. **4th, Inhalation:**—Gases of all medical virtues. Atmosphere medicated and of varied densities.

APPARATUS—1st, **Three Buildings :**—Steam Heat—Gas—Artesian Water and Sewer Connections. 2d, **Baths :**—In every form and character—Douche—Sitz—Shower—Plunge—Pool—Russian—Turkish—Roman—Packs and Thermo-Electricity—Hot Sand—Hot Clay or Mud Bath—Sulphur, etc.—Medicated Water Baths—Pine Needle and Rheumatic.

CASES RECEIVABLE—1st, Light Mental Troubles. 2d, Nervous Prostration. 3d, The Opium or Alcohol Habit. 4th, Nervous Troubles—Neuralgia, Paralyses, Rheumatisms, and Hyperæsthesios. 5th, Catarrhs of Throat and Head. 6th, Lung, Liver, and Kidney Troubles. 7th, Dyspepsias and Chronic Intestinal Disorders. 8th, Scrofulous and other Constitutional Diseases. 9th, Troubles resulting from Pneumonia, Scarlet and other Fevers. 10th. Malarias.

SPECIAL WORK—**Gynecology :**—The Surgery of the Institute will be confined to Gynecological cases, except in emergencies.

THE OPTICAL DEPARTMENT—Chronic Troubles for the Eye, Fitting and Supplying Glasses, and Treating such Acute Conditions as are liable to arise at the Sea Shore.

Acute or Contagious Diseases Will Not be Received, except Children's Troubles, at our option.

Rates :—For Board, $7.00 to $15.00 per week. For Board, Massage, and Full Baths, $20.00 to $30.00 per week. Medical Examination, upon request, with advice as to condition and Bath, $5.00. Medical Care and Treatment, not including Surgical Operations, $5.00 to $15.00 per week. Special charge for operations or special cases.

D. M. BARR, M.D., Proprietor,

Member of the Pennsylvania State Medical Society, Philadelphia County Medical Society, Philadelphia Obstetrical Society, Consulting Physician to Philadelphia Methodist Orphanage, Surgeon to Post 77, G. A. R., Philadelphia.

IF I CAN ONLY
AFFORD TO TAKE ONE WEEKLY PAPER

THIS IS WHAT I WANT:

I WANT
To keep abreast of the current of
Religious thought and of the progress

I WANT
Of all the great reform movements.
All the latest Home News,
All the latest Foreign News,
All the Latest Political News.

I WANT
News of the doings of the Republican party,
News of the doings of the Democratic part .

I WANT
The best Market Reports,
The most reliable quotations of Farm Products.
Live Stock Markets, Financial and Commercial.

I WANT
Sensible and seasonable Editorials
On Political, Social, and Moral Questions.

I WANT
The Cream of the Best Editorials
In the New York and other daily and weekly papers
To let me know what they think of matters.

I WANT
Good, Reliable Farm and Garden Articles
Written by Practical Men.

I WANT
To know something of the Home Life of
The American people, and of their
Life, thoughts, and experiences.

I WANT
Pleasant moral stories for the Young People,
Then the children will look for the paper
As they do for a friend.

I WANT
Stories of Interest for us Elders,
For we, too, like our hours of leisure.

THIS IS WHAT I DON'T WANT:

I DON'T WANT
Long, padded News Articles;
The padding doesn't add to the value,
And I haven't time to read them.

I DON'T WANT
Fierce, one-sided Editorials,
Written by special pleaders,
Who cannot see anything good
In any other side but their own.

NOW, WHAT PAPER WILL FILL THE BILL?
WE ANSWER:
THE NEW YORK WEEKLY WITNESS
EVERY TIME.

$1 A YEAR. $1 A YEAR. $1 A YEAR.

The WITNESS is just the paper for Farmers, Farmers' Wives, Farmers' Sons, Farmers' Daughters, Country Merchants, Country Store-Keepers, Blacksmiths, Carpenters, Builders, Stone Masons, and all other laborers who form the backbone of our Country and who want to be thoroughly posted in what is going on in the World.

Sample copies sent free to any address. Write to us for copies for free distribution.

Address JOHN DOUGALL & CO.,
No. 150 Nassau St., New York City.

Saratoga Kissingen Water.

A FINE TABLE WATER AND A PLEASANT BEVERAGE.

THIS popular Water was discovered in 1872, and is rapidly crowding out all other table waters.

It is bottled only with its own natural carbonic acid gas, and is put up for family, hotel, and bar use, in quart and pint bottles. The Saratoga Kissingen has more fixed gas than any other natural spring water known in this country. It mixes well with wines, and when drank with meals, or soon after, is a great aid to digestion; when taken at night, before retiring, it is quieting in its effects.

Send for Circulars and Price-List.

The Saratoga Kissingen Spring Co.,

Office, 369 and 371 Broadway,

SARATOGA SPRINGS, N. Y.

H. F. CARY, Sup't and Treas.

WASHINGTON, D. C.

T. E. ROESSLE, - - - Proprietor.

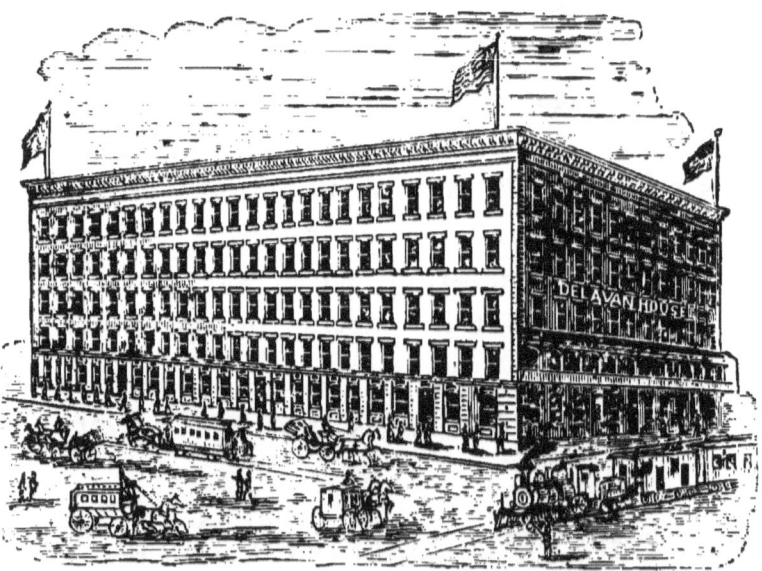

DELAVAN HOUSE, Albany, N. Y.,

T. E. ROESSLE, Proprietor.

FORT WILLIAM HENRY HOTEL.

Opens June 1st. Board for the season, $15, $17.50, $21, $25 and $28 per week, according to the location of rooms.

T. E. ROESSLE, Proprietor, Lake George, N. Y.

Also proprietor of the "The Arlington," Washington, D. C., and the Delavan House, Albany, N. Y.

CLARENDON SPRINGS, VERMONT.

CLARENDON HOUSE AND COTTAGES.

OPEN FROM JUNE TO OCTOBER. Accommodations for 200 guests. Farm of 170 acres connected with the Hotel.

CLARENDON SPRINGS WATER.

THE "UPPER SPRING" is a specific for Cutaneous Diseases, Dyspepsia, Gout, and Rheumatism. THE "LOWER SPRING" is wonderful as a Diuretic. THE "NORTH SPRING" is a Laxative Water. When used freely will cure constipation. ☞ Table Water of Highest Excellence.

A few extracts from Letters and Testimonials:

NEW YORK, August 30, 1887.
Messrs. MURRAY BROTHERS—I have been troubled for forty-five years with salt rheum, and for the past twenty years have had from one to three attacks yearly of erysipelas. Four weeks at your Springs, drinking the water and bathing in it, has completely restored me, and my skin is now cleaner from eruption than it has been for forty-five years. Yours truly, CYRUS PALMER, 193 Temple Court.

CAMBRIDGE, MASS., September 20, 1887.
Messrs. MURRAY BROTHERS—After an experience of more than fifty years in the use of Clarendon Spring Water, I can speak with confidence of their value as remedial agents. While the waters of all the springs are tonic, that of the North Spring is a laxative, acting mildly upon the intestinal canal, and is a sovereign cure for constipation. MASON D. BENSON, Treasurer Fitchburg R. R. Co.

MIDDLEBURY, VT., November 8, 1884.
Messrs. MURRAY BROTHERS—Having prescribed Clarendon Spring Water in several obstinate cases of eczema and catarrh of the bladder with good success, I can heartily recommend it to those who may be suffering from obstinate skin diseases, accompanied or caused by a torpid condition of the liver and kidneys.
Respectfully, M. D. SMITH, M.D.

RUTLAND, VT., February 24, 1885.
Messrs. MURRAY BROTHERS—In the last thirty years I have seen an army of sufferers cured by the wonderful healing powers of this most delicious of waters. People broken down by overwork and shattered nerves are rapidly restored, dyspeptics are cured, while those who suffer from any affection of the mucous membranes, stomach, kidneys, skin, etc., quickly improve. I know of no place where so many good combinations exist, of pure water, exhilarating air, fine drives, quiet and freedom from all annoyances, as are found at Clarendon Springs.
Yours cordially, E. A. POND, M.D.

THE "CHRISTIAN UNION" EDITORIAL ROOMS,
NEW YORK, January 28, 1885.
Messrs. MURRAY BROTHERS—For all persons who are in a quandary as to what they shall drink, such water as the Clarendon Springs Water seems to me a great benefaction. Yours sincerely, LYMAN ABBOTT.

BROOKLYN, N. Y., February 11, 1885.
Messrs. MURRAY BROTHERS—I regard the Clarendon Springs Water worthy of being ranked in the first class of table waters. HENRY WARD BEECHER.

NEW YORK, February 12, 1885.
Messrs. MURRAY BROTHERS—The Clarendon Springs Water I find very refreshing and wholesome. It has a special appetizing power at a meal.
Yours very truly, HOWARD CROSBY.

For pamphlet containing numerous letters and testimonials in full, hotel rates, etc., address **MURRAY BROTHERS, Proprietors,**
Clarendon Springs, Vermont.

FOR SUMMER READING.

BOYESEN.   **VAGABOND TALES.**
Vagabond Tales, by Hjalmar Hjorth Boyesen, is a collection of seven of the best and latest novelettes of this prince of story-tellers. Strong, simple, manly, tender, pathetic, dramatic, and pure. $1.25.

LUNT.   **ACROSS LOTS.**
Across Lots, by Horace Lunt, is just the book for the Summer outing. No better companion for a stroll by pond and river, roadway and hillside, could be selected. It is charming, helpful, suggestive, and poetic. $1.25.

THOMPSON.   **THE STORY OF LOUISIANA.**
The Story of Louisiana, by Maurice Thompson, is a history made romantic, and information made entertaining. A strong but picturesque presentation of one of the most dramatic of American commonwealths. $1.50.

LUSKA.   **MY UNCLE FLORIMOND.**
My Uncle Florimond, by Sidney Luska (Henry Harland), though written for young people, has been even more thoroughly enjoyed by the thousands of older readers who know the fascinating work of the author of "As It Was Written," and "Grandison Mather." A capital character study. $1.00.

MOODEY.   **ALAN THORNE.**
Alan Thorne, by Martha Livingston Moodey, tells a simple story in a straightforward way, and should be read by the mass of readers who have been fascinated by the brilliancy of "Robert Elsmere." It shows "the other side" in a way to enlist sympathy and awaken thought. $1.25.

HEATON.   **THE STORY OF VERMONT.**
The Story of Vermont, by John L. Heaton, is a practical but picturesque presentment of the history of that most sturdy American commonwealth—the noble Green Mountain State. The first history of the State in forty years. $1.50.

LOTHROP'S SUMMER SERIES FOR 1889.
PAPER COVERS.
Some of the Best Things in Recent Fiction at 35c each.

TILTING AT WINDMILLS.   **Connelly.**
A story of Northern endeavor in Southern fields. An interstate romance.

THE DOCTOR OF DEANE.   **Palmer.**
A tender and captivating love story of good women at cross purposes.

A MODERN JACOB.   **Stuart.**
One of the best of recent stories of New England village life.

THE RUSTY LINCHPIN and LUBOFF ARCHIPOVNA.   **Kokhanovsky.**
Two exquisite idyls of Russian rural life.

Send for a catalogue; 2000 live American books, representing every department of literature.

THE LOTHROP MAGAZINES.
WIDE AWAKE.
The best Magazine for Young People and the Family. Over 80 pages of choicest reading matter and fine art every month. The best writers and artists contribute to make it a success. Serials by Charles R. Talbot and Margaret Sidney now running. **Only $2.40 a year.**

BABYLAND.
The one Magazine in the world for babies. Dainty stories, beautiful pictures, tender and amusing poems. **Only 50 cents a year.**

OUR LITTLE MEN AND WOMEN.
The little folks' own Magazine, which they can read for themselves. Little stories, games, pieces to speak, full-page pictures, large print. **Only $1.00 a year.**

THE PANSY.
Edited by "Pansy"—Mrs. G. R. Alden. Devoted to young people from eight to fifteen. Adapted to both Sunday and week-day reading. Full of "Pansy's" magnetic spirit. **Only $1.00 a year.**

Specimens of the four Magazines, 15 cents; any one, 5 cents.

D. LOTHROP COMPANY, Boston,

(Opposite Bromfield Street.)   **364 and 366 Washington Street.**

WILLARD'S HOTEL,

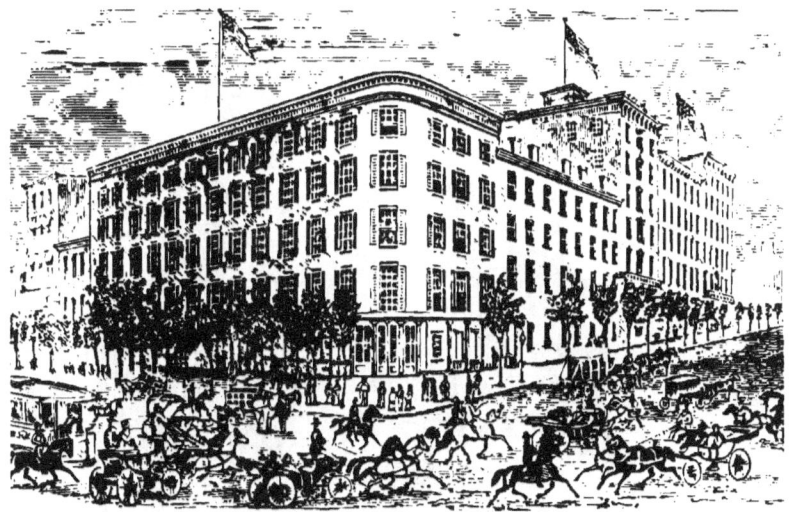

WASHINGTON, D. C.

  This old-established and chosen rendezvous and favorite abiding-place of the most famous men and women of America has, under the present management, been thoroughly renovated at an expense of over $100,000, and is now pronounced as the model Hotel in regard to luxurious apartments, cuisine, service and system for heating and ventilation.

  The "WILLARD" is located within a stone's-throw of the Executive Mansion, Treasury, War, Navy and State Departments, the Department of Justice, Corcoran Art Gallery, and other numerous points of interest, and can justly be called the most convenient Hotel for tourists and other travelers in Washington City.

        O. G. STAPLES, Proprietor.
          Formerly of the Thousand Island House

Also HOTEL POMENAH, Milford Springs, N. H. Post Office and Telegraph address, Amherst Station, N. H., B. & L. R. R., 48 Miles from Boston. Open from July to November.

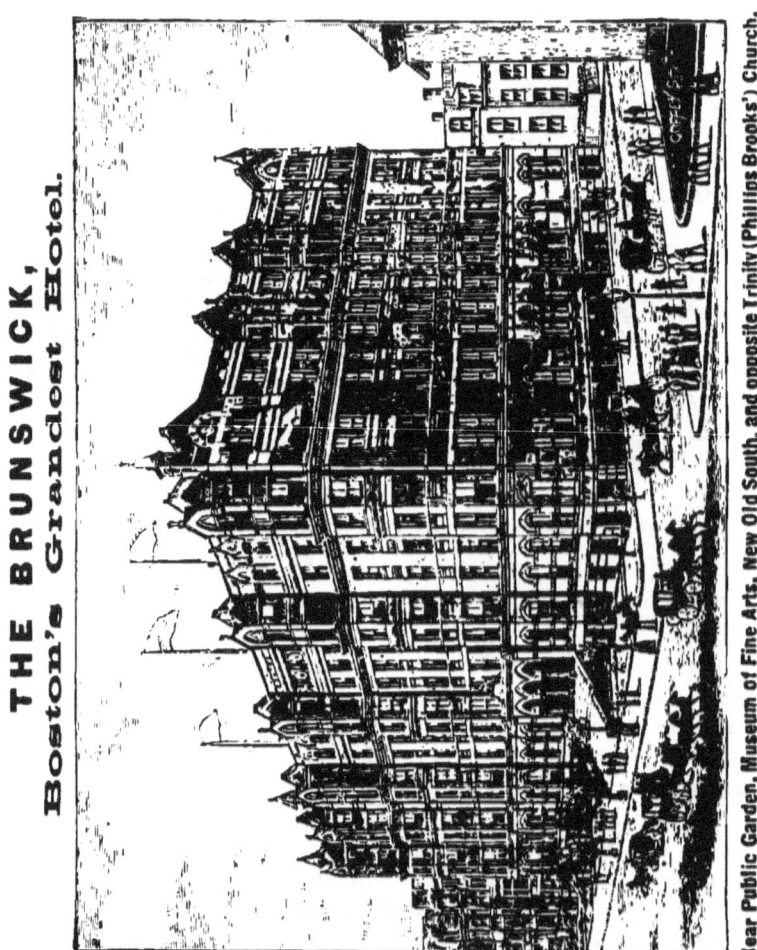

THE BRUNSWICK, Boston's Grandest Hotel.

Near Public Garden, Museum of Fine Arts, New Old South, and opposite Trinity (Phillips Brooks') Church. Dartmouth, Huntington Ave., and all "Back Bay" Cars pass the Hotel.

BARNES & DUNKLEE, Proprietors.

HOTEL POMENAH—Milford Springs, N. H. Post Office and Telegraph address, Amherst Station, N. H., B. & L. R. R. 48 Miles from Boston. Open July to November.

THE VICTORIA,
Dartmouth and Newbury Streets, Boston.
EUROPEAN PLAN.
In the Centre of the Back Bay District.
BARNES & DUNKLEE, of the Brunswick, Proprietors.
C. A. GLEASON, Manager.

THE CONGREGATIONALIST.

[ESTABLISHED 75 YEARS.]

The Oldest Religious Newspaper in the World.
The National Denominational Organ.

TERMS: $3.00 IN ADVANCE.

The CONGREGATIONALIST is a family religious journal (weekly) which, in all its various departments, aims to keep fully abreast of the times. It makes a specialty of the prayer meeting, giving a topic which is used by multitudes of churches, and commenting on the same each week. It has a staff of seven editors in the home office, besides an editor in New York and in Chicago, and a list of contributors which includes many eminent men and women in all departments of Christian thought and activity.

The following classification will give some idea of the great variety of matter furnished by THE CONGREGATIONALIST. The endeavor is made to meet the tastes of each member of the family, young and old, so far as possible.

News from the Churches.
    Literary Review.
        The Home.
           Our Young People.
                Editorials.
Diary of Events.   **Poetry.**
    Notes from Abroad.   **Education.**
        The Sunday School.
           The Prayer-Meeting.
Sketches.   **Farm and Garden.**
    Missions.   **Selections.**
        Secular News.   **Commercial.**
           Public Opinion.
                New York Letter.
                    Chicago Letter.
                        Washington Letter.

All these departments are edited with great care, it being our constant aim to furnish only the choicest reading on every page.

For club rates, premiums, trial subscriptions, write to

W. L. GREENE & CO., Publishers,
1 Somerset Street, Boston.

COMMONWEALTH AVENUE, Showing the Brattle-square Church and the Vendome.

The Successful Remedy for Nasal
CATARRH
AND
HAY-FEVER.

Must be non irritating, easy of application, and one that will, by its own action, reach all the remote sores and ulcerated surfaces. The efforts to treat catarrh during the past few years demonstrate that only one remedy has met these conditions, and that is Ely's Cream Balm. This safe and pleasant remedy has mastered catarrh as nothing else has ever done, and both physicians and patients freely concede this fact. The more distressing symptoms quickly yield to it, and a multitude of persons who have for years borne all the worry and pain that catarrh can inflict, testify to radical and permanent cures wrought by it.

Ely's Cream Balm is soothing, excites no dread, dissolves the hardened accumulations, lessens the extreme sensibility of the membrane to cold and all external irritants, and is followed by no reaction whatever.

A cold in the head is an inflammation of the lining membrane of the nasal passages, which, when unchecked, is certain to produce a catarrhal condition—for catarrh is essentially a "cold" which nature is no longer able to resolve or throw off.

I suffered from catarrh 12 years. The droppings into my throat were nauseating. My nose bled almost daily. Since the first day's use of Ely's Cream Balm have had no bleeding, the soreness is entirely gone.—D. G. Davidson, with "The Boston Budget."

For eight years I suffered from catarrh. After using Ely's Cream Balm for six weeks I believe myself cured. It is a most agreeable remedy.—Joseph Stewart, 624 Grand Avenue, Brooklyn, N. Y.

I had catarrh very badly and could hardly breathe. Suffered over ten years. I am using Ely's Cream Balm; it is working a cure, surely. I have induced several friends to use it, and with happy results in every case.—R. W. Sperry, Hartford, Conn.

I used Ely's Cream Balm and consider myself cured. I suffered 20 years from catarrh and catarrhal headache. This is the first remedy that afforded lasting relief.—D. T. Higginson, 145 Lake St., Chicago.

I suffered from severe cold in my head for months without relief. Ely's Cream Balm has worked like magic in its cure, after using it one week.—S. J. Harris, Wholesale Grocer, 119 Front St., N. Y.

I was so much troubled with catarrh it seriously affected my voice. One bottle of Ely's Cream Balm did the work. My voice is fully restored.—B. F. Liepsner, A.M., Pastor of the Olivet Baptist Church, Philadelphia.

I have been a great sufferer from dry catarrh for many years. Ely's Cream Balm completely cured me.—M. J. Lally, 39 Woodward Avenue, Boston.

Ely's Cream Balm is not a liquid, snuff, or powder. Applied into the nostrils it is quickly absorbed. It cleanses the head, allays inflammation, heals the sores, restores the senses of taste and smell. Sold by druggists or sent on receipt of price.

50c ELY BROTHERS, 56 Warren St., New York. **50c**

www.ingramcontent.com/pod-product-compliance
Lightning Source LLC
Chambersburg PA
CBHW021354230426
43666CB00006B/520